PROPHET MUHAMMAD: ASPECTS OF HIS LIFE

BY

M. FETHULLAH GÜLEN

VOL. 2

Published by The Fountain

9900 Main St. #504

Fairfax, Virginia 22031 USA

www.fountainlink.com

Translated by Ali Ünal

Library of Congress Cataloging-in-Publication Data

Gülen, M. Fethullah, 1938-

[Sonsuz nur. English.]

Prophet Muhammad: aspects of his life / M. Fethullah Gülen.

p. cm.

Includes index.

ISBN

1. Muhammad, Prophet, d. 632--Biography.   I. Title.

BP75 .G8213 2000

297.6'3--dc21

00-010842

Printed and bound in Turkey

Table of Contents

About the Author i

A General Introduction ix

Chapter 1: Prophet Muhammad as Educator 1

The educational atmosphere 1
Islam addresses all human faculties 3
Educating by example 7
Essentials of a good education 8
Further remarks 15

Chapter 2: The Military Dimension .21

Jihad 23
Early military expeditions 38

Chapter 3: A General Evaluation 47

The Battle of Badr 49
The Battle of Uhud 56
The Battle of the Trench 71
Toward the conquest of Makka 77
The conquest of Makka and its aftermath 79
The Battle of Hunayn 82
The expedition to Tabuk 83
A general evaluation of his military achievements 85

Chapter 4: A Universal Leader 93

His appointment of competent people 93
He knew his people 94
His wisdom 97
Merging two different communities 98
Consultation 102
A manifest victory: The Treaty of Hudaybiya 105
Ending racism 111
The last word 112

Chapter 5: Other Dimensions of His Prophethood 117

His prayers and supplications 117
The Prophet of universal mercy 122
His mildness and forbearance 130
His generosity 137
His modesty 142
The ethos created by the Messenger 146
Endnote 154

Chapter 6: The Sunna and Its Place .157
        in Islamic Legislation

The Sunna and its role 159
Categories of the Sunna 161
The Sunna in the Qur'an 163
The Sunna in the Traditions 166
The Sunna's role 167
Establishing the Sunna 172
Other motives 175
The Companions and the Sunna 179
Further remarks on the Sunna's importance 184

Chapter 7: Relating the Traditions

The Messenger's warning and the Companions' self-control 187
Literal narration 189
Verification 191
Ensuring authenticity 198
Examples 201
The number of authentic Traditions 213
Recording the Traditions 218

Chapter 8: The Companions and the Tabi'un 227

The Companions 227
Factors in their greatness 230
The Tabi'un 253

Index 265

About the Author

Known by his simple and austere lifestyle, Fethullah Gülen, affectionately called Khodjaefendi by those who love him, is a scholar of remarkable proportions. He was born in Erzurum, eastern Turkey, in 1938. Upon graduation from Divinity school in 1958, he obtained his license to preach and teach. Ever since, he has striven to communicate to society at large the importance of human understanding and tolerance in the quest to solve society's ills and our spiritual needs. His social reform efforts, begun in the 1960s and showing no signs of stopping, have made him one of the most well-known and respected public figures in Turkey, and has led numerous people throughout the world to do their best to implement his vision.

Though simple in outward appearance, he is considerably original in his ideas and activity. He embraces all humanity, and is deeply adverse to unbelief, injustice, and deviation. His belief and feelings are profound, as are his wise and rational ideas and approaches to problems. An example of love, ardor, and feeling, he remains extraordinarily balanced in thought, deed, and treatment of matters.

Contemporary intellectuals and scholars in Turkey who know him, whether tacitly or explicitly, acknowledge Fethullah Gülen as one of the most serious and important thinkers and writers, and among the wisest activists, of twentieth-century Turkey. Some even attribute this status to him throughout the Muslim world. Despite this and his leadership of a new intellectual, social, and spiritual of Islam and its community, which has the potential to embrace a considerable part of the world, he considers himself no more than a humble servant of God Almighty and a most modest friend among other people. *Desire for fame is the same as show and ostentation, and is a poisonous honey extinguishing the spiritual liveliness of the heart, is one of the golden rules he follows.*

Gülen has spent his life trying to voice the cries and laments of Muslims, in particular, and of humanity, in general, as well as their beliefs, hopes, and aspirations. While bearing his own sorrows, he feels crushed by the sorrows arising from the suffering of others. He feels each blow falling upon humanity as if it were delivered first to his own heart, and is so deeply and inwardly connected to creation that once he said: *Whenever I see a leaf fall from its branch in autumn, I feel as much pain as if my arm were amputated. That is why he always suffers inwardly.*

A brief biography

Fethullah Gülen was born in Korucuk, Erzurum Province, Turkey. After completing his education, he was posted to Edirne, where he began his career in teaching and providing religious and social service. He then fulfilled military service, returned to Edirne to teach again, and then was transferred to Izmir, Turkey's third largest province. This proved to be a turning point. Since childhood, he had dedicated himself to the religious life and taken a deep interest in the conditions of Muslims and of humanity in general. While in Izmir, he traveled from city to city to give lectures on subjects ranging from Darwinism to social justice in Islam, and visited places frequented by average people to convey his message.

He had long dreamed of a young generation that would combine intellectual "enlightenment" with pure spirituality, wisdom, and continuous activism. Being extraordinarily knowledgeable in religious and social sciences and quite familiar with the principles of material sciences, he instructed his students in almost all of them.

The first students who attended his courses in Izmir became the vanguard of the revived generation willing to serve his ideals. The small group attracted to his opinions by the end of 1960s has increased rapidly and steadily ever since. The generation captivated by his tears, sincerity, altruism, and love has served, and continues to serve, people without expecting any material reward. Having the support of the majority of the Turkish people, they preach, teach, and establish private schools all over the world; publish books and magazines, dailies and weeklies; broadcast television and radio programs; fund scholarships for poor students; and avoid politics and political ambition.

He is well-known for his ardent endeavor to strengthen bonds among all people, for, as he puts it so eloquently, the bonds that join us are far more than those that separate us. As a step toward this goal, he was a founding member of the Journalists' and Writers' Foundation, which promotes dialogue and tolerance among all social strata and is welcomed warmly by almost everyone. On a personal level, he visits and receives leading Turkish and international figures. He also meets regularly with leading journalists, columnists, and intellectuals of all persuasions.

One of his unequivocal beliefs is that *if you wish to keep the masses under control, deprive them of knowledge, for only through knowledge can tyranny be overthrown.* Totally dedicated to solving social problems, he believes that justice can only appear and be maintained through an adequate universal education. Only this development will engender sufficient understanding and tolerance in society for the need to respect the rights of others. To this end, he continually encourages society's elite and local leaders, industrialists, and businesspeople in his community to support quality education for the needy.

His tireless efforts have begun to bear fruit, as students graduating from the schools opened in Turkey and Central Asia have taken top honors in university placement tests and consistently finish at the top in International Knowledge Olympics. These schools, all of which are financed by private donations and run as trusts, already have produced a number of world champions, especially in physics, chemistry, biology, and mathematics.

Gülen maintains that *if a nation wishes to remain ignorant and free, while others enter a state of civilization, it expects what has never been and can never be.* In the area of education, he has inspired the use of mass media, notably television, to inform the public, especially those without a formal education, of pressing social matters. He believes that democracy, as a political and governing system and despite its shortcomings, is the only viable choice at this time. We must make it work, for people shall always demand freedom of choice when it comes to their own affairs and how they express their spiritual and religious values.

Do not despair in the face of adversity, and do not yield to anarchists, he emphasizes time and again, *and never despair, for despair buries human progress, kills the will to succeed, and chokes and drowns us.*

Perceiving a positive change in the global spiritual climate, he is optimistic about the future. He envisions a twenty-first century of spiritual dynamism that will dust off our long-dormant moral values, an age of tolerance and understanding leading to the cooperation of civilizations. The human spirit shall triumph on the way to intercivilizational dialogue and the sharing of values.

Gülen bridges the past with his view of the future. His deep desire to solve social problems presents itself, in his writings, as a row of sentences set one after another like priceless pearls on a string. In his inimitable style and choice of vocabulary, he offers a way out of the "material quicksand" in which we find ourselves today.

People today are searching for their Creator and the purpose of their creation, Gülen contends. We ask such questions as Why was I born? What is the purpose of my life? What is the meaning of death, and what does it demand from me?, and he provides practical and convincing answers. In his speeches and writings, one encounters statements like: *Humanity has come to a crossroads: one leads to despair, the other to salvation. May God give us the wisdom to make the right choice.* He also discusses how we can search for the truth.

He does not believe that there is any material shortage in the world, and sees no justifiable reason why millions of people should starve to death. Calling for inequitably distributed wealth to be channeled through private charities to the needy, he has spearheaded the establishment of charitable organizations to help the needy directly.

A unique social reformer, Gülen has synthesized positive science with divinity by reconciling their "differences." In his writings and public speeches, he brings the ideologies and philosophies of the East and the West closer together. He states that the days of gaining supporters through brute force are over, for in today's enlightened world persuasion and convincing argument are what count: *Those who resort to brute force to reach their goal are intellectually bankrupt souls.*

In our daily life, we must maintain the delicate balance between material and spiritual values if we want to enjoy serenity and true happiness. Thus, we must guard against unbridled greed.

A true leader who leads by example, he lives as he preaches and thus presents humanity with an ideal model to emulate. As a student of hadith, *tafsir* (Qur'anic commentary), *fiqh* (Islamic jurisprudence), Sufism, and philosophy he occupies his rightful place among his contemporaries in the Islamic sciences.

His works

Fethullah Gülen has passed his life in studying, teaching, traveling, writing, and speaking in order to alleviate the suffering engendered by the spiritual wasteland of the twentieth century. He contributes to several journals and magazines, and writes the editorials for *Yeni Umit, Sizinti, Yagmur,* and *The Fountain* magazines. His sermons and discourses have been recorded on thousands of tape and video cassettes, and many books have been compiled from his articles, sermons, and answers to questions. Some of his books are as follows:

- *Asrın Getirdiği Tereddütler* (4 vols.; vol. 1 has appeared as Questions and Answers about Faith)
- *Kalbin Zümrüt Tepeleri* (translated as :Key Concepts in the Practice of Sufism)
- *Çağ ve Nesil* (This Era and the Young Generation)
- *Ölçü veya Yoldaki Işıklar* (4 vols.; vol. 1 has appeared as Pearls of Wisdom)
- *Zamanın Altın Dilimi* (The Golden Part of Time)

- *Renkler Kuşağında Hakikat Tomurcukları* (2 vols.; vol. 1 has appeared as Truth through Colors)
- *Kırık Mızrap* (Broken Plectrum), a collection of verse

- *Fatiha Üzerine Mülahazalar* (Reflections on *Surat al-Fatiha*)
- *Sonsuz Nur* (2 vols., Prophet Muhammad: Aspects of His Life)
- *Yitirilmiş Cennet'e Doğru* (Towards the Lost Paradise)
- *İnancın Gölgesinde* (The Essentials of Islamic Faith).

Some of his books, such as *Asrın Getirdiği Tereddütler*, *İnancın Gölgesinde*, *Sonsuz Nur*, *Kırık Mızrap*, have been translated into German, Russian, Albanian, and Bulgarian.

The present book is a compilation of the sermons he gave every Friday of 1989 to introduce young people to Prophet Muhammad in all his aspects. In this translation, to be published in two volumes, you will meet the *Rahmat li al-'Alamin* (the Mercy for all the worlds) as Prophet, educator, statesman, commander, sociologist, economist, psychologist, moralist, preacher, orator, father, and husband; a most humble, compassionate, brave, wise, gracious, gentle, and truthful member of humanity; and the most sincere and beloved servant of God. Also, you will find out how to follow his example.

A General Introduction

I would like to introduce the reader to the exemplary life of the blessed Prophet Muhammad[1] and his distinguished, exalted personality. The "water of life" for the salvation of humanity should be made known to everyone.

Prophet Muhammad is the pride of humanity. For the past 14 centuries, many thinkers, philosophers, scientists, and scholars, each a radiant star in our intellectual world, have stood behind him in respect and admiration, and taken pride in belonging to his community.

It is enough to appreciate and understand his greatness that even after so many attacks, we still hear the words "I bear witness that Muhammad is the Messenger of God" from minarets five times a day. We rejoice while his name is being proclaimed from minarets, as do the dead and other spiritual beings. Despite concerted efforts to corrupt our young people and lead them astray, they continue to hasten to him, although they cannot perceive the full reality of Muhammad.

---

[1] In any publication dealing with the Prophet Muhammad, his name or title is followed by the phrase "upon him be peace and blessings," to show our respect for him and because it is a religious requirement to do so. A similar phrase is used for his Companions and other illustrious Muslims: "May God be pleased with him (or her)." However, as this practice might be distracting to non-Muslim readers, these phrases do not appear in this book, on the understanding that they are assumed and that no disrespect is intended.

Time has not caused us to forget the truth about him. He is so fresh in my mind that if I mention his holy name, it is as if I am about to meet him. Once, while on pilgrimage to his radiant city, Madina, I felt that he was about to appear and welcome us. As time progresses, some thoughts become obsolete, but he remains as fresh as a rosebud in our hearts. And so whenever we hear his name mentioned from the minaret, we immediately abandon our work and, accepting his invitation, hasten to mosque.

If we had been allowed to describe him as others have been described, if we had used the social and educational institutions, then perhaps our young people would be following his way. Despite our shortcomings, many pick up their "glasses" and run to fill them from this "pure spring." In every part of the world, including the United States, England, France, and Germany, an Islamic revival is occurring. Muslims are sowing these lands with the seeds of a happy future. Islam is everywhere healthy and flourishing as it did during the Time of Happiness—the time of Muhammad.

The same is true of predominantly Muslim lands. Those Muslims whose devotion to Islam was largely unconscious and devoid of deep perception or research have given way to a new generation who are consciously following Muhammad in the light of science and advances in knowledge. Those who were previously exploiting schools and universities on behalf of unbelief are now running to him. Even such well-known people as Maurice Bucaille and Roger Garaudy have seen the falsehood of their systems and are hastening to him.[2]

----

[2] Maurice Bucaille is a French physician and scientist who accepted Islam about 25 years ago. Roger Garaudy is one of the ideologues of communism of our age, and a previous general secretary of the French Communist Party. He chose Islam about 20 years ago.

Muhammad as the most beloved of hearts

I wonder whether we have fully recognized the most beloved of hearts. Even I, who have been performing five daily prayers since the age of 5 and striving to be a servant at his door, wonder if I can recognize him. Have we been able to enthuse love into the hearts of our recent generations by describing the ultimate source of all love and enthusiasm?

If only humanity had known Muhammad, they would have fallen in love with him as Majnun fell in love with Layla.[3] Whenever his name is mentioned, they would tremble with joy in anticipation of entering the ethos that surrounds him and those following his way wholeheartedly.

We can love only those whom we know and only to the extent of our knowledge. Our enemies have tried to make us forget him, to ensure that his name is no longer mentioned. Since he is supported by God, all obstacles have been torn down, and the younger generation submits to him as joyfully as one dying of thirst does upon finding water. His mighty tenderness and compassion will embrace every "thirsty" person who comes to him.

You must have noticed that when you come to the Friday prayers, the congregation consists mainly of young people. Have you ever asked why, despite the prevalence of misguidance and rebellion, young people come to mosques and sit despite cold and other difficulties? There is only one attraction: Muhammad. Whether we can grasp it or not, souls and hearts rush to him as moths to a candle. Even those "winter flies" who have not been so fortunate will soon turn to him. Scientists and great thinkers will study him. Those who

---

[3] Majnun and Layla are two legendary figures in who loved each other very deeply. (Tr.)

are currently enemies will soon be bosom friends, and will take refuge in his warm welcome. In his time, even his enemies admired him.

He once related a dream: "They weighed me against ten people of my community, and I outweighed them. Then they weighed me against a hundred and then a thousand, and I outweighed them all." [4] He also related: "I was weighed against my whole community, and I outweighed it." [5] He outweighs all people of intellect, piety and spirituality, and faith and knowledge, for all other beings were created because of him. It is reported that God said to him: But for you, I would not have created the spheres. [6]

Muhammad describes the meaning of creation

The universe is a book. If Muhammad had not been created, this book would not have been understood. To create an incomprehensible book is a waste of time and effort. As God is beyond such things, He created Muhammad to describe the meaning of creation to humanity. God would be his teacher, and the Earth and firmaments would be subjected to him. He would answer all the eternal questions: "Who and where am I?" "Why have I been created?" "What is my ultimate destination?" and "Who is my guide during this journey?"

Muhammad provides creation with meaning and answers such questions. If he had been fully recognized, he would have been truly loved. Although we only know him a little, we still love him.

---

[4] Qadi Iyad, *Shifa' al-Sharif*, 1:173.

[5] Ahmad ibn Hanbal, *Musnad*, 2:76.

[6] Al-Ajluni, *Kashf al-Khafa'*, 2:232.

Let me narrate an incident that occurred during a visit to Muhammad's holy city. The atmosphere was overpowering. Something occurred to me: I pray to God every morning, saying seven times: "O my God, save me from Hellfire and make me enter Paradise among the company of the godly people." There can be no believer who does not wish to enter Paradise. However, in this environment I asked myself: "If they were to invite you to Paradise through any of its seven gates, would you prefer entering into the *rawdah* (the area in the mosque next to the Prophet's tomb) or entering Paradise?" Believe me, I swear by God that I said to myself: "This place is more appealing to me. I have had the chance to rub my face against the soil of my master, at whose door I prefer to be a chained slave rather than anything else in the world. I do not want to miss this chance."

I believe this is the desire of every believer. When I was blessed with this great opportunity, I was with a member of the Turkish Parliament, Mr. Arif Hikmet. He told me he had promised himself that he would roll in the soil like a donkey when he stepped across the border and entered the land of Madina. This great man kept his promise. When I remember this incident, I cannot prevent my eyes from watering.

Muhammad's message embraces humanity and jinn

Since Prophet Muhammad came with a sacred Law that will never be abrogated, a Message that embraces humanity and jinn, and has hundreds of miracles excelling those of all other Prophets, he is the head of all Prophets. Therefore, he has the core of all their miracles and their unanimous confirmation. In other words, all other Prophets' agreement on the same faith and the testimony of their miracles support Muhammad's honesty and truthfulness. He is, at the same time, the master and leader of all saints and scholars of purity and profound knowledge who have attained perfection through his teaching and guidance, and through the light of his sacred Law.

In addition, he has the core of their wonders, their unanimous affirmation, and the strength of their verified conclusions. Since the way they have followed to reach the truth was the one opened and left open by him, all of their wonders and conclusions established through meticulous research and intuition, as well as their consensus on the same faith, support his Prophethood and truthfulness. This is why his coming was promised by all the Prophets before him. God made a covenant with them that they would believe in him and support him.

> God took a covenant with the Prophets: I have given you of Book and Wisdom; then there shall come to you a Messenger confirming what is with you—you shall believe in him and help him. He said: "Will you affirm this, and take My load on you in this matter?" They answered: "We affirm it." He said: "Bear witness, and I shall be with you among the witnesses." (3:81)

All of the Prophets led their lives in perfect loyalty to their promise. When Prophet Muhammad was about to make his *mi'raj* (Ascension to the Heavens), he led the prayers before the souls of all the other Prophets.[7] All of them, including Abraham, Moses, Noah, and Jesus, displayed their desire to become his *muezzin* (the one who calls to prayer).

In the Bible, Jesus repeatedly gave his disciples the glad tidings of Muhammad's coming. According to John (see 14:16, 26, 30; 16:7), he said:

---

[7] Ibn Jarir al-Tabari, *Jami' al-Bayan 'an Ta'wil Ay al-Qur'an*; Ibn Kathir, *Al-Bidaya wa al Nihaya*, 3:139.

It is better for you that I go away, because if I do not go, the helper will not come. I have much more to tell you, but for now it would be too much for you to bear. When, however, the spirit of the Truth, the lord of the world, who reveals the truth about God comes, he will lead you to the truth.

I wonder if we realize how unique he was as the head of family. Do we know how he brought up his children or grand-children, each of whom would have been a great leader in any succeeding century? He dealt with his wives so successfully that there was no serious disagreement among them. He is beyond all comparison as father, husband, or human being.

He had such sublime virtues in his blessed being, such exalted qualities in his Messengership, and such precious merits in the religion and sacred Law that he preached, that even his bitterest enemies could find no fault with him. Since he combines function, religion, and the most praiseworthy virtues in his personality, he is certainly the embodiment, master, and representative of all perfections and high, laud-able virtues found in creation.

This perfect a commander challenged the world with only a few followers. He repelled all who opposed his teachings and was never defeated, although he had no mortal teachers and never attended a military academy. He was so informed about science that he told his followers about almost all the major events that would occur until the Last Day. It was as if he were watching television or reading from an unseen tablet.[8]

Some time ago, a friend brought me a video cassette in which Keith Moore, a Canadian pediatrician who had real-ized how the Qur'an describes the development of the human

---

[8] *Sahih al-Muslim*, "Fitan, 22-25"; *Ibn Hanbal*, 1:4.

embryo in the womb, declared his conversion to Islam. On the same tape, a Japanese psychologist who had discovered that Islam explains many problems that baffle modern scientists, was trying to get his tongue around the Arabic words to make the same declaration.

Who taught all these scientific facts to Muhammad? Certainly he did not speak on his own. Whatever he spoke was a Revelation revealed to him by his teacher, the One Who knows everything, Who is All-Knowing and All-Aware. As science advances, humanity will come to discover a new aspect of his personality and will regret not having known him earlier.

His Companions knew him and loved him more than they loved themselves. They were prepared to sacrifice their lives to protect him. For example, he dispatched a group of teachers to the Hudayl tribe at their request. The Hudayli unbelievers betrayed their teachers and killed most of them. Zayd ibn Dasina and Hubayb were handed over to the Quraysh, then enemies of the Muslims.

When they were about to be executed, someone asked Hubayb: "Don't wish that Muhammad were in your place so that you could be with your family in Madina?" Hubayb was startled, and replied: "I would rather be cut into pieces than wish Muhammad were in my place. I don't want even a thorn to hurt his blessed foot in exchange for my being returned to my family." Hubayb prayed that God would convey his wish of peace and greetings to His Messenger, and inform him that he had remained loyal to him until he died. Meanwhile, the Prophet informed his Companions of Hubayb's martyrdom and returned his greetings.[9]

---

[9] Ibn Kathir, *Al-Bidaya*, 4:76.

Sumayra, from the Dinar tribe, hurried to the battlefield when she learned that the Muslims had experienced a reverse in Uhud. They showed her her father's corpse, and those of her husband and sons, but she ignored all of them. She just kept asking what had happened to the Prophet. When somebody guided her to him, she threw herself to the ground at a short distance from his feet and exclaimed: "All misfortunes mean next to nothing to me, provided that you are alive, O Messenger of God!" [10]

He was so loved that his Companions would have given their lives if it meant that he could live forever. But, of course, he was mortal like other created beings. The appointed hour drew near, and he had to say farewell to his friends of 23 years. Mu'adh ibn Jabal had been shuttling between Madina and Yemen carrying the Prophet's Message. On the day he was about to leave, the Messenger of God told him: "Mu'adh, leave now for Yemen. When you come back, you will probably visit my mosque and my tomb." These words were enough to bring Mu'adh to the point of emotional collapse. [11]

Our problems can be solved only by following his way

The problems of our time will be solved by following the way of Muhammad. This has been acknowledged by unbiased Western and Eastern intellectuals. As Bernard Shaw once admitted, humanity can solve its accumulated problems by turning to Prophet Muhammad, who solved the most complicated problems as easily as one drinks coffee.

---

[10] Ibn Kathir, *Al-Bidaya,* 4:54; al-Haythami, *Majma' al-Zawa'id,* 6:115.

[11] Ibn Hanbal, 5:235.

Humanity is waiting for the return of the Muhammadan spirit, for the Message of Muhammad. When they turn to him to solve their problems, they will be saved from exploitation, freed form misery, and attain true peace and happiness. This second revival has already begun, despite the aversion of unbelievers:

> They desire to extinguish the light of God with their mouths; but God will perfect His light, even though unbelievers are averse. He has sent His Messenger with the guidance and the religion of truth, that He may uplift it above every religion, even though the polytheists are averse (61:8-9).

God will uplift His religion, and people will run to Prophet Muhammad. In him, they will find peace and happiness. Humanity finally will learn to live in security through him, and it will seem as if they are already living in Paradise despite still being in this temporary world. This will take place despite the presence in every country of unbelievers, wrongdoers, hypocrites, and those who ignore him. The lord of the Prophets, whose name we proclaim from our minarets five times a day, sooner or later will enter the hearts of all human beings. And since Prophet Muhammad was a man of peace, humanity will attain happiness through the Message he brought: Islam.

CHAPTER 1

Prophet Muhammad as Educator

The educational atmosphere

Consider the following verse:

> It is He who has sent among the unlettered a
> Messenger of their own, to recite to them His signs, to
> purify them, and to instruct them in Scripture and
> Wisdom, although they had been, before, in manifest
> error. (62:2)

Some of these words are very interesting. God is mentioned in the third person, because the ignorant, primitive, and savage Arabs did not know Him. As there was no "He" in their minds, God first emphasizes the darkness of their nature, their great distance from Him, and indicates that they cannot be addressed directly by Him.

Then God calls them *unlettered*. They were not all illiterate, but they had no knowledge of God and the Messenger. God, by His infinite Power, sent to this trifling community a Messenger with the greatest willpower, the most sublime nature, the deepest spirituality, and the highest morality, by means of whom He would instruct them in how to become geniuses who would one day govern humanity.

The word *among* shows that the Messenger was one of them, but only in the sense of being unlettered. Being chosen by God, he could not possibly belong to the Age of Ignorance (pre-Islamic Arabia). However, he had to be unlettered so that God would teach him what he needed to know. God would remove him from his people, educate him, and make him a teacher for all unlettered people.

The phrases *to recite to them His signs* and *to purify them* point out that He teaches them about the meanings of the Qur'an and of creation in a gradual manner, and informs them how to become perfect human beings by striving for spiritual perfection. He guides them to higher ranks by explaining the Qur'an and the universe to them, and showing them in minute detail how to lead a balanced and exemplary life in every sphere of activity.

The sentence *although they had been, before, in manifest error* indicates that God would purify and educate them even though they had gone astray. He did all of this through an unlettered Messenger and by teaching them the Qur'an. Throughout history and even today, this Book has met the needs of countless brilliant scientists, scholars, and saints.

After the Prophet, humanity saw his flag waving every-where for centuries. Those who follow him, both now and in the past, reach the highest spiritual realms on wings of saint-hood, piety, righteousness, knowledge, and science. Those who climbed the steps of good conduct and spirituality, and knowledge and science, both now and in the past, saw in each step the "footprints" of Prophet Muhammad and greet him with "God bless you."

They will do the same again in the near future. All so-called original ideas will disappear one by one, like candles blown out, leaving only one "sun"—the Qur'an—that will never set. Its flag will be the only one waving on the horizon, and every generation will rush to it, breaking the chains around their necks.

Islam addresses all human faculties

As is explicit in the above-mentioned verse, the Messenger's method of education does not just purify our evil-commanding selves; rather, it is universal in nature and raises human hearts, spirits, minds, and souls to their ideal level. He respected and inspired reason; in fact, he led it to the highest rank under the intellect of Revelation.

The universal truths of the Qur'an also state this fact. Moreover, the Message touches all of our inner and outer senses, makes its followers rise on the wings of love and compassion, and takes them to places beyond their imagination. His universal call encompasses, in addition to the rules of good conduct and spirituality, all principles of economics, finance, administration, education, justice, and international law. He opened the doors of economic, social, administrative, military, political, and scientific institutions to his students, whose minds and spirits he trained and developed to become perfect administrators, the best economists, the most successful politicians and unique military geniuses.

If there had been any lack in his teaching of humanity, the aim of his Prophethood could not have been realized so fully. He said:

> Each Prophet before me built some part of this marvelous building, but there was a gap that needed to be closed. Every person passing by would say: "I wonder when this building will be completed." The one who completes it is me. After me, there is no longer any defect in the structure.[12]

The Qur'an affirms this: *This day I have completed your religion for you* (5:3). In short, the Prophet reformed, com-

---

[12] *Bukhari*, "Manaqib," 18; *Muslim*, "Fada'il," 20-23.

pleted, and perfected the ways of life that had been lacking, had become deficient, or had deviated from the Will of God.

All previous Prophets were sent to a certain people and for a fixed time. However, as God chose Prophet Muhammad and Islam for all times and peoples, Islam is the perfection of His universal favor upon His creation. He fashioned Islam in such a way that it pleases everybody. Therefore, rather than trying to find fault with the Message and the principles relayed by the Messenger, people should seek these truths and principles in order to design their lives according to them.

The Prophet was a man who completed, perfected, and reformed. He transformed an illiterate, savage people into an army of blessed saints, illustrious educators, invincible commanders, eminent statesmen, and praiseworthy founders of the most magnificent civilization in history.

An educator's perfection depends on the greatness of his or her ideal and the quantitative and qualitative dimensions of his or her listeners. Even before Prophet Muhammad's death, the instructors and spiritual guides he dispatched were traveling from Egypt to Iran and from Yemen to Caucasia to spread what they had learned from him. In succeeding centuries, peoples of different traditions, conventions, and cultures (e.g., Persians and Turanians, Chinese and Indians, Romans and Abyssinians, Arabs and some Europeans) rushed to Islam. An educator's greatness also depends on the continuation of his or her principles. No one can deny that people all over the world accept Islam and adopt his principles. By God's Will and Power, most of humanity will embrace Islam soon.

Remember that the Messenger appeared among a wild and primitive people. They drank alcohol, gambled, and indulged in adultery without shame. Prostitution was legal, and whorehouses were indicated by a special flag. Indecency was so extreme that a man would be embarrassed to be called a man. People were constantly fighting among themselves, and no one had ever been able to unify them into a strong nation. Everything evil could be found in Arabia. However, the Prophet eradicated these evils and replaced them with such deep-rooted values and virtues that his people became the leaders and teachers of the civilized world.

Even today we cannot reach their ranks. This has been acknowledged by such Western intellectuals as Isaac Taylor,[13] Robert Briffault, John Davenport, M. Pickhtal, P. Bayle, and Lamartine.[14]

---

[13] Isaac Taylor, who spoke at the Church Congress of England, relates how Islam changes the people who accept it:

> The virtues which Islam inculcates are temperance, cleanliness, chastity, justice, fortitude, courage, benevolence, hospitality, veracity, and resignation... Islam preaches a practical brotherhood, the social equality of all Muslims. Slavery is not part of the creed of Islam. Polygamy is a more difficult question. Moses did not prohibit it. It was practiced by David, and is not directly forbidden in the New Testament. Muhammad limited the unbounded license of polygamy. It is the exception rather than the rule... (Abu'l-Fazl Ezzati, *An Introduction to the History of the Spread of Islam*, London) (Tr.)

[14] To give just one example, Lamartine asks:

> Philosopher, orator, apostle, legislator, warrior, conqueror of ideas, restorer of rational dogmas, of a cult without images; the founder of twenty terrestrial states and of one spiritual state, that is Muhammad. As regards all standards by which human greatness may be measured, we may well ask: Is there any man greater than he? (*Historie de la Turquie*, 2:276-77.) (Tr.)

God creates living things from lifeless things. He grants life to soil and rock. The Prophet transformed "rocks, soil, coal, and copper" into "gold and diamonds." Just consider the cases of Abu Bakr, 'Umar, 'Uthman, 'Ali, Khalid, 'Uqba ibn Nafi', Tariq ibn Ziyad, Abu Hanifa, Imam Shafi'i, Bayazid al-Bistami, Muhyi al-Din ibn al-'Arabi, Biruni, Zahrawi, and hundreds of thousands of others, all of whom were brought up in his school. The Messenger never allowed human faculties to remain undeveloped. He developed them and replaced weakness with marvelous competency. As a great thinker recalled:

> 'Umar had the potential to be a great man even before he embraced Islam. After his conversion, he became a powerful yet very gentle man who would not step on an ant or kill even a grasshopper. Such was his compassion, sensitivity, and understanding of justice and administration that he used to say: 'If a sheep falls into the Tigris because of a destroyed bridge, God will ask me about it.'

We cannot eradicate such a small habit as smoking, despite all our modern facilities and practically daily symposia and conferences to combat it. Medical science says smoking causes cancer of the larynx, mouth, esophagus, windpipe, and lungs; however, people insist on smoking. On the other hand, the Messenger eradicated countless ingrained bad habits and replaced them with laudable virtues and habits. Those who saw them used to say: "My God, his followers are superior even to the angels." When these people pass over the Bridge above Hell with their light spreading everywhere, even the angels will ask in awe: "Are they Prophets or angels?" In fact, they are neither Prophets nor angels; they are the educated people of the Prophet's nation.

Prophet Muhammad had a holistic view of each individual. He took all of their mental and spiritual capacities and developed them, turning his own wretched people into paragons of virtue. His wisdom in assessing such potential is another proof of his Prophethood.

Educating by example

The Messenger represented and expressed what he wanted to teach through his actions, and then translated his actions into words. How to be in awe of God, how to be humble, how to prostrate with deep feelings, how to bow, how to sit in prayer, how to cry to God at night—all of these he first did himself and then taught to others. As a result, whatever he preached was accepted immediately in his house and by his followers, for his words penetrated all of their hearts. After him, humanity saw his standard carried everywhere by people raised on the wings of sainthood, purification, devotion to God, and desire to be close to Him. Wherever they went, they walked in the footsteps of Prophet Muhammad. Others will do so in the future.

In the house of the Messenger there was a permanent sense of awe. Those who caught a glimpse of him could feel the allure of Heaven and the terror of Hell. He swayed to and fro during prayer, trembling with the fear of Hell and flying on wings of the desire of Heaven. All who saw him remembered God. Imam al-Nasa'i narrates: "While the Messenger was praying, a sound, like a boiling pot, was heard."[15] He always prayed with a burning and weeping heart. 'A'isha often found him in the presence of his Master, prostrating and trembling.[16]

---

[15] *Nasa'i,* "Sahw," 18.

[16] Ibid., "Ishrat al-Nisa'," 4.

His behavior inspired and benefited everyone around him. The children and wives of every Messenger had the same awe and fear, as the Messengers preached, ordered, related what they practiced and experienced, and gave examples through their actions. We can assess a person's impact through his or her behavior while at home. If all pedagogues gathered and merged their acquired knowledge about education, they could not be as effective as a Prophet.

Many of his descendants have shone among their respective generations like a sun, a moon, or a star. He brought up his Companions so perfectly that almost none of them became heretics.[17] None of his progeny has ever become a heretic, which is a distinction unique to him. Heretics and apostates have appeared among the households and descendants of many saintly people, but none of Muhammad's descendants have betrayed the roots of their household. If there have been a few exceptions unknown to us and history, they do not negate the rule.[18]

Essentials of a good education

A real educator must have several virtues, among them the following:

First: Give due importance to all aspects of a person's mind, spirit, and self, and to raise each to its proper perfection. The Qur'an mentions the evil-commanding self that drags people, like beasts with ropes around their necks, wher-

---

[17] Those who became apostates after the Prophet's death were not Companions. (Tr.)

[18] There is a rule in logic: Exceptions do not invalidate the rule. We do not know of any heretics among his descendants. But this does not mean that there will not be, because it is possible. Considering this possibility, we speak with caution.

ever it wants to go, and goads them to obey their bodily
desires. In effect, the evil-commanding self wants people to
ignore their God-given ability to elevate their feelings,
thoughts, and spirits.

The Qur'an quotes the Prophet Joseph as saying: *Surely
the self commands evil, unless my Master has mercy* (12:53).
Commanding evil is inherent in the self's nature. However,
through worship and discipline, the self can be raised to higher ranks, to a position where it accuses itself for its evils and
shortcomings (75:2), and then still higher where God says to
it: *O self at peace! Return unto your Master, well-pleased,
well-pleasing* (89:27-28).

Higher than the self at peace (at rest and contented) is the
self perfectly purified. Those who rise to this degree of attain-
ment are the nearest to God. When you look at them you
remember God, for they are like polished mirrors in which all
of His attributes are reflected. The Companions' desire to follow the training provided by Prophet Muhammad enabled
almost all of them to reach this degree of moral and spiritual
perfection; millions of people have followed and continue to
follow their example.

Second: An education system is judged by its universali-
ty, comprehensiveness, and quality of its students. His students were ready to convey his Message throughout the
world. The Message they conveyed, being universal in nature
and valid for all times and places, found a ready acceptance
among people of different races, religious background, intellectual levels, and age differences from modern-day Morocco
and Spain to the Philippines, from the Russian steppes to the
heart of Africa. Its principles remain valid. Despite numerous
upheavals and changes, as well as social, economic, intellectual, scientific, and technological revolutions, his system

remains the most unique and original, so much so that it is the hope of the future of humanity.

Third: An education system is judged by its ability to change its students. The example of smoking was mentioned earlier, as was that of how Islam and the Prophet's spread of it transformed the tribes of Arabia into their exact opposite within the space of just two or three decades. To those who deny or question his Prophethood, we challenge them to go anywhere in the world and accomplish, within 100 years, even one-hundredth of what he accomplished in the deserts of Arabia 1,400 years ago. Let them take all of the experts they can gather, and then we will wait to see their results.

When Prophet Muhammad was conveying the Message, Arabia was isolated from its neighbors by vast deserts. In terms of its cultural, intellectual, and moral life, it rightfully could be considered one of the most backward areas of the world. The Hijaz, where the Prophet was born, had experienced no social evolution and had attained no intellectual development worthy of mention. Dominated by superstitions, barbarous and violent customs, and degraded moral standards, people lived in savagery. They drank wine, gambled, and indulged in what even average societies consider immoral sexual activities. Prostitutes advertised their services by hanging a flag on the doors of their houses.[19]

It was a land without law and a government. Might was right, as in many areas today, and looting, arson, and murder were common. Any trivial incident could provoke intertribal feuding, which sometimes grew into peninsula-wide wars.

These were the people Prophet Muhammad appeared among. With the Message he relayed from God and his way

---

[19] *Bukhari*, "Nikah," 36; *Abu Dawud*, "Talaq," 33.

of preaching it, he eradicated barbarism and savagery, adorned Arabia's wild and unyielding peoples with all praise-worthy virtues, and made them teachers of the world. His domination was not physical or military; rather, he conquered and subjugated them by becoming the beloved of their hearts, the teacher of their minds, the trainer of their souls, and the ruler of their spirits. He eradicated their evil qualities, and implanted and inculcated in his followers' hearts exalted qualities in such a way that they became second nature to all of his followers.

But this transformation was not limited only to the people of his own time and place, for this process continues even today wherever his Message spreads. It was not only quickly accepted in Arabia, Syria, Iraq, Persia, Egypt, North Africa, and Spain at its first outburst, but, with the exception of the now-vanished brilliant civilization of Islamic Spain, it has never lost its vantage ground. Since it first appeared, it has never stopped spreading.[20]

---

[20] A nineteenth-century Western writer notes his impressions of the influence of Islamic moral values on Africans:

> As to the effects of Islam when first embraced by a Negro tribe, can there, when viewed as a whole, be any reasonable doubt? Polytheism disappears almost instantaneously; sorcery, with its attendant evils, gradually dies away; human sacrifice becomes a thing of the past. The general moral elevation is most marked; the natives begin for the first time in their history to dress, and that neatly. Squalid filth is replaced by some approach to personal cleanliness; hospitality becomes a religious duty; drunkenness, instead of the rule, becomes a comparatively rare exception. Chastity is looked upon as one of the highest, and becomes, in fact, one of the commoner virtues. It is idleness that henceforward degrades, and

Many world-renowned individuals have been raised in the school of Muhammad. Certainly, we come across numerous great historical figures in other schools of education as well. God has honored humanity with great heroes, eminent statesmen, invincible commanders, inspired saints, and great scientists. However, most of them have not made a deep impression on more than one or two aspects of human life, for they confine themselves to those fields.

But since Islam is a Divine way for all fields of life, a Divine system encompassing all aspects of life—"like a perfect work of architecture all of whose parts are harmoniously conceived to complement and support each other, nothing lacking, with the result of an absolute balance and solid composure," according the Muhammad Asad,[21] a Jewish convert—its students usually combine within themselves the spiritual and the rational, the intellectual and the material, the worldly with the otherworldly, the ideal with the real, and the scientific and the revealed (by God).

At its very outset, Islam abolished tribal conflicts and condemned racial and ethnic discrimination. The Prophet put the Qurayshi chiefs under Zayd's command (an emanci-

---

industry that elevates, instead of the reverse. Offenses are henceforward measured by a written code instead of the arbitrary caprice of a chieftain—a step, as everyone will admit—of vast importance in the progress of a tribe. The mosque gives an idea of architecture at all events higher than any the Negro has yet had. A thirst for literature is created and that for works of science and philosophy as well as for commentaries on the Qur'an. (Waitz quoted by B. Smith, Muhammad and Muhammadanism, 42-3.) (Tr.)

[21] Al-Ezzati, *An Introduction to the History of the Spread of Islam.*

pated black slave), and innumerable scholars and scientists, commanders, and saints appeared among conquered peoples. Among them was Tariq ibn Ziyad, an emancipated Berber slave who conquered Spain with 90,000 valiant warriors and laid the foundations of one of the most splendid civilizations of world history. After this victory, he went to the palace where the defeated king's treasury was kept. He said to himself:

> Be careful, Tariq. Yesterday you were a slave with a chain around your neck. God emancipated you, and today you are a victorious commander. However, you will change tomorrow into flesh rotting under earth. Finally, a day will come when you will stand in the Presence of God.

The world and its pomp could not attract him, and he continued to live a very simple life. What kind of education could transform a slave into such a dignified and honorable person?

However, his conquest of Spain was not his real victory. This came when he stood before the treasury of the Spanish king and reminded himself that one day he would die and face God. As a result of this self-advice, he took none of the treasure for himself.

'Uqba ibn Nafi' was another great commander who conquered northern Africa and reached the Atlantic coast. There he stood and said: "O God, if this sea of darkness did not appear before me, I would convey Your Name, the source of light, to the remotest corners of the world."[22]

Before his conversion, 'Abd Allah ibn Mas'ud took care of 'Uqba ibn Abi Mu'ayt's sheep. He was a weak, little man

---

[22] Ibn al-Athir, *Al-Kamil fi al-Tarikh*, 4:106.

who everyone ignored.[23] After becoming a Muslim, however, he was one of the most senior Companions. During his caliphate, 'Umar sent him to Kufa as a teacher. In the scholarly climate he established there, the greatest figures of Islamic jurisprudence grew up, among them Alqama, Ibrahim al-Nakha'i, Hammad ibn Abi Sulayman, Sufyan al-Thawri, and especially Imam Abu Hanifa, the founder of the largest Islamic legal school.

Ikrima was the son of Abu Jahl, the harsh and inflexible leader of the Qurayshi unbelievers. Finally, after the Conquest of Makka, he converted to Islam. This event so changed him that he welcomed martyrdom 3 years later at the Battle of Yarmuk. His son, Amir, was martyred with him.

Hansa was one of the finest poetesses before Islam. Becoming a Muslim, she abandoned poetry because: "While we have the Qur'an, I cannot write poems." She lost her four sons at the Battle of Qadisiyya. This great woman, who had lamented her brother's death before the appearance of Islam with a great poem, did not lament this loss. Instead, she deepened her submission to God and said only: "O God, all praise be to You. You have bestowed on me while alive the possibility of offering you as martyrs my four sons that you gave me."[24]

The school of Prophet Muhammad also produced the most just rulers in history. Besides Abu Bakr, 'Uthman, 'Ali and many others who succeeded them, 'Umar has been recognized in almost every age as one of the world's most just

---

[23] Kufa, a famous city in the early history of Islam, is located on the west branch of the river Euphrates, south of the ruins of Babel (Iraq). (Tr.)

[24] Ibn al-Athir, *Usd al-Ghaba*, 7:88-90; Ibn Hajar, *Al-Isaba*, 4:287.

and greatest statesmen. He used to say: "If a sheep falls from a bridge even on the river Tigris and dies, God will call me to account for it on the Day of Judgment."[25] When you compare the pagan 'Umar to the Muslim 'Umar, you easily see the sharp contrast between the two and understand how radically Islam changes people.

Further remarks

Due to misconceptions and secular tendencies, especially in the West in recent centuries, most people define religion as blind faith, meaningless acts of worship, a consolation for life's problems. Such mistaken ideas have developed in Christendom partly due to Christianity's historical mistakes and shortcomings. Some secularized, worldly Muslims have compounded this mistake by reducing Islam to an ideology, a social, economic, and political system. They ignore one fact stated in the Qur'an, the Traditions, and throughout Islamic history: Islam, the middle way between all extremes, addresses itself to all human faculties and senses, as well as to each individual's mind, heart, and feelings, and encompasses every aspect of human life. That is why Prophet Muhammad stressed learning, trading, agriculture, action, and thought.

Moreover, he encouraged his people to do perfectly whatever they did, and condemned inaction and begging. For example, he said: "God loves a believing, skilful servant."[26] The Qur'an declares: *Say: "Work; and God will surely see your work, and the Messenger and the believers"* (9:105). As all of our actions will be displayed on the Day of Judgment, we cannot be careless and do something half-

---

[25] Tabari, *Tarikh*, 5:195; Ibn Sa'd, *Tabaqat*, 3:305; Abu Nu'aym, *Hilya*, 1:53.

[26] Munavi, *Fayd al-Qadir*, 2:290.

heartedly just to get rid of it. Moreover, The Messenger declares: "When you do something, God likes you to do it perfectly."[27]

Islam encourages people to work, and considers our lawful attempts to earn our living and support our family acts of worship. Unlike medieval Christianity, it does not idealize (nor even advise) life as a hermit. It forbids dissipation and luxury on the grounds that if we live a self-indulgent life here and neglect our religious duties, our prosperity in both worlds will be in jeopardy. The Messenger declares, in a concise saying that summarizes the essentials of a happy economic and social life and prosperity in both this world and the next:

> When you are involved in speculative transactions, occupied only with animal-breeding, content with agriculture, and abandon striving in the way of God to preach His religion, God will subject you to such a humiliation. He will not remove it until you return to your religion.[28]

This *hadith* is gives a very accurate description of the pitiable condition of Muslims over the last few centuries. Speculative transactions signify the dying of a healthy economic life and the resort to unlawful, self-abandoned ways of earning one's living. Contentment with agriculture and animal breeding is the sign of laziness and abandoning scientific investigation—the Qur'an explicitly states that God created humanity as His vicegerent and entrusted us with knowledge of the names of things.

This means that we are to establish science and exploit natural resources by discovering the Divine laws of nature

---

[27] Muttaqi al-Hindi, *Kanz al-'Ummal*, 3:907.

[28] *Abu Dawud*, "Buyu'," 54; Ibn Hanbal, *Musnad*, 2:84.

and reflecting on natural phenomena. However, while doing this, we should seek God's good pleasure and practice Islam.

The Qur'an contains many verses, such as: *Say: "Are they equal—those who know and those who don't know?"* (39:9), that emphasize the importance of knowledge and learning. It also warns that *among His servants, only those who have knowledge truly fear God* (35:28), meaning that true piety and worship is possible only through knowledge. Confining knowledge to religious sciences devoid of reflection and investigation inevitably results in contentment with animal breeding and agriculture, in idleness and the neglect of striving in the way of God. The ultimate result is misery, poverty, and humiliation.

The Messenger drew attention to this important fact in some other Traditions, such as: "An hour of reflection and contemplation is better than a year of (supererogatory) religious worship,"[29] and "A powerful believer is better and more lovable to God than a weak one."[30] Being powerful requires both spiritual and physical health as well as scientific and technical competence. Restricting the meaning of being powerful to physical strength shows one's total lack of understanding of what true power is based on.

In conclusion, being a good Muslim is possible only through being a good student in the school of Prophet Muhammad. This attitude was displayed by Ja'far ibn Abi Talib, the Prophet's cousin, who emigrated to Abyssinia to escape severe Qurayshi persecution. He once told the Negus,

---

[29] Ajluni, *Kashf al-Khafa'*, 1:370.

[30] *Muslim*, "Qadar," 34; *Ibn Maja*, "Muqaddima," 10; Ibn Hanbal, 3:366.

ruler of Abyssinia: "O king, we used to drink blood, eat carrion, fornicate, steal, kill each other, and plunder. The powerful used to oppress the weak. We used to do many other shameful and despicable things."[31]

Prophet Muhammad set the best example for his people in belief, worship, and good conduct—in short, in all aspects of life. His people considered having daughters a source of shame, and so buried them alive. When the Prophet came with the Divine Message, women enjoyed their rights fully. Once a girl came to The Messenger and complained: "O Messenger of God, my father is trying to force me to marry my uncle's son. I don't want to marry him." The Messenger sent for her father and warned him not to do this. The man promised that he would not do so. The girl then stood up and said: "O Messenger of God, I didn't intend to oppose my father. I came here only to find out whether Islam allows a father to marry his daughter to somebody without her consent."[32]

The Messenger warned his Companions not to beg. However poor and needy they were, the Companions did not beg from anybody. They were so sensitive in this matter that they even refrained from asking help. If, for example, one of them dropped his whip while on a mount, he would dismount and pick it up himself rather than ask someone to pick it up and hand it to him.[33]

Prior to Islam, people worshipped idols and did not give due respect to their parents. God's Message told them: *Your*

---

[31] *Bukhari*, "Wasaya," 9.

[32] *Nasa'i*, "Nikah," 36.

[33] *Muslim*, "Zakat," 108; *Ibn Maja*, "Jihad," 41.

Master has decreed that you shall not worship any but Him, and to be good to parents (17:23). This Divine decree changed them so radically that they began asking the Messenger if they would be punished if they did not return the looks of their parents' with a smile. The Qur'an ordered them *not to usurp an orphan's property* (17:34) and forbade theft. This made them so sensitive to others' rights that history does not record more than one or two thefts in that blessed period of the Prophet's rule.

Murder was extremely widespread in pre-Islamic Arabia. However, when the Prophet came with the prohibition: *Slay not the soul God has forbidden* (17:33), this evil was all but eradicated. The Messenger also forbade fornication. This ended all kinds of sexual immorality. However, we do find one incident of fornication during that period. It is as follows:

> One day a pale and exhausted man came to the Messenger and exclaimed: "O Messenger of God, cleanse me!" The Messenger turned his face from him, but the man insisted, repeating his demand four times. At last, the Messenger asked: "Of what sin shall I cleanse you?" The man replied that he had fornicated. This sin weighed so heavily on his conscience that he desired to be punished. The Messenger asked those present: "Is he insane?" When told he was not, he told them to see if he was drunk. They examined him and found him sober. In the face of his insistent confession, the Messenger had to order the man to be punished. After it, he sat and wept.

> A few days later, the man's partner appealed to the Messenger to cleanse her. Many times he turned away from her and sent her back. In utmost remorse, she insisted on being punished. The Messenger sent her back once more, saying: "You may be pregnant. Go and give birth to your child." The woman did so, and then returned with the same request. The Messenger excused her: "Go back, for perhaps your child needs feeding."

After the child had been weaned, the woman came again. When someone reproved her while the punishment was being carried out, the Prophet frowned at him and said: "By God, this woman repented of her sin so much that if her repentance were shared out among all the people of Madina, it would be enough to cover them with forgiveness also."[34]

Prophet Muhammad established such a magnificent system and formed such an excellent community that not even a Plato, a Thomas Moore, a Campanella, or any other utopian has been able to imagine its equal. Among thousands of other examples, the following illustrates this fact:

Abu Hurayra, one of the poorest Companions, came to the Messenger. He had not eaten anything for some days. Abu Talha (an Ansari) took him home to feed him. But there was no food in his house except some soup that his wife had made for the children. She asked her husband what she should do, and they decided upon the following: They would put their children to bed without feeding them. As the soup was too little to satisfy all of them, only the guest should have it. While they were sitting at the table and getting ready to eat, Abu Talha's wife would knock the candle over, extinguishing it apparently by mistake. In the resulting darkness, they would act as if they were eating, although Abu Hurayra would be the only one eating. This is what they did. Abu Hurayra ate until he was satisfied, and then left, unaware of what had really happened.

The following day, they went to pray the morning prayer in the mosque. At the end of the prayer, the Messenger turned to them and asked: "What did you do last night, that caused this verse to be revealed in praise of you: *They prefer others above themselves, even though poverty be their portion.* (59:9)?"[35]

---

[34] *Muslim*, "Hudud," 22-23.

[35] *Bukhari*, "Tafsir," 6; *Muslim*, "Ashriba," 172.

CHAPTER 2

The Military Dimension

Islam is the religion chosen by God for humanity's individual and collective welfare in this world and the next. It is based on belief in and worship of God, and does not countenance associating any partners with Him, whether in the form of something created, a person, or a concept. True belief and worship requires a deep concern for all animate and inanimate things. The deeper their belief in and submission to God is, the deeper is their concern for all creatures. Belief in God's Unity prevents humanity from enjoying and exercising absolute freedom in dealing with creatures.

Islam is derived from the Arabic root *s-l-m*, which means salvation, peace, and submission. In its religious context, it is the expression of God's Grace flowing in the universe's arteries, the Divine system to which all creatures (except humanity) have submitted willingly. The universe displays perfect order, for everything therein is *muslim*, in the sense that it submits to God's laws. Even people who reject belief in God or worship that which is not God are *muslims*, as far as their bodily existence is concerned. While we journey between being an embryo and a corpse, every bodily tissue and every limb follows the course prescribed for them by God's law.

The fundamental Islamic principle of Divine Unity implies that humanity necessarily must be in harmony with the surrounding world. The vast *muslim* universe displays a coherence and harmony of which our world is a part. Although our world is subject to laws special to itself and to the general "laws of nature," it is also in harmony with other laws governing surrounding phenomena. Human beings, unlike other creatures who tread "the path of nature," have free will. We bear the gift of freedom and the obligation to harmonize our life with nature. This harmony is also the path of our exaltation and progress, the path upon which God created human nature:

> Set your face to the religion, a man of pure faith—God's original nature in which He originated humanity. There is no changing God's creation. That is the right religion, but most of humanity know it not. (30:30)

To harmonize our lives with nature, we first should realize our personal integrity. To do this, we must apply our free will to our energies (e.g., desires, thoughts, and actions) to keep them within the limits established by God. If we do not recognize such limits, we might usurp another's property, seek illicit sexual relations, and indulge in other sins. If we do not recognize such limits with respect to our intellect, we may use it to deceive others. Our powers must be held in check, our intellect used with wisdom, and our desire and anger restrained by lawful behavior and moderation. In addition, we should remember that we are social beings; if we do not restrain ourselves as God demands, wrongdoing, injustice, exploitation, disorder, and revolution will occur in society.

God does not approve of wrongdoing and disorder. Rather, it is His Will that we live in peace and justice. Therefore, those who believe in God and worship Him faithfully are obliged to work for justice in this world. Islam calls this responsibility *jihad*.

Jihad

Jihad has the literal meaning of exerting our best and greatest effort to achieve something. It is not the equivalent of war, for which the Arabic word is *qital*. Jihad has a much wider connotation and embraces every kind of striving in God's cause. A *mujahid* is one who is sincerely devoted to his or her cause; who uses all physical, intellectual, and spiritual resources to serve it; who confront any power that stands in its way; and, when necessary, dies for this cause. Jihad in the way of God is our struggle to win God's good pleasure, to establish His religion's supremacy, and to make His Word prevail.

A related principle, that of enjoining good and forbidding evil (*amr bi al-maʿruf wa nahy ʿan al-munkar*) seeks to convey the message of Islam and establish a model Islamic community. The Qur'an introduces the Islamic community as a model community required to inform humanity of Islam and of how the Prophet lived it: Thus We have made you a community justly balanced, that you might be witnesses for all humanity, and the Messenger may be a witness for you (2:143).

The greater and lesser jihad. There are two aspects of jihad. One is fighting to overcome carnal desires and evil inclinations—the greater jihad. The other is encouraging others to achieve the same objective—the lesser jihad.

The Muslim army was returning to Madina after they had defeated the enemy, when the Messenger of God said to them: "We are returning from the lesser jihad to the greater one." When the Companions asked what the greater jihad was, he explained that it was fighting with the carnal self.[36]

---

[36] Ajluni, *Kashf al-Khafa'*, 1:424.

The aim of either jihad is that the believer be purified of sins and so attain true humanity. The prophets were sent for this purpose. God says in the Qur'an:

> Thus We have sent unto you a Messenger from among you, who recites unto you Our revelations (and makes Our signs known to you), and who purifies you and instructs you in the Book and in the Wisdom, and also instructs you in what you don't know. (2:151)

Human beings are in some sense like raw minerals to be worked upon by Prophets, who purify and refine them by removing the seal from their hearts and ears, by lifting the veils from their eyes. Enlightened by the Prophets' message, people can understand the meaning of the laws of nature, which are signs of God's Existence and Unity, and can penetrate into the subtle reality behind things and events. Only through the guidance of Prophets can we attain the high status expected of us by God.

In addition to teaching the signs, Prophets also instructed their people in the Book and in Wisdom. As the Qur'an was the last Revelation to the Last Prophet, God means the Qur'an when He speaks of the Book, and the Sunna when He speaks of Wisdom. We must therefore follow the Qur'an and the Prophet's Sunna if we desire to be rightly guided.

The Prophet also teaches us what we do not know, and so humanity will continue to learn from the Prophet until the Day of Judgment. We learn from him how to purify ourselves of sin. By following his way, many great saints have attained their distinctions as saints. Among them, 'Ali says that his belief in the pillars of Islam is so firm that even if the veil of the Unseen were lifted, his certainty would not increase.[37]

---

[37] Imam Rabbani, Ahmad Faruq al-Sarhandi, *Maktubat*, 1:157.

'Abd al-Qadir al-Jilani is said to have had insight into the mysteries of the seventh heaven. These and many others, such as Fudayl bin 'Iyaz, Ibrahim bin Adham, and Bishr al-Khafi might well have been endowed with Prophethood, if God had not already set a seal on Prophethood.

The dark clouds of ignorance have been removed from our intellectual horizon through the guidance of Prophet Muhammad, and many more advances will be made in science and technology as a result of the light he brought from God.

Jihad is the legacy of the Prophets, and Prophethood is the mission of elevating men to God's favor by purifying them. Jihad is the name given to this prophetic mission, which has the same meaning as bearing witness to the truth. Just as judges listen to witnesses to settle a case, so those who have performed jihad have borne witness to God's Existence and Unity of God by striving in His way. The Qur'an says: *God bears witness that there is no god but He and so do the angels and the people of learning, maintaining justice. There is no god save He, the All-Mighty, the Wise* (3:18). Those who have performed jihad will also bear witness to the same truth in the heavenly court, where the case of unbelievers will be settled.

Those who bear witness to God Existence and Unity the remotest parts of the world and preach this truth. This was the duty of the Prophets as stated in the Qur'an, and it should be our duty as well:

> ...Messengers who brought good news to humanity and who admonished them, so that they might have no argument against God after their coming. God is the All-Mighty and the All-Wise. God Himself bears witness by what He has revealed to you that it has been revealed with His knowledge; and so do the angels. There is no better witness than God. (4:165-66)

God has sent a Prophet to every people, so that every people can have an idea of Prophethood. As the term used to describe the activity of Prophethood, jihad is deeply engraved on the heart of every believer so that he or she feels a profound responsibility for preaching the truth in order to guide others to the Straight Path.

The lesser jihad, usually taken to mean fighting in God's cause, does not refer only to military struggle. The term is comprehensive, for it includes every action done for God's sake. Whether speaking or keeping silent, smiling or making a sour face, joining or leaving a meeting, every action taken to ameliorate the lot of humanity, whether by individuals or communities, is included in its meaning.

While the lesser jihad depends on mobilizing all material facilities and is performed in the outer world, the greater jihad means a person's fighting against his or her carnal soul. These two forms of jihad cannot be separated from each other.

The Messenger of God has taught us how to perform both forms of the jihad. He has established the principles of preaching the truth, which have application until the Day of Judgment. When we scrutinize the way he acted, we shall see that he was very systematic. This is actually another proof of his Prophethood and a wonderful example of following the way of God in behavior.

The believers kept their belief vigorous and active by means of jihad. Just as a tree keeps its leaves as long as it yields fruits, so believers can preserve their vigor as long as they perform jihad. Whenever you encounter a hopeless pessimist, you soon realize that he or she is one who has abandoned jihad. Such people have been deprived of the spirit, and are sunk in pessimism because they have abandoned preaching the truth. Whoever performs jihad unceasingly does not lose his or her enthusiasm and always tries to increase the scope of his or her activities. Every good deed results in a new one, so that believers never become deprived of a good: *As for those who strive for us We surely guide them to our path. God is with the good* (29:69).

There are as many paths leading to the Straight Path as the number of breaths drawn in creation. Whoever strives for His cause is guided, by God, to one of these paths and is save from going astray. Whoever is guided to His Straight Path by God lives a balanced life. They neither exceed the limits in their human needs and activities or in their worship and other religious observances. Such balance is the sign of true guidance.

All sacrifices made in fighting oppressive unbelievers, no matter how great, only constitute the lesser jihad of striving to discharge religious obligations as perfectly as possible. The greater jihad is much harder to accomplish, since it requires us to fight against our own destructive drives and impulses, such as arrogance, vindictiveness, jealousy, selfishness, self-conceit, and the carnal desires.

Although the person who abandons the lesser jihad is liable to spiritual deterioration, he or she may recover. Everything in the universe praises and glorifies God with each breath and is, accordingly, a sign of God's Existence and Unity. A person may be guided to the Straight Path through one of these signs. For this reason, it is said that there are as many paths leading to the Straight Path of God as the breaths of all His creatures. A person returning from the lesser jihad is vulnerable to worldly weaknesses. Pride, love of comfort and ease may captivate that person. Thus the Prophet warned us through his Companions by saying, while returning to Madina after a victory: "We are returning from the lesser jihad to the greater."

The Companions were fearless on the battlefields, and as sincere and humble as dervishes in worshipping God. Those victorious warriors used to spend most of their nights praying to God. Once, when night fell during battle, two of them took turns in standing guard. One rested while the other prayed. Having become aware of the situation, the enemy shot a shower of arrows at him. He was hit and bled profusely, but did not abandon his prayer. When he finished his devotions, he woke his friend, who asked him in amazement why he had not done so sooner. He replied: "I was reciting *Surat al-Kahf*, and I did not wish the deep pleasure I found in this prayer to be interrupted."[38]

The Companions went into a trance-like state of ecstasy when in prayer, and would recite the Qur'an as if it were being revealed directly to them. Thus, they did not feel the pain caused by arrows which penetrated their bodies. Jihad, in its lesser and greater aspects, found complete expression in them.

The Prophet combined these two aspects of jihad in the most perfect way in his own person. He displayed monumental courage on the battlefields. 'Ali, one of the most courageous figures of Islam, confesses that the Companions took shelter behind the Prophet at the most critical moments of fighting. To give an example, when the Muslim army experienced a reverse and began to scatter in the first phase of the Battle of Hunayn, the Prophet urged his horse toward the enemy lines and shouted to his retreating soldiers: "I am a Prophet, I do not lie! I am the grandson of 'Abd al-Muttalib, I do not lie!"[39]

---

[38] Ibn Hanbal, *Musnad*, 3:344; 359.

[39] *Bukhari*, "Jihad," 52, 61, 67.

Jihad's stages and main principles. The first Revelation to the Messenger was the command: *Read!* This command, coming at a time when there was nothing readily available to read, meant that believers should use their intellectual and spiritual faculties to discern God's acts in the universe and His laws related to its creation and operation. Through such discernment, believers seek to purify themselves and their minds of all ignorance-based superstitions and to acquire true knowledge through observation and contemplation.

We are not composed only of our minds. God has endowed us with many faculties, each of which needs satisfaction. So while feeding our minds with the Divine signs in the universe, we seek to cleanse our hearts of sin. We live a balanced life in awareness of Divine supervision, and continuously seek His forgiveness. In this way, we eventually conquer our desire for forbidden things and, through prayer, ask God to enable us to do good deeds.

Thus *Read!* signifies action. For the Messenger, who already was absolutely pure in spirit and devoid of superstition, it meant that it was time to start his mission as a Messenger of God. He was to recite the Revelation in public and instruct people about His signs. By doing this, he would purify their minds of superstitions carried over from the Age of Ignorance, and their hearts of sin. He would enlighten them, intellectually and spiritually, by instructing them in the Revealed Book of God (the Qur'an) and His Created Book (the universe):

> We have sent among you, of yourselves, a Messenger who recites Our signs to you, purifies you, and instructs you in the Book and in the Wisdom, and also instructs you in what you don't know (2:151).

After he received this first revelation, the Messenger returned home in great agitation. He was sleeping wrapped in a cloak, enwrapped by his people's suffering and this heavy responsibility, when God commanded him:

> O enwrapped one, keep vigil the night long, save a little (a half of it, or diminish or add a little), and chant the Qur'an in measure, for We shall charge you with a weighty word. (73:1-5)

The short period between the first revelation and the spreading of Islam, marked by such verses as those mentioned above, was a preliminary stage for the Messenger. He had to prepare himself to convey the Qur'an by keeping long night vigils and reciting the Qur'an in measure.[40]

In addition to conveying the Message, jihad, as discussed above, entails the believers' struggles with their carnal selves to build a genuine spiritual character, one overflowing with belief and inflamed with love. These two dimensions of jihad continue until the believer dies (the individual sphere) and until the Last Day (the collective sphere). Therefore, soon after this verse was revealed, the Messenger received the following revelation:

> O enshrouded one, arise and warn! Magnify your Master, purify your robes, and flee defilement! Do not show favor, seeking worldly gain! For the sake of your Master, be patient! (74:1-7)

These revelations ordered the Prophet to begin preaching Islam. He started with his family members and nearest relatives and, after *Warn your tribe of nearest kindred* (26:214) was revealed, spread this call throughout his tribe. His subsequent public preaching was met with derision, threats, torture, enticing bribes if he would stop, and boycott.

---

[40] As is known, night vigils are times when impression is more keen and recitation more penetrating.

In Makka, the Messenger never resorted to or allowed retaliation. Islam came not to spread trouble or cause dissention, but, in the words of Amir ibn Rabi', to bring people out of the darkness of unbelief into the light of belief, to free them from serving that which is not God so that they can serve the One True God, and to elevate them from the pits of the Earth to the heights of Heaven.[41]

As Islam literally means "peace, salvation, and submission," it obviously came to establish peace. This is established first in our inner worlds, so that we are at peace with God and natural environment, and then throughout the world and the universe. Peace and order are fundamental in Islam, which seeks to spread in a peaceful personal and collective atmosphere. It refrains from resorting to force as much as possible, never approves of injustice, and forbids bloodshed:

> Whoever kills someone, other than in retaliation for murder or corruption on the Earth, in effect has killed humanity; whoever saves a life in effect has saved humanity (5:32).

Coming to eradicate injustice and corruption, and to "unite" the Earth with the Heavens in peace and harmony, Islam calls people with wisdom and fair exhortation. It does not resort to force until the defenders of their corrupt order, which is rooted in injustice, oppression, self-interest, exploitation, and usurpation of others' rights, seek to prevent its preaching in peaceful ways and to suppress it. Thus, force is allowed in the following cases:

• If unbelievers, polytheists, or those who cause trouble and corruption actively resist the preaching of Islam and pre-

---

[41] The Muslim envoy to the Persian commander during the war of Qadisiya. This took place in 637 CE, during 'Umar's caliphate.

vent others from listening to its message. As Islam is a Divine religion seeking to secure human well-being and happiness in both worlds, it has the right to present itself. If this is not allowed, theoretically, its opponents are given three alternatives: accept Islam, allow its preaching in peaceful ways, or admit its rule. If they reject these alternatives, force is allowed.

However, there is an important point to mention. In order to use force, there must be an Islamic state. It was allowed only after the Prophet emigrated to Madina and established an independent state, for the Muslims had been wronged. The verses revealed to give this permission explain the Islamic view of just war:

> (Fighting is) permitted to those who are fought against, because they have been wronged. God is able to give them victory. Those who have been driven from their homes unjustly only because they said: "Our Master is God." For had it not been for God's repelling some people by means of others, cloisters and churches and synagogues and mosques, wherein the Name of God is much mentioned, would have been pulled down. God helps one who helps Him [His religion]. God is All-Strong, All-Mighty. Those who, if We give them power in the land, establish worship and pay zakat and enjoin the good and forbid the evil. And God's is the sequel of events. (22:39-41)

It is clear from these verses and from history that Islam resorts to force only to defend itself and establish freedom of belief. Under Muslim rule, Christians, Jews, Zoroastrians, Hindus, and adherents of other religions are free to practice their religion. Even many Western historians and writers have agreed that Christians and Jews experienced the most prosperous and happiest period of their history under Muslim rule.

- Islam, being the true religion revealed by God, never approves of injustice. As declared in: *We have written (decreed) in the Psalms after the Torah (and remind once more in the Qur'an) that My righteous servants will inherit the Earth* (21:105), God's righteous servants must submit the Earth to His rule, which depends on absolute justice and worship of the One God. They also are obliged to strive until persecution, as well as any worship of and obedience to false deities and unjust tyrants, is ended. Thus Muslims are to fight for the feeble and oppressed:

> How should you not fight for the cause of God and of the feeble and oppressed men and women and children, who cry: "Our Master! Bring us out of this town whose people are oppressors! Give us from Your presence some protecting friend! Give us from Your presence some defender!" (4:75)

Some rules. As believers cannot transgress God's limits, they must observe His rules related to fighting. Some are deduced direct from the Qur'an and Sunna, and are as follows:

- A believer is *one from whom God has bought his or her life and wealth in exchange for Paradise* (9:111). They are dedicated solely to His cause and seek only His good pleasure. Therefore, whoever fights for other causes (e.g., fame, wealth, racial or ideological considerations) is excluded from God's good pleasure.

- *Fight in the way of God against those who fight you, but do not transgress. God does not love transgressors* (2:190). Believers are told not to fight neutral parties, and to reject unscrupulous methods or indiscriminate killing and pillage, which characterize all wars waged by non-Muslims. The excesses alluded to consist of, but are not limited to, fighting women and children, the old and the injured, mutilating enemy corpses, destroying fields and livestock, and other acts of injustice and brutality. Force is to be used *only* when unavoidable, and *only* to the extent absolutely necessary.

• When fighting cannot be avoided, the Qur'an tells believers not to avoid it. Rather, they must prepare themselves, both morally and spiritually, and take precautions. These are:

- Strive for that spiritual stage when 20 Muslims can overcome 200 of the enemy:

> O Prophet! Exhort the believers to fight. Twenty steadfast men shall overcome 200; 100 hundred steadfast men shall overcome 1,000 unbelievers, because unbelievers have no understanding or sound judgment. (8:65)

> When those who will meet their Master exclaim: How often a small company has overcome a mighty host by God's leave! God is with the steadfast. (2:249)

To attain such a rank, Muslims must have an unshakable belief and trust in God and avoid all sins as much as possible. Belief and piety or righteousness are two unbreakable weapons, two sources of inexhaustible power: *Don't faint or grieve, for you shall gain the upper hand if you are true believers* (3:139), and *The sequel is for the righteous people* (7:128).

- In addition to moral strength, believers must equip themselves with the latest weaponry. Force is vital to obtaining the desired result, so believers cannot ignore it. Rather, they must be further advanced in science and technology than unbelievers so that the latter cannot use their superiority for their own selfish benefit. As Islam states that "right is might," believers must be able to prevent unbelievers and oppressors from showing that "might makes right":

> Make ready for them all you can of armed force and
> tethered horses, that thereby you may dismay the
> enemy of God and your enemy, and others beside them
> whom you don't know; God knows them. Whatever
> you spend in the way of God will be repaid to you in
> full, and you will not be wronged. (8:60)

An Islamic state should be powerful enough to deter the attacks of unbelievers and oppressors, as well as their plans to subject weaker people. It should be able to secure peace and justice, and to prevent any other power from causing trouble or corruption. This will be possible when Muslims equip themselves with strong belief and righteousness, and with scientific knowledge and the latest technology. They must combine science and technology with faith and good morals, and then use this force for the good of humanity.

Belief in God calls for serving people. Greater belief means a greater concern for the created's welfare. When Muslims attain this rank, *God will not allow unbelievers to defeat believers* (4:141). Otherwise, what the Prophet predicted will happen: "(The forces of unbelief) will unite to make a concerted attack upon you. They will snatch the morsel out of your mouths and pillage your table."[42]

- When fighting is necessary, Muslims must report for duty, for:

> O you who believe! What ails you that when you are
> told: "Go forth in the way of God," you sink down

---

[42] *Abu Dawud*, "Malahim," 5; Ibn Hanbal, 5:278.

heavily to the ground? Are you so content with the life of the world, rather than the world to come? Yet the enjoyment of the life of the world, compared with the world to come, is a little thing. If you don't go forth, He will afflict you with a painful doom. He will replace you with another people; and you will not hurt Him. God is powerful over everything. (9:38-39)

God loves those who battle for His cause in ranks, as if they were a solid structure. (61:4)

O you who believe! Shall I show you something that will save you from a painful doom? You should believe in God and His Messenger, and strive for the cause of God with your wealth and your lives. That is better for you, if you only knew. He will forgive your sins and admit you into Gardens underneath which rivers flow, and to dwelling places goodly in Gardens of Eden. That is the mighty triumph; and other things you love, help from God, and a nigh victory. Give good tidings to believers. (61:10-13)

- A community is structured and functions like a body, for it demands a "head" having "intellect." Therefore, obedience to the head is vital for communal prosperity. When the Messenger was raised in Arabia, people resembled a broken rosary's scattered beads and were unaware of the need for obedience and the benefits of collective life. The Messenger inculcated in them the feeling of obedience to God, His Messenger, and their superiors, and used Islam as an unbreakable rope to unite them:

O you who believe! Obey God, the Messenger, and those of you who are in authority. If you have a dispute concerning anything, refer it to God and the Messenger if you believe in God and the Last Day. That is better and more seemly in the end. (4:59)

O you who believe! When you meet an army, hold firm and remember and mention God much, so that you

may be successful. Obey God and His Messenger, and
don't dispute with each other lest you falter and your
strength departs. Be steadfast, and God is with the
steadfast. (8:45-46)

The Companions' consciousness of obedience made
many previously impossible things possible. For example, when he appointed the 18-year-old son of his emancipated (black) slave as commander of an army containing many elders, among them Abu Bakr, 'Umar, and
'Uthman, no Companion objected.[43] In another case,
during a military expedition the commander ordered his
soldiers to throw themselves into a fire. Even though
this was not an Islamic order, some tried to obey it.
However, others prevented them from committing suicide and persuaded them to ask the Messenger whether
they had to obey such un-Islamic orders.[44] Although it is
unlawful to obey sinful orders, obedience to law is vital-
ly important to a community's collective life, particularly if it wants to win a war.

- Believers must remain steadfast and are forbidden to
  flee the battlefield:

> O you who believe! When you meet unbelievers in
> battle, don't turn your backs to them. Whoever does
> so on that day, unless maneuvering for battle or
> intending to join a company, has incurred God's
> wrath, and his habitation will be Hell—an evil home-
> coming! (8:15-16)

Fleeing the battlefield is one of the seven major sins,
for it causes disorder in the ranks and demoralizes the
others. Their belief in God and the Hereafter cannot be

---

[43] *Muslim*, "Fada'il al-Sahaba," 63; Ibn Kathir, *Al-Bidaya*, 6:336.

[44] *Muslim*, "'Imara," 39; *Ibn Maja*, "Jihad," 40.

firm, for their actions show they prefer this life to the Hereafter. Believers may leave the battlefield only to maneuver, as a tactic, or to join another company.

In the Battle of Yarmuk (636), 20,000 valiant Muslims fought and defeated 200,000 Byzantines.[45] Qabbas ibn Ashyam, one of the heroes, realized that he had lost a leg (around noon) only when he dismounted from his horse hours later. His grandson later introduced himself to Caliph 'Umar ibn 'Abd al-'Aziz, saying: "O Caliph, I am the grandson of the one who lost his leg at noon but became aware of it only toward evening."

During the Battle of Mu'ta (629), the Muslim army consisted of 3,000 soldiers; the opposing Byzantine forces had about 100,000 soldiers. The Muslims fought heroically, and both armies retreated at the same time. Despite this, the Muslims thought that they had fled the battlefield and so were ashamed to meet the Messenger. However, he welcomed and consoled them: "You did not flee; you retreated to join me. You will collect strength and fight with them again."[46] It happened just as he said, for just before his death the Muslim army raided southern Syria; 2 years later, the Muslims dealt the Byzantines a deadly blow at Yarmuk.

Early military expeditions

With the arrival of the Messenger in Madina, the struggle between Islam and unbelief entered a new phase. In Makka the Prophet had devoted himself almost exclusively to

---

[45] This battle took place during Abu Bakr's caliphate. (Tr.)

[46] *Abu Dawud*, "Jihad," 96; *Tirmidhi*, "Jihad," 36; Ibn Hanbal, 2:70, 86.

expounding Islam's basic principles and to his Companions' moral and spiritual training. After the Emigration (622), however, new Muslims belonging to different tribes and regions began to gather in Madina. Although the Muslims held only a tiny piece of land, the Quraysh allied itself with as many tribes as possible to exterminate them.

In these circumstances, the small Muslim community's success, not to mention its very survival, depended upon several factors. In order of importance, there were:

- Propagate Islam efficiently and effectively to convert others.

- Demonstrate the unbelievers' falsehoods so convincingly that nobody could doubt Islam's truth.

- Face exile, pervasive hostility and opposition, economic hardship, hunger, insecurity, and danger with patience and fortitude.

- Regain their wealth and goods usurped by the Makkans after they emigrated.

- Resist, with courage and weapons, any assault launched to frustrate their movement. While resisting, they should ignore the enemy's numerical or material superiority.

In addition to threats from Makka and its allies, the young community had to contend with Madina's three Jewish tribes, which controlled its economic life. Although they had been waiting for a Prophet, they opposed the Messenger because he was not Jewish. One of the first things the Messenger did in Madina was to sign a pact with the Jews.[47] Despite this, the

---

[47] Such modern historians as Muhammad Hamidullah tend to regard as the first constitution in Islamic history.

Jews continued to harbor considerable ill-will toward the Messenger and plot against him and Islam. For example, the skilled Jewish poet Ka'b ibn Ashraf composed poems satirizing the Messenger and instigating his enemies.

In Madina, another hostile element began to emerge: hypocrisy. The Hypocrites can be divided into four broad groups, as follows:

• Those who had no faith in Islam but entered the Muslim community to cause trouble within its ranks.

• Those who understood political realities and so sought some advantage by seeming to convert. However, they maintained contacts with anti-Islamic forces in the hope that they could benefit from contacts with both sides and thus not be harmed.

• Those who had not made up their minds yet, but seemed to have converted because those around them were doing so.

• Those who accepted Islam as the true religion but found it difficult to abandon their inherited way of life, superstitions, and customs, as well as to exercise the self-discipline required by Islam.

Military expeditions. In such severe circumstances, the Messenger decided to dispatch military expeditions into the desert's heart. He had several goals in mind, some of which were as follows:

• Unbelievers tried *to extinguish the Light of God with their mouth, but, although they were averse, God willed to perfect His Light* (61:8). The Messenger wanted to prove that unbelievers could not exterminate Islam, and to show that Islam could not be ignored.

- Makka enjoyed a central position in Arabia. As the peninsula's most formidable power, all other tribes felt some sort of adherence to it. By sending military expeditions to neighboring areas, the Messenger wanted to display Islam's power and break the Quraysh's dominance. Throughout history, the concept of "might is right" has usually been a norm, for "right" is often too weak to rule. In Arabia, the Quraysh had might and wealth, and so neighboring tribes obeyed them. Islam came to make right prevail, and so the Messenger had to break Makka's grip.

- His Mission was not restricted to a fixed period or nation, for he was sent as a mercy for all the worlds. Thus he was charged with conveying Islam as far as possible. To succeed, he had to know what was going on in the peninsula. These expeditions served as vanguards providing him with the information he needed to pave the way for the preaching of Islam.

- One of the most effective ways to crush your enemies is to drive them to unpremeditated, premature actions, for this allows you to retain the initiative. The Messenger surely was informed of the Quraysh's contacts with 'Abd Allah ibn Ubayy ibn Salul, leader of Madina's Hypocrites. He also was alert to their possible attacks on Madina. After a Qurayshi military force entered Madina's suburbs and the returned to Makka with its plunder, the Messenger dispatched military expeditions to encourage the Quraysh to act before thinking. He then could thwart their plots.

- The Quraysh lived on trade with the international markets in Syria and Yemen, and so had to secure their trade routes. But now that the Muslims were in Madina, these routes could be threatened. While strengthening his position, the Prophet also was dispatching military expeditions to paralyze the Quraysh's hopes and plans of defeating him.

- Islam's commandments seek to guarantee security of life and property, chastity and belief, as well as physical, mental, and spiritual health. Given this, murder and theft, robbery and plundering, usurpation and interest (or usury), gambling, alcohol, illicit sexual relations, anarchy, and the propagation of atheism are forbidden.

The Arabic word for belief, *iman*, means giving security. Thus a *mu'min* (believer) never cheats, and all are safe from a believer's tongue and hand. Believers do not lie, break their promise, or betray a trust. They do not earn their livelihood through stealing, usurpation, and interest-based transactions. In addition, they seek to harm no one, for they are convinced that those who kill even one person are like those who kill humanity.

When the Messenger was raised as a Prophet, Arabia had no security of life or property, chastity, health, or belief. One of his tasks, therefore, was to establish absolute security in every aspect of life. Once he said to Adiy ibn Khatam: "A day will come when a woman will travel, riding in a litter, from Hira to Makka and fear nothing except God and wolves."[48] By dispatching military expeditions, the Messenger sought to establish security therein and show everyone that only Islam would bring them security.

---

[48] *Bukhari*, "Manaqib," 25.

Expeditions. The first post-Emigration military expedition, led by Hamza, was sent toward Sif al-Bahr. It arrived
just as a Qurayshi trade caravan was returning from
Damascus. The Quraysh had usurped all the Emigrants' possessions and traded them in Damascus. The Messenger used
this situation to display Muslim power and directly threaten
Quraysh's economic well-being. No clash took place in this
first confrontation, but the desert tribes witnessing the incident were inclined to acknowledge another source of power
in the peninsula.

This expedition was followed by another one commanded by 'Ubayda ibn Harith. With the same purpose in mind,
'Ubayda went as far as Rabigh, a valley on the way to
Makka. The 60 Muslim cavalrymen encountered a Qurayshi
force of 200 armed men. An exchange of arrows took place
and, fearing defeat, the Makkan force eventually withdrew
toward Makka.[49]

Military expeditions, some led by the Messenger, now
followed one another. In two of the expeditions he commanded, the Messenger went to Abwa and Buwat, respectively, with the intention of threatening Qurayshi trade caravans and intimidating the Quraysh.[50] In Abwa, he concluded a treaty with the Banu Damra tribe: neither side would
fight the other, and Banu Damra would not aid the Muslims'
enemies.

Shortly before the Battle of Badr (624), the Messenger
sent an expedition of about 10 people, commanded by 'Abd
Allah ibn Jahsh, to Nakhla, located a few miles from Makka
on the way to Ta'if. He told them to follow the Quraysh's

---

[49] Ibn Hisham, *Sira*, 2:241; Ibn Sa'd, *Tabaqat*, 2:7.

[50] Ibn Hisham, 2:241, 248.

movements and gather information about their plans. While they were in Nakhla, a Qurayshi trade caravan coming from Ta'if halted there. Something happened unexpectedly, and the Muslims killed one Makkan and captured the rest (except one) and their belongings. These were taken to Madina.

This event occurred toward the end of Rajab and the beginning of Sha'ban. Therefore, it was uncertain whether the sanctity of Rajab, one of the four holy months, had been violated. The Quraysh, those Jews secretly allied with them, and the Hypocrites made full use of this possible violation in their anti-Muslim propaganda campaign. They claimed that the Muslims shed blood in a sacred month, a time when doing so is prohibited.

Since the incident had taken place without his approval, the Messenger explained to its participants that he had not ordered them to fight. Other Muslims also reproached them. However, a Revelation consoled them on account of their pure intention with hope for God's mercy:

> They question you concerning the holy month, and fighting in it. Say: "Fighting in it is a heinous thing, but to bar from God's way, and unbelief in Him, denying entry into the Holy Mosque, expelling its people from it are more heinous in God's sight. Persecution is more heinous than killing." They will not cease to fight with you till they turn you from your religion, if they are able; and whoever of you turns from their religion and dies unbelieving—their works have failed in this world and the next. Those are the inhabitants of the Fire; therein they shall dwell forever. But the believers, and those who emigrate and struggle in God's way—those have hope of God's Mercy. God is All-Forgiving, All-Compassionate.[51] (2:217-18)[51]

---

[51] Ibn Hisham, 2:252.

The verses answered the objections of the anti-Muslim forces. In short, fighting during the holy months is an evil act. However, those who had subjected the believers to continual and indescribable wrong for 13 years merely because they believed in the One God had no right or justification to raise such an objection. Not only had they driven the Muslims from their homes, they had placed the Holy Mosque beyond their reach, a punishment unknown in the Ka'ba's approximately 2,000-year known history. With such a record, who were they to raise such an outcry over a small incident, especially one that had taken place without the Prophet's approval?

CHAPTER 3

A General Evaluation

About 20 military expeditions preceded the Battle of Badr. Through these activities, the Messenger seized control of the desert and paralyzed Makka's morale. In addition, most of the desert tribes began to acknowledge Islam's power and come to some agreement with the Muslims. Only one expedition resulted in the Muslims actually killing or wounding enemy soldiers. To prove that Islam guaranteed security, they neither plundered caravans nor usurped the bedouins' property.

The Messenger formed an intelligence network to inform him of everything happening in the desert and in Makka. This system was so sophisticated that probably most of his Companions in Madina did not know, for example, that his uncle 'Abbas was left in Makka as an intelligence agent. When the Messenger set out on a military campaign, no one knew his real intention and destination.[52] He used couriers to communicate with his soldiers fighting at the front, and news reached him through a series of relay stations. With this system, his information was always up-to-date.

Only Emigrants participated in these expeditions. First of all, the Quraysh were at war with the Emigrants and did not

---

[52] Ibn Hisham, 4:39-42; Ibn Kathir, *Al-Bidaya*, 4:332-35.

want them to be sheltered in Madina. Besides, it was the Emigrants who had been forced out and made to leave all their possessions behind. As the Helpers had sworn allegiance to the Messenger, they were expected to realize on their own that they also should fight in the way of God.

The military genius of the Messenger showed itself in his choice of military commanders. His uncle Hamza led the first military expedition. Besides his courage and strength, Hamza had sound judgment, good opinions, and a high administrative ability. Until his community adopted his ideas and opinions, the Messenger chose to practice them through his relatives. Since his mission's military dimension was displayed for the first time in Madina, the Messenger put his own relatives on the front line until everyone became used to this. It should be noted, however, that these commanders were capable and eminent generals who were highly qualified for the post. In addition, they were wholly devoted to Islam.

Hamza was martyred at Uhud after killing more than 20 enemy soldiers. 'Ubayda ibn Harith, the Prophet's cousin, eventually died from wounds he received at Badr. Before he died, he asked the Messenger: "O the Messenger, I did not die fighting at the front. Am I considered a martyr?"[53]

The expedition sent to Nakhla was commanded by 'Abd Allah ibn Jahsh, the son of the Prophet's paternal aunt. In the second stage of the Battle of Uhud, he fought heroically. He came across Sa'd ibn Abi Waqqas and told him:

> "Come on and pray, and I'll say amen for your prayer. Then I'll pray and you say amen for mine." Sa'd prayed: "O God, make me encounter one of the strongest enemy soldiers, and let me defeat him." Ibn

---

[53] Hakim, *Mustadrak*, 3:188; Ibn Kathir, 3:334.

Jahsh said *amen* and then prayed: "O God, let me encounter one of the strongest enemy soldiers. After I wound him severely, let him kill me, and cut off my ears and nose and lips so that I shall come to Your Presence bleeding profusely. You will ask me: 'Abd Allah, where are your ears, nose, and lips?' and I'll respond: 'O God, I was ashamed to come to Your Presence with my members with which I had sinned, so I sacrificed them while fighting in the way of Your Beloved One.'"

When the battle ended, 'Abd Allah was found lying with his ears, nose, and lips cut off and his abdomen lanced.[54]

Lastly, by sending a series of military expeditions, the Messenger agitated the Quraysh into an unpremeditated action. On the pretext of recapturing their trade caravan, 1,000 Makkan soldiers left for Badr, some 90 miles toward Madina.

The Battle of Badr

As Muslim power solidified in Madina, the Quraysh began to worry about a possible threat to their trade route to Syria. In a letter addressed to 'Abd Allah ibn Ubayy ibn Salul,[55] the Quraysh threatened to kill all Madinese men and enslave their women unless they expelled the Messenger. The Prophet put a timely end to this, and Ibn Ubayy did not pursue the matter. Next, when Sa'd ibn Mu'adh went to Makka to perform the minor pilgrimage (*'umra*), he was stopped at the Ka'ba's entrance and prevented from performing the cir-

---

[54] Ibn Hajar, *Al-Isaba*, 1:286-7.

[55] He had been on the verge of becoming king of Madina when the Emigration began. Seeing that many people had accepted the Prophet as the new leader of Madina, he eventually converted to Islam. However, his lost kingship continued to gall him inside and caused him to become a leading Hypocrite and thorn in the side of the Muslim community.

cumambulation. The Makkans also sent quite regular invading parties.

Given such incidents, the Muslims had to extend their control over the Syrian trade route to force the Quraysh and other unfriendly tribes to reconsider. It also was time for the Prophet to show the forces arrayed against him that the preaching of Islam could not be stopped or eradicated from its adherents' hearts, and that polytheism and unbelief would surrender to Islam.

At the beginning of 624, a large Qurayshi caravan en route to Makka from Syria, and escorted by no more than 40 security guards, arrived at a place within reach of the Muslims. It contained goods that had been purchased with the Emigrants' property. Naturally Abu Sufyan, the caravan's leader, feared a Muslim attempt to retrieve their stolen property. And so he sent a messenger to Makka asking for help and reinforcements.

This caused an uproar throughout Makka. Leading Qurayshi chiefs decided to fight the Prophet. About 1,000 fighters left Makka, amidst much pomp and show, to crush the Muslims' rising power. They also wanted, as always, to terrorize neighboring tribes to ensure their trade caravans' continued safety.

The Messenger, always informed of developments that could affect his mission, realized that if an effective step were not taken right then, the preaching of Islam might suffer a blow. Had the Quraysh taken the initiative and attacked Madina, the city's small Muslim community might have perished. Even if they only brought their caravan safely to Makka by dint of their military strength, the Muslims' political and military prestige would be undermined. Once this happened, their lives, property, and honor would be jeopardized.

Deciding to use his available resources, the Prophet left Madina. Although he may have wanted a decisive battle with the Quraysh, most Muslims wanted to capture the caravan and retrieve their property. The Prophet assembled the people and told them that the Qurayshi trade caravan was in the north and its invading army was in the south, moving toward Madina. He also informed them that God had promised that they would be able to seize either party.[56] It was for them to choose which target to attack.

Aware of the Prophet's intention, an Emigrant named Miqdad ibn 'Amr replied:

> "O Messenger of God. Proceed as God has command-
> ed you. We are with you wherever you go, even as far
> as Bark al-Ghimad. We shall not say, as the Children
> of Israel said to Moses: 'Go forth, you and your
> Master, and fight. We shall remain here sitting.' We
> rather say: 'Go forth, you and your Master, and fight,
> and we shall fight on your side as long as the eyelid of
> any one of us keeps moving.'"[57]

Until the Battle of Badr, the Messenger had not sought military aid from the Ansar. This was the first time they would prove their commitment to Islam. Without addressing them directly, the Messenger again put the two alternatives before his audience. Realizing what the Messenger was doing, an Ansari named Sa'd ibn Mu'adh, the leader of the Aws tribe, rose and said:

---

[56] *God promised you that one of the two hosts would be yours, and you wished that the one with no power should be yours. But God willed to establish the truth through His words and to annihilate the unbelievers to the last remnant, that He might prove the truth to be true and falsify false-hood, even if the sinful are averse* (8:7-8).

[57] Ibn Sa'd, 3:162.

O Messenger of God. I think your question is directed
to the Ansar. We believe in you, affirm that you are the
Messenger of God, and bear witness to the truth of
your teachings. We took the oath of allegiance to you
that we would hear and obey you. O Messenger of
God, do as you wish! By the One Who has sent you
with the truth, if you were to take us to the sea and
plunge into it, none of us should remain behind. So
take us along to the battlefield with God's blessings.[58]

The decision was made to fight. This was also the decree
of God, as mentioned above.

The Makkan army consisted of 1,000 fighters, including
600 soldiers in coats of mail and 200 cavalrymen, and was
accompanied by singers and dancers. Dancing and drinking
parties were held whenever it halted. The soldiers arrogantly
vaunted their military power and numerical strength to the
tribes and settlements it passed, and boasted of their invincibility.[59] Even worse, they were fighting for no lofty ideal;
rather, they sought to defeat the forces of belief, truth, justice,
and good morals.

The Muslim army was made up of 313 fighters: 86
Emigrants and 227 Ansar. Only two or three Muslims had
horses, for resources were scarce. There were no more than
70 camels, so three or four persons took turns riding each
camel. The Messenger took turns with two others. When
they asked him to ride the camel and exclude them from the
turns, the Messenger answered: "You are not stronger than
me. And as for the reward, I need it just as much as you
do."[60]

---

[58] *Muslim*, "Kitab al-Jihad wa al-Siyar," 30; Waqidi, *Maghazi*, 1:48-49.

[59] Tabari, *Tarikh al-Umam wa al-Muluk*, 2:430.

[60] Ibn Hanbal, 1:411, 418.

The Muslim soldiers were fully devoted to and ready to die for the cause of Islam. To accomplish what He had decreed, God made the Messenger dream that the number of Makkan soldiers was small, just as He made the number of the Muslims appear smaller in the eyes of the Makkans (8:44).

The two armies met at Badr. The Makkans outnumbered the Muslims by three to one and were far better equipped. However, the Muslims were fighting for the most sublime cause: to establish God's religion, based on belief, good morals, and justice. Deeply convinced of Islam's truth and eager to die for it, they were ready for battle.

Being the first to reach the battlefield, they positioned themselves around the wells. They also benefited from the heavy downpour of the previous night, for it provided them with an abundant supply of water that they quickly stored in large containers. The rain also compacted the loose sand in the upper part of the valley in which they pitched their tents. This allowed them to plant their feet firmly and move with less difficulty. In the valley's lower part, however, where the Quraysh army stationed itself, the ground was marshy. In addition to these Divine blessings, God sent a feeling of drowsiness over the Muslims and gave them a feeling of peace and security (8:11).

From their campsite, the Muslim army could see the whole battlefield. It was divided into three parts: one center and two flanks. The central force consisted of the leading Emigrants and Ansar who were foremost in devotion to the Messenger. Mus'ab ibn 'Umayr, a member of one of Makka's richest families who had accepted Islam as a youth, carried the standard of the Messenger. He was so handsome that when he would go out wearing his silk clothes, before his conversion, Makkan girls would stare at him from their windows. After he embraced Islam, however, he followed the Messenger wholeheartedly. He sacrificed whatever he had in the way of God, and was martyred at Uhud, during which he again bore the Prophet's standard. When he lost his right arm, he took the standard in his left hand; when he lost his left arm, he was left with a "head" to protect the Messenger, before whom he was finally martyred.[61]

The flanks were commanded by 'Ali and Sa'd ibn Mu'adh. 'Ali was famous for his courage and deep devotion to the Messenger. He had been only 9 or 10 years old when he told the Messenger: "I will help you," after the Messenger had gathered his kinsmen at the outset of his mission to seek their conversion and support.[62] On the night of the Prophet's Emigration, 'Ali had slept in the Prophet's bed so he could leave Makka in safety.[63] By the time those surrounding the house discovered this ruse, the Messenger had reached Thawr cave. 'Ali was wholly dedicated to the cause of God.

The Messenger took all necessary precautions and made the best possible preparations. He mobilized his resources and chose his best and most qualified men as commanders. He stationed his army at the valley's upper part. He then pitched his tent where he could see the whole battlefield and have his commands conveyed instantaneously. As the final prerequisite, he prayed with great earnestness and humility:

> "O God, here are the Quraysh who in their vainglory seek to deny and cry lies against Your Messenger. O God, support us with the help You promised me. O

---

[61] Ibn Sa'd, 3:120.

[62] Ibn Hanbal, 1:159.

[63] Ibn Hisham, 2:127.

> God, were this small group of Muslims to perish, no
> one in the world would remain to worship You."[64]

After the prayer, he threw a handful of dust at the enemy saying: "May their faces be scorched."[65]

Badr was a severe test for the Muslims. They would either
win or be martyred, for they were ordered not to flee. They
could retreat in orderly fashion under strong enemy pressure,
as a stratagem to seek reinforcements or to regroup with
another party in the rear (8:15), but not because of cowardice
and defeatism. Such a disorderly flight would reveal that they
preferred their lives over Islam, a major and deadly sin.

The battle begins. In the Quraysh's first frontline were
'Utba ibn Rabi'a, his brother Shayba, and his son Walid.
They challenged the Muslims to single combat. Three young
Ansar went forward. "We will not fight Madina's farmers and
shepherds!" 'Utba shouted arrogantly. This was, in fact, what
the Messenger expected. He ordered 'Ali, Hamza, and
'Ubayda ibn Harith forward for single combat. Hamza fought
and killed 'Utba, and 'Ali killed Walid with two blows.
'Ubayda, who was old, fought Shayba and was wounded on
his knee. Hamza and 'Ali rescued him, killed Shayba, and
carried 'Ubayda away.[66]

The Quraysh were shocked by such an unexpected beginning. The Muslims' belief and sincerity won them God's
help. The Quraysh, who had exulted in their power, were
decisively defeated by the ill-equipped Muslims. Seventy
Qurayshis were killed. 'Awf and Mu'awwidh (two young

---

[64] Ibid, 1:621.

[65] Ibid, 1:668; Ibn Hanbal, 1:368.

[66] Ibn Hisham, 2:277.

Ansari brothers) joined with 'Abd Allah ibn Mas'ud to kill
Abu Jahl, who the Messenger called the "Pharaoh of the
Muslim Community."[67] Almost all Qurayshi leaders were
killed: Abu Jahl, Walid ibn Mughira, 'Utba ibn Rabi'a, 'As
ibn Sa'id, Umayyah ibn Khalaf, and Nawfal ibn Khuwaylid.
Prior to the battle, the Messenger had indicated the spots
where they would die, saying: "'Utba will be killed here; Abu
Jahl here, Umayyah ibn Khalaf here," and so on.[68]

Seventy Qurayshis were captured. God allowed the
Muslims to ransom them, and some were released. Those
who were literate were to be released only after teaching
these skills to the unlettered Muslims. This policy had several benefits: captives who had expected execution gladly
paid the ransom; Madina's low literacy rate was raised, making the newly literate Muslims more effective in preaching
Islam and gaining people's respect; literate captives could
learn about Islam and be in close contact with Muslims,
which would bring more people into Islam; and the captives'
families and relatives were so glad to see their presumed-
dead family members that they became much more receptive
to Islam."

The decisive victory made Islam a force to be reckoned
with throughout Arabia, and many hardened hearts were
inclined to accept Islam.

The Battle of Uhud

The victory of Badr alerted the peninsula's hostile forces.
The Muslims were in a state of unease, and endured the wrath
of most neighboring societies.

---

[67] Ibn Hisham, 2:280-7; Ibn Kathir, 3:350.

[68] Abu Dawud, 2:53; Muslim, 5:170.

Madina's Jewish tribes were not eager to honor their agreements with the Messenger after his Emigration. During the Battle of Badr, they favored the Makkan polytheists; afterwards, they openly encouraged the Quraysh and other Arab tribes to unite against the Muslims. They also collaborated with the Hypocrites, who were apparently an integral part of the Muslim body politic.

To sabotage the spread of Islam, they began to fan the flames of old animosities between the Aws and Khazraj, the two tribes of Madinan Muslims. Ka'b ibn Ashraf, chief of Banu Nadir, went to Makka and recited stirring elegies for the Makkans killed at Badr to provoke the Quraysh into renewed hostilities. He also slandered the Muslims and satirized the Messenger in his poems.

The Jewish tribes' violation of their treaty obligations exceeded all reasonable limits. A few months after Badr, a Muslim woman was treated indecently by some Jews of Banu Qaynuqa, the most anti-Muslim Jewish tribe. During the ensuing fight, a Muslim was martyred and a Jew was killed. When the Messenger reproached them for this shameful conduct and reminded them of their treaty obligations, the Jews threatened him: "Don't be misled by your encounter with a people who have no knowledge of warfare. You were lucky. By God, if we fight you, you will know that we are the men of war."

Finally, the Messenger attacked the Banu Qaynuqa, defeated them, and banished them from Madina's outskirts. In addition, upon the order of the Messenger, Muhammad ibn Maslama killed Ka'b ibn Ashraf and ended his trouble-making activities.[69]

---

[69] Ibn Hisham, 3:58.

The reasons for the battle. The Quraysh were still smarting from their defeat at Badr. Their women were mourning their dead warriors almost daily, and encouraging the survivors to revenge themselves. In addition, the Jewish efforts to rouse their feelings of revenge were like pouring oil on flames. Within a year, the Quraysh attacked Madina with an army of 3,000 soldiers, including 700 in coats of mail and 200 cavalrymen.

Informed of the Makkans' march upon Madina, the Messenger consulted with his Companions about how to meet this threat.[70] He had dreamed that he was in his coat of mail with his sword notched, and that some oxen were being

---

[70] An advisory system of government is an indispensable article of the Islamic constitution. Those who are learned, pious, and have sound judgment and expert knowledge, and who enjoy the people's confidence, are to be sought. In turn, they are expected to express their opinions, according to the dictates of their conscience, with precision and integrity. This advisory system is so important that God praises the first, exemplary Muslim community as one whose affair is by counsel among them (42:8).

This importance becomes more explicit when the Prophet's leadership is considered. He never spoke out of caprice and on his own authority, but only spoke what God revealed (53:3-4). Thus, he preferred the majority opinion to his own. But since he had to execute their decision in full submission to and confidence in God, he could not change his decision for several reasons: First, this would cause some to pressure others to accept their opinions; second, leaders who change their decisions according to individual feelings and fancies can lose their authority and reliability; third, any resulting hesitation passes fear, anxiety, and confusion to the followers; fourth if the Messenger had changed his decision and defended the Muslims from within Madina, a defeat would have caused his opponents to criticize him and the leading Companions.

In his every word and deed, the Messenger set an example to be followed. All the above reflections refer to his behavior prior to Uhud and his words: "It does not befit a Prophet to take off his coat of mail after he has put it on."

slaughtered. He interpreted this to mean that they should defend themselves within Madina's boundaries, and that a leading member of his kinsmen, together with some Companions, would be martyred.[71] He also knew that the Makkan army was coming to fight on open ground. Thus, if the Muslims defended themselves within Madina, the Makkan army could not mount a long siege. He stressed once more that Muslims represent peace and security, and that they should resort to force only to eliminate an obstacle to the preaching of Islam or to defend themselves, their faith, or their country.

However, several young people longed for martyrdom. Upset that they had not fought at Badr, they wanted to fight the enemy outside of Madina. The Messenger gave in to this ultimately majority demand. When these young people repented, upon warning from their elders about their insistence, and the elders informed the Messenger of this, the Messenger replied: "It does not befit a Prophet to take off his coat of mail once he has put it on."[72]

Having decided to follow the majority, the Messenger and 1,000 warriors left Madina for Uhud, a volcanic hill only a few miles from its western outskirts. Its main feature was a plain that stretched out before it. When they were only half way there, however, 'Abd Allah ibn Ubayy ibn Salul turned back with his 300 men.[73] This event, coming just before the battle began, caused such perplexity and confusion that the Banu Salama and Banu Haritha tribes also wanted to turn back. Eventually, they were persuaded to remain.

---

[71] Ibid. 3:664-67.

[72] *Bukhari*, "I'tisam," 28; Ibn Hisham, *Sira*, 3:68.

[73] Ibn Hisham, 3:68.

The Messenger advanced with the remaining ill-equipped 700 Muslims. He lined them up at the foot of Mount Uhud so that the mountain was behind them and the Qurayshi army in front of them. The enemy could launch a surprise attack from only one mountain pass. The Messenger posted 50 archers there under the command of 'Abd Allah ibn Jubayr. He told him not to let anyone approach or move from that spot, adding: "Even if you see birds fly off with our flesh, don't move from this place."[74]

Mus'ab ibn 'Umayr was the standard bearer, Zubayr ibn 'Awwam commanded the cavalry, and Hamza commanded the infantry. The army was ready to fight. To encourage his Companions, the Prophet brought forth a sword and asked: "Who would like to have this sword in return for giving its due?" Abu Dujana asked: "What is its due?" "To fight with it until it is broken," the Prophet said. Abu Dujana took it and fought.[75] Sa'd ibn Abi Waqqas and 'Abd Allah ibn Jahsh prayed to God to let them meet the strongest enemy soldiers. Hamza, the Prophet's uncle and "Lion of God," wore an ostrich feather on his chest. The verse revealed to describe the godly persons around previous Prophets pointed also to them:

> Many a Prophet there was, with whom a large number of God-devoted men fought. They fainted not for anything that befell them in the way of God, neither weakened nor abased themselves. God loves the steadfast. Nothing else did they say but: "Our Master, forgive our sins, and that we exceeded in our affair. Make our feet firm, and help us against the unbelievers." God gave them the reward of the world and the good reward of the Hereafter. God loves those who do good. (3:146-48)

---

[74] *Bukhari*, "Jihad," 164; *Abu Dawud*, "Jihad," 6.

[75] *Muslim*, "Fada'il al-Sahaba," 128; Ibn Hanbal, 3:123.

In the first stage, the Muslims defeated the enemy so easily that Abu Dujana, with the sword the Prophet had given him, pushed into the center of the Qurayshi army. There he met Abu Sufyan's (the Qurayshi commander) wife Hind. He tried to kill her but, "in order not to dirty the sword given by the Prophet with a woman's blood," spared her.[76] 'Ali killed Talha ibn 'Abi Talha, the enemy's standard-bearer. All who carried the Qurayshi standard were killed by 'Ali, 'Asim ibn Thabit, or Zubayr ibn 'Awwam. After that, such self-sacrificing heroes of the Muslim army as Hamza, 'Ali, Abu Dujana, Zubayr, and Miqdad ibn 'Amr flung themselves upon the enemy and routed them.

When the enemy began to flee, the Muslims gathered the spoils. The archers on the mountain pass saw this and said to themselves: "God has defeated the enemy, and our brothers are collecting the spoils. Let's join them." 'Abd Allah ibn Jubayr reminded them of the Prophet's order, but they said: "He ordered us to do that without knowing the outcome of the battle." All but a few left their posts and began to collect booty. Khalid ibn Walid, still an unbeliever and commander of the Qurayshi cavalry, seized this opportunity to lead his men around Mount Uhud and attacked the Muslims' flank through the pass. 'Abd Allah ibn Jubayr's depleted forces could not repel them.

The fleeing enemy soldiers came back and joined the attack from the front. Now, the battle turned against the Muslims. Both of these sudden attacks by superior forces caused great confusion among the Muslims. The enemy wanted to seize the Messenger alive or kill him, and so attacked him from all sides with swords, spears, arrows, and stones. Those who defended him fought heroically.

---

[76] Haythami, *Majma' al-Zawa'id*, 6:109.

Hind, having lost her father and brothers at Badr, urged Wahshi, a black slave, to kill Hamza. When the scales turned, Hamza fought like a furious lion. He had killed almost 30 people when Wahshi's lance pierced him just above the thigh. Hind came forward and ordered Hamza's stomach split open. She then mutilated his body and chewed his liver.[77]

Ibn Kami'a martyred Mus'ab ibn 'Umayr, the Muslims' standard-bearer who had been fighting in front of him. Mus'ab resembled the Messenger in build and complexion, and this caused Ibn Kami'a to announce that he had killed the Messenger. Meanwhile, the Messenger had been wounded by a sword and some stones. Falling into a pit and bleeding profusely, he stretched his hands and prayed: "O God, forgive my people, because they do not know (the truth)."[78]

The rumor of the Prophet's martyrdom led many Companions to lose courage. In addition to those like 'Ali, Abu Dujana, Sahl ibn Hunayf, Talha ibn 'Ubaydullah, Anas ibn Nadr, and 'Abd Allah ibn Jahsh, who fought self-sacrificingly, some Muslim women heard the rumor and rushed to the battlefield. Sumayra, of the Banu Dinar tribe, had lost her husband, father, and brother. All she asked about was the Messenger. When she saw him, she said: "All misfortunes mean nothing to me as long as you are alive, O Messenger!"[79]

Umm 'Umara fought before the Messenger so heroically that he asked her: "Who else can endure all that you endure?" That pride of womanhood took this opportunity to ask him to pray for her: "O Messenger of God, pray to God that I may

---

[77] Ibn Sa'd, *Tabaqat*, 3:12; Waqidi, *Maghazi*, 221.

[78] Qadi 'Iyad, *Shifa'*, 1:78-9; Hindi, *Kanz al-'Ummal*, 4:93.

[79] Ibn Hisham, 3:99.

be in your company in Paradise!" The Messenger did so, and she responded: "Whatever happens to me from now on does not matter."[80]

Anas ibn Nadr heard that the Messenger had been martyred. He fought so valiantly that he suffered 80 wounds.[81] They found Sa'd ibn Rabi' dying with 70 wounds on his body. His last words were: "Convey my greetings to the Messenger. I sense the fragrance of Paradise from behind Uhud."[82]

Besides Abu Dujana and Sahl ibn Hunayf, 'Ali stood in front of the Messenger and defended him. Three times the Messenger pointed to some of the enemy who were advancing toward them; each time 'Ali attacked and routed them.[83]

Despite the indescribable resistance of the Muslim warriors around the Messenger, defeat seemed inevitable until Ka'b ibn Malik, seeing the Messenger, shouted: "O Muslims! Good tidings for you! This is the Messenger, here!" The scattered Companions advanced toward him from all sides, rallied around him, and led him to the safety of the mountain.

The reasons for the setback at Uhud. Before explaining the reasons for this setback, it should be pointed out that the Companions, after the Prophets, are superior to everybody else in virtue. They are honored with being the comrades and trainees of Prophet Muhammad, the greatest of creation, the one for whose sake the universe was created and who was sent as a mercy for all the worlds. Therefore, according to

---

[80] Ibn Sa'd, *Tabaqat*, 8:413-15.

[81] Ibn Hanbal, 3:201; Bayhaqi, *Sunan*, 9:44.

[82] Ibn Kathir, *Al-Bidaya*, 4:35-6.

[83] Tabari, *Tarikh*, 3:17; Ibn Athir, *Al-Kamil*, 2:74; Ibn Hisham, *Sira*, 3:100.

the rule "the greater the blessing, the greater the responsibility," they had to be the most obedient to God and His Messenger.

We read, for example, *whoever of the Prophet's wives commits manifest indecency, the punishment for her will be doubled ... you are not like any other women* (33:30, 32). Likewise, even a small sin committed by a Companion deserves severe punishment. They are all included in those "foremost in belief and nearness to God," and their conduct is an example to be followed by later generations. Therefore, they must be pure in belief and intention, sincere in worship and devotion, upright in conduct, and extremely careful in refraining from sin and disobedience.

God raised the community of Muhammad *as the best community to enjoin the good and forbid the evil, and believe in One God* (3:110) and appointed them as *a middle nation so that they may be witnesses to humanity, and the Messenger may be a witness to them* (2:143). In the early years of the Madinan era, the Companions consisted of true believers and Hypocrites. Therefore, God wanted to sift His true witnesses against all humanity, and see who strove hard in His Way and remained steadfast (3:141-42). The Battle of Uhud, therefore, was a decisive test to sift out the sincere and steadfast from the hypocritical and wavering, and served to make the Islamic community more stable and formidable.

After these preliminary notes, we can summarize why the Muslims experienced a setback as follows:

- The Messenger, the commander-in-chief, thought they should stay within Madina. The younger Companions, inexperienced and excited, urged him to march out of the city. This was a mistake, even though for the sake of martyrdom in the way of God, since the Messenger tended to apply different tactics in battles and knew in advance that the Quraysh army was coming to fight in an open field.

• The archers posted to defend the army left their posts. They misinterpreted the Messenger's order not to leave for any reason and went to collect booty.

• The 300 Hypocrites, one-third of the army, deserted half-way and returned to Madina. This undermined the morale of the Banu Salama and Banu Haritha tribes, who were persuaded only with difficulty not to leave. Moreover, a small group of Hypocrites demoralized the Muslims during the battle.

• Several Companions became impatient. They acted, in certain respects, inconsistently with the dictates of piety and were lured by material wealth.

• Some believers thought that as long as the Messenger was with them, and as long as they enjoyed God's support and help, the unbelievers could never beat them. However true this was, the setback taught them that deserving God's help requires, besides belief and devotion, deliberation, strategy, and steadfastness. They also perceived that the world is a field of testing and trial:

> Many ways of life and systems have passed away before you; journey in the land, and see the end of those who did deny (the Messengers). This is an exposition for humanity, and a guidance and an admonition for the God-fearing. Don't faint or grieve, for you shall gain mastery if you are true believers. If a wound has touched you, a like wound already touched the (unbe-lieving) people (at Badr); such days We deal out in turn among humanity, that God may see who are the believ-ers, and that He may take witnesses from among you; God loves not the evil-doers; and that God may prove the believers, and blot out the unbelievers. (3:137-41)

- Those who had not taken part in Badr sincerely prayed to God for martyrdom. They were deeply devoted to Islam and longed to meet God. Some, like 'Abd Allah ibn Jahsh, Anas ibn Nadr, Sa'd ibn Rabi', 'Amr ibn Jamuh, and Abu Sa'd Haysama tasted the pleasure of martyrdom; the martyrdom of the others was delayed. The Qur'an sings the praises of them as follows:

  > Among the believers are men who were true to their covenant with God; some of them have fulfilled their vow by death (in battle), and some are still awaiting, and they have not changed in the least. (33:23)

- Any success or triumph lies with God, Who does whatever He wills and cannot be questioned. Belief in God's Unity means that believers must always ascribe their accomplishments to God and never appropriate anything good for themselves. If the decisive victory of Badr gave some Muslims a sort of self-pride, and if they imputed the victory to their own prudence, wise arrangement, or some material causes, this would have been part of the reason for their setback.

- Among the Qurayshi army were several eminent soldiers and commanders (such as Khalid ibn Walid, Ikrima ibn Abi Jahl, 'Amr ibn al-'As, and Ibn Hisham) who were destined by God to be great servants of Islam in the future. They were the ones most esteemed and respected among the people. For the sake of their future service, God may not have willed to hurt their feelings of honor completely. So, as expressed by Bediuzzaman Said Nursi, the Companions of the future defeated the Companions of the present.[84]

---

[84] Said Nursi, *Lemalar* (Istanbul: 28).

• The following verses explain the reasons for that setback together with its aftermath, and the lessons to be taken from it:

Did you suppose you should enter Paradise without God displaying which of you have struggled and who are patient? (3:142)

Muhammad is naught but a Messenger; Messengers have passed away before him. Will you, if he should die or is slain, turn back on your heels? Whoever should turn back on his heels will not harm God in any way; and God will recompense the thankful. It is not given to any soul to die save by the leave of God, at an appointed time. Whoso desires the reward of this world, We will give him of this; and whoso desires the reward of the other world, We will give him of that; and We will recompense the thankful. (3:144-45)

God fulfilled His pledge to you when by His leave you blasted them, until you lost heart, and quarreled about the matter, and disobeyed, after He had shown you that you longed for. Some of you sought this world and some of you sought the next. Then He turned you from them, that He might try you; and He has pardoned you. God is bounteous to the believers. When you were going up, not twisting about for anyone, and the Messenger was calling you in your rear; so He rewarded you with grief after grief that you might not sorrow for what escaped you neither for what smote you. God is aware of the things you do. (3:152-35)

Those of you who turned away on the day two hosts encountered—Satan made them slip because of some of their lapses; but God has pardoned them. God is All-Forgiving, All-Clement. (3:155)

O believers, be not as the unbelievers who say concerning their brothers, when they journey in the land, or are upon expeditions: "If they had been with us, they would not have died and not been slain"—that God may make that an anguish in their hearts. For God

gives life, and He makes to die; and God sees all that
you do. If you are slain or die in God's way, forgiveness and mercy from God are a better thing than what
they amass; if you die or are slain, it is unto God that
you shall be mustered. (3:156-58)

If God helps you, none can overcome you; if He for-
sakes you, who can help you after Him? Therefore let
the believers put all their trust in God. (3:160)

Why, when an affliction visited you, and you had visited twice over the like of it, did you say: "How is this?"
Say: "This is from your own selves; God is powerful
over everything." And what visited you, the day the two
hosts encountered, was by God's leave, that He might
mark out the believers and that He also might mark out
the Hypocrites, to whom it was said: "Come, fight in
the way of God, or repel!" They said: "If only we knew
how to fight, we would follow you." They that day were
nearer to unbelief than to belief. (3:165-67)

Count not those who were slain in God's way as dead.
They are alive with their Master, by Him provided,
rejoicing in the bounty that God has given them, and
joyful in those who remain behind and have not joined
them yet. No fear shall be on them, neither shall they
sorrow, joyful in blessing and bounty from God, and
that God leaves not to waste the wage of the believers.
(3:169-71)

God will not leave the believers in the state in which
you are, till He shall distinguish the corrupt from the
good, and God will not inform you of the Unseen; but
God chooses out of His Messengers whom He wills.
Believe then in God and His Messengers; if you
believe and avoid disobeying God, there shall be for
you a mighty wage. (3:179)

*The last stage of the Battle of Uhud and the campaign of
Hamra' al-Asad.* After this confusion ended, his Companions
rallied around the Prophet, who was wounded and had faint-
ed. Many Companions also were wounded. They retreated to

mountain's safety. The Qurayshi army began to leave the battlefield, thinking they had revenged themselves for Badr. Seeing that they could not crush the Muslims' resistance, they mounted their camels and, leading their horses, headed for Makka.

The Messenger worried that the Makkans might return and launch another attack on Madina. On the second day of Uhud, therefore, he ordered those who had fought the day before to gather together and pursue the unbelievers. Some of the Banu 'Abd al-Qays, appointed by Abu Sufyan, tried to discourage this line of action by saying: "The people have gathered against you, therefore fear them." But this only increased the faith of the believers, who retorted: *God is sufficient for us; what an excellent Guardian He is!* (3:173).[85]

Most were seriously wounded; some could not stand and had to be carried by their friends.[86] At this highly critical moment, they girded up their loins and prepared to lay down their lives at the Messenger's behest. They accompanied him to Hamra' al-Asad, eight miles from Madina. The Makkan polytheists had halted and were talking about a second attack on Madina. However, when they saw the believers they had supposedly just defeated coming toward them, they could not muster sufficient courage and so continued on to Makka.

The Messenger's prudence and military genius turned a defeat into a victory. The enemy did not have enough courage to confront the Muslims' resolution yet again by marching upon Madina, and so retreated to Makka. God revealed the following verses in praise of the Muslim heroes:

---

[85] Ibn Hisham, 3:120-1; Ibn Kathir, *Al-Bidaya*, 4:43.

[86] Ibn Hisham, 3:101.

Those who answered God and the Messenger after the
wound had smitten them—to all those of them who did
good and behaved in utmost devotion to God, shall be
a mighty wage; those to whom the people said: "The
people have gathered against you, therefore fear them."
But it increased them in faith, and they said: "God is
sufficient for us; what an excellent Guardian He is!" So
they returned with blessing and bounty from God,
untouched by evil. They followed the good pleasure of
God, and God is of bounty abounding. (3:172-74)

Toward the Battle of the Trench. The Jewish Banu Nadir
tribe was originally the sworn ally of the Muslims in Madina.
However, its members secretly intrigued with the Makkan
pagans and the Madinan Hypocrites. They even tried to kill
the Prophet while he was visiting them, breaking the laws of
hospitality and their treaty. The Messenger asked them to
leave their strategic position, about three miles south of
Madina, and they agreed to do so. But when 'Abd Allah ibn
Ubayy, the Hypocrites' chief, promised them help in case of
war, the Banu Nadir demurred.

The Muslim army then besieged them in their fortresses.
The Banu Nadir, seeing that neither the Makkan polytheists
nor the Madinan Hypocrites cared enough to help them, left
the city. They were dismayed, but their lives were spared.
Given 10 days to leave, along with their families and all they
could carry, most of them joined their brethren in Syria and
others in Khaybar.

While returning from Uhud, Abu Sufyan had challenged
the Muslims to a rematch at Badr the following year.[87] But
when the appointed time arrived, his courage failed him. As
a face-saving device, he sent Nu'aym ibn Mas'ud (then an
unbeliever) to Madina to spread the rumor that the Quraysh

---

[87] Ibn Hisham, 3:94; Ibn Sa'd, 2:59.

were making tremendous war preparations and gathering a huge and invincible army. However, when the Prophet reached Badr with an army of 1,500 fighters, there was no enemy to meet him. They stayed there for 8 days, waiting for the threatened encounter. When no sign of the Quraysh army appeared, they returned to Madina. This campaign was called *Badr al-Sughra* (Badr the Minor).

In 627, the Messenger was told that the desert tribes of Anmar and Sa'laba had decided to attack Madina. He went to Zat al-Riqa' with 400 fighters and, hearing that the enemy tribes had fled, returned to Madina.[88] After this, he marched upon the pagan Banu Mustaliq tribe, which had made preparations to fight the Muslims. He attacked and defeated them with 700 warriors.[89] On the way back to Madina, the Hypocrites tried, and failed, to cause dissension among the Emigrants and the Ansar. The verses sent down revealed all their secrets and how polluted their inner world was (63:1-11).

The Battle of the Trench

In 627, a group of the expelled Banu Nadir Jews, including Sallam ibn Abi al-Huqayq, Huyayy ibn Akhtab, and some of the Banu Wa'il, went to Makka. They met with the Quraysh, urged them to continue the fight, and promised their help and support. These Jews then went to Ghatafan and Qays Aylan tribes and, promising them help, encouraged them to fight against the Messenger.[90] These intrigues resulted in a great anti-Muslim confederacy of Makkan polytheists, the desert tribes of central Arabia, the Jews (both already expelled

---

[88] Ibn Hisham, 3:213.

[89] Ibn Kathir, 4:178-79.

[90] Ibn Hisham, 3:225-26; Waqidi, 441-43.

and those still resident) in Madina, and the Hypocrites. The last two constituted a fifth column within Madina.

When the Messenger was informed of this anti-Muslim gathering of confederates through his intelligence service, he consulted his Companions. It was their unanimous view that they should remain in Madina and fight from there. Salman al-Farisi suggested digging a trench around the city. It took 6 days of feverish labor to dig this trench. The Messenger divided the Muslims into groups of ten and told them to compete with each other. It was a hard task, there was not much time, and hunger was rampant. Yet all the Companions worked enthusiastically. In order to not feel the hunger, each fastened a rock around his stomach and recited, while digging:

> We are those people who
> Took the oath of allegiance to Muhammad;
> Therefore we shall fight in the way of God
> As long as we live.
> By God, if God had not enabled us to,
> We would have neither been guided
> Nor given alms, nor performed prayers.
> Send down unto us calmness and tranquility
> And make our feet firm if we confront the enemy![91]

The Messenger, digging alongside them with two rocks fastened around his stomach, answered them with the couplet:

> O God, the real life is the life of the Hereafter
> So, forgive the Helpers and the Emigrants.[92]

While digging the ditch, the Companions unearthed a huge rock that they could not break. Informing the Messenger of this, he began to strike it with his pickaxe. In the light of the

---

[91] *Bukhari*, "Manaqib al-Ansar," 9; "Maghazi," 29; *Muslim*, "Jihad," 123-25.

[92] *Bukhari*, "Manaqib," 9; *Muslim*, "Jihad," 127.

resulting sparks, he predicted: "I have been given the keys to Persia; my community will conquer it." He struck the rock a second time and, in the light of the resulting sparks, declared: "God is the Greatest. I have been given the keys to Byzantium. My community will conquer it."[93]

Madina under threat. The allies advanced against Madina in the hope of destroying the Muslims on an open battlefield. However, when they faced this new strategy, they took the first blow. Numbering around 20,000, they camped near the ditch. The Madinans had no more than 3,000 soldiers. Moreover, the Jewish Banu Qurayza and the Hypocrite fifth columns already had contacted the enemy. As stated in Qur'an 33:12-20, when the Hypocrites first saw the enemy, they were already in a defeatist mood. Not content with disloyalty themselves, they tried to infect others, who made feeble excuses to withdraw. If the enemy could gain entrance, they would betray the city.

The Messenger once again displayed his sagacity and military genius: He kept the soldiers within the city and stationed them so that they could safeguard their homes against possible Banu Qurayza attacks. The most critical moment came when the Banu Qurayza sent a man into Madina to learn the conditions of the Muslim women. However, their hopes were frustrated when this man was killed by Safiyya, the Prophet's aunt.[94]

While the war was continuing with exchanges of arrows and stones, the Messenger engaged in diplomatic attempts to split the Allies. He contacted the Ghatafan's leaders and, offering them peace, urged them to withdraw their people.

---

[93] Ibn Hisham, 3:230; Ibn Kathir, *Al-Bidaya*, 4:116.

[94] Ibn Hisham, 3:239.

Nu'aym ibn Mas'ud, an Ally leader who before the battle had come to Madina to sow discord, already was inclining toward Islam. During the battle, he secretly entered Islam and followed the Messenger's order to stir up the Banu Qurayza. Nu'aym set them against the Quraysh by asserting that the Makkans would abandoned them and so they should withhold their help until the Quraysh gave them hostages. Then he told the Quraysh that the Banu Qurayza would not fulfill their promise and would try to stall by asking for Qurayshi hostages to share their plight in the case of defeat. This stratagem succeeded, and dissension grew among the Allies.[95]

The Messenger, supported by Sal mountain behind the city, had ordered a narrow point to be made in the trench, as he expected that leading Qurayshi horsemen would try to cross there. This is what happened, for some of the most renowned Qurayshi warriors tried to cross for single combat with Muslim fighters. Among them were 'Amr ibn 'Abd Wudd, Ikrima ibn Abi Jahl, Hubayra ibn Abi Wahb, Dirar ibn al-Khattab, and Nawfal ibn 'Abd Allah ibn al-Mughira.

Boasting of his strength and fighting ability, 'Amr dismounted from his horse and faced 'Ali, who was ordered by the Messenger to fight him. 'Amr advanced with his sword drawn. He brought his sword quickly against 'Ali, but it caught in 'Ali's shield. 'Ali struck him with such strength that dust rose around them. Then the words *Allahu akbar* (God is the Greatest) were heard: 'Ali had killed his opponent.[96] He also killed Dirar, Hubayra, and Nawfal.[97] No other Qurayshi horsemen or generals could get across at that spot.

---

[95] Ibid., 3:240-42.

[96] Ibid., 3:235-36.

[97] Ibn Kathir, 4:123.

The siege lasted 27 days. The Muslims suffered greatly from hunger, cold, unending barrages of arrows and stones, attempts and concentrated assaults to cross the trench, and betrayals and intrigues within Madina. The Qur'an describes this situation as follows:

> When they came against you from above and from below, and when your eyes swerved and your hearts reached your throats, while you thought thoughts about God; there it was that the believers were tried, and shaken most mightily. And when the Hypocrites, and those in whose hearts is sickness, said: "God and His Messenger promised us only delusion." And when a party of them said: "O people of Yathrib, there is no abiding here for you, therefore return!" And a party of them were asking leave of the Prophet, saying: "Our houses are exposed"; yet they were not exposed. They desired only to flee. (33:10-13)

After almost 4 weeks, during which the enemy was disheartened by it failure and the believers proved their steadfastness and loyalty, there was a piercing blast of cold wind from the east. The enemy's tents were torn up, their fires were extinguished, and sand and rain beat their faces. Terrified by the portents against them, and already riven by discord, they soon gave up. Hudayfa al-Yamani, sent by the Messenger to spy on the enemy's movements, heard Abu Sufyan shout: "Come on, we're going home!"[98]

The Muslims were victorious by God's help, for hidden forces (the angels) were helping them:

> O believers, remember God's blessing upon you when hosts came against you, and we loosed against them a wind, and hosts you didn't see. God sees the things you do. (33:9)

---

[98] Ibn Hisham, 3:243.

The Battle of the Trench was the last Qurayshi attempt to destroy Islam and the Muslims. Following their withdrawal in defeat and humiliation, the Messenger declared: "From this moment we will march upon them; they will no longer be able to raid us."[99]

After the Allies were routed and returned to their homes, the Messenger focused on to the Banu Qurayza, who had betrayed their agreement with the Messenger and allied themselves with the Quraysh. They also had given asylum to the Banu Nadir's leaders, like Huyay ibn Akhtab, who had been expelled from Madina and continued to conspire against the Muslims.

No sooner had the Messenger returned from this battle than Archangel Gabriel came and said: "I have not taken off my coat of mail, and I am going to the Banu Qurayza."[100] The Messenger ordered his Companions to march upon this Jewish tribe, and had his tent pitched opposite their fortresses. He would have forgiven them if they had asked, but they preferred to resist. The Messenger besieged them for 25 days. At last they asked for surrender terms, agreeing that they should submit to Sa'd ibn Mu'adh's judgment, who decreed the sentence according to the Torah. This was the end of the Banu Qurayza's conspiracies, as well as of the Jewish presence in Madina.[101]

Sa'd ibn Mu'adh, a leader of the Ansar, had been wounded in the Battle of the Trench. He prayed: "O God, if I am able to fight once more beside the Messenger, make me live.

---

[99] Bukhari, "Maghazi," 29; Ibn Hanbal, 4:262.

[100] Bukhari, "Maghazi," 30.

[101] Ibn Hisham, 3:249-51.

Otherwise, I am ready to die." He died a martyr shortly after the Jewish conspiracies ended.[102]

Toward the conquest of Makka

As will be elaborated later, the treaty of Hudaybiya was a clear victory that opened a door to new and greater victories. The Makkan threat ended, and the Messenger sent envoys to neighboring countries to invite them to Islam. He also set out to solve the other problems he faced within Arabia.

Most of the Banu Nadir Jews had resettled in Khaybar. Together with them, the Jews of Khaybar continued to work against Islam in league, at various times, with either the Quraysh or the Banu Ghatafan. The Banu Nadir had been instrumental in forming the 20,000-man anti-Muslim alliance defeated during the Battle of the Trench. Seeking to end this continually hostile Jewish presence so that Arabia could be made secure for the future and free preaching of Islam, the Muslims acted.

The Banu Qurayza's punishment roused the Jews of Khaybar to ally themselves with the Banu Ghatafan and attack Madina.[103] They were making preparations for this when, after the treaty of Hudaybiya, the Messenger marched upon Khaybar. He made as if to attack the Banu Ghatafan, and forced them to shelter in their confines without daring to help the Jews in Khaybar. Then he suddenly turned toward Khaybar. The village's farmers, who had left their homes early with their farming tools, saw the Muslim army approach the city and began running and taking shelter in their formidable citadels.

---

[102] Ibn Hisham, 3:238, 262; Ibn Sa'd, 3:423-24; Tabari, *Tarikh*, 3:49.

[103] Ibn Hisham, 3:226; Diyarbakri, *Khamis*, 1:540.

The Messenger besieged Khaybar for 3 weeks. Toward the end of the siege, he gathered his soldiers and told them: "Tomorrow I will hand the standard to him who loves God and His Messenger and is loved by God and His Messenger. God will enable us to conquer Khaybar through him."[104] On the next day, almost everyone was hoping to receive the standard. However, the Messenger asked for 'Ali. Told that "he has sore eyes," the Messenger sent for him, applied his saliva to 'Ali's sore eyes, and gave him the standard.[105] 'Ali went to the fortress and, after a fierce battle, Khaybar was conquered. Among the prisoners was Safiyya, a noble woman and daughter of Huyay ibn Akhtab, the Banu Nadir's chief. By marrying her, the Messenger established a relationship with the conquered people.

The Battle of Mu'ta. In the peaceful atmosphere brought about by the treaty of Hudaybiya, the Messenger sent letters to neighboring kings inviting them to the fold of Islam. King Shurahbil of Busra, a Christian Arab, killed the envoy (Harith ibn 'Umayr). This was an unforgivable breach of international custom and the prestige of Islam, and could not remain unanswered. The Messenger formed an army of 3,000 men, with Zayd ibn Haritha as commander, and said: "If something happens to Zayd, Ja'far ibn Abi Talib will assume the command. If Ja'far is martyred, 'Abd Allah ibn Rawaha will assume the command. In case something happens to 'Abd Allah, choose one among you as the commander."

When the Muslim army reached Mu'ta, it confronted a 100,000-man Byzantine army. Obviously it would be a fierce battle. Each Muslim would have to fight about 33 of the

---

[104] *Bukhari*, "Maghazi," 38.

[105] Bukhari, 5:77; Muslim, 4:1872.

enemy. In the meantime, the Messenger was in the mosque, relating the fighting to those around him. Zayd took the standard. He thrust himself into the enemy ranks and was martyred. The standard passed to Ja'far ibn Abi Talib. He also rose up to Paradise. 'Abd Allah ibn Rawaha took the standard and was martyred. Now the standard was in the hands of one of the "swords of God,"[106] meaning Khalid ibn Walid, who would, from then on, be called "the Sword of God."[107]

When it was night, Khalid stationed the troops at the rear in the front rank, and changed the wings, positioning those on the right to the left and vice versa. Seeing new troops before them in the morning, the Byzantine army was demoralized. When night fell, the sides parted with each other and retreated. The Muslim army returned to Madina with only 12 losses. Although this was a victory for the Muslims, they were ashamed to meet the Messenger. However, he welcomed and consoled them: "You didn't flee. You retreated to join me, and will go against them later."

The conquest of Makka and its aftermath

In 627, the Messenger had a dream or a vision that he and his Companions would enter the Holy Mosque of Makka in safety, with their heads shaven or trimmed, and without fear. As will be explained later, earlier they had been prevented from entering Makka and so made a treaty with the Quraysh at Hudaybiya. At first, the Muslims did not like the conditions, but the verses revealed after the treaty called it a clear victory.

The 2 years following this event proved the truth of these words. Such leading Qurayshi figures as Khalid ibn Walid and

---

[106] *Bukhari*, "Maghazi," 44.

[107] Ibn Hanbal, 5:299; Tabari, 3:110.

'Amr ibn al-'As became Muslims, and Islam spread across Arabia. Jewish conspiracies were ended, and Islam crossed into other lands through the letters sent to neighboring kings. At the end of this period, the Banu Bakr (a Qurayshi ally) attacked the Banu Khuda'a (the Muslims' ally) and killed some of them. The truce between the Muslims and the Quraysh was now over. No longer able to resist the Muslims, Abu Sufyan came to Madina in the hopes of renewing it. However, the Messenger refused to meet with him.[108]

The Messenger began to prepare for war. As always, he kept the affair quite secret and no one, including his wives and closest friends, knew where the campaign would be. When Abu Bakr asked his daughter 'A'isha (a wife of the Messenger) where the Messenger intended to march, she told him that she did not know.[109] However, an Emigrant named Khatib ibn Abi Balta'a guessed his intention and sent a letter to the Quraysh informing them of the Messenger's preparations. The Messenger, learning of this through Revelation, ordered 'Ali and Zubayr to take the letter from the woman to whom Khatib had entrusted it. They did this successfully.[110]

The Messenger left Madina with 10,000 men. Two years before, they had numbered 1,600 when his attempted minor pilgrimage ('umra) resulted in the treaty of Hudaybiya. The resulting peaceful atmosphere caused many to reconsider and accept Islam.

The Companions did not know the destination until they were ordered to head for Makka. When they approached this

---

[108] Ibn Hisham, 4:31.

[109] Ibid., 4:39.

[110] Ibid., 4:41.

holy city, the Messenger ordered each soldier to light a fire, for the Makkans would light a fire for every tent while traveling in the desert.[111] As a result, they estimated the Muslim army to consist of about 30,000 men. Having no realistic way to resist, they surrendered. Abu Sufyan, who had been invited by the Messenger to see the Muslim army, also advised this.

The Messenger did not desire bloodshed. Dividing his army into six columns, each one entered Makka through a different route. He ordered the commanders to avoid bloodshed unless they were attacked. To realize this goal and conquer Makka peacefully, he announced: "Those who shelter in the Ka'ba are safe, those who shelter in Abu Sufyan's house are safe, and those who stay in their own houses are safe."[112]

Being a Prophet of absolute mercy who came to secure the happiness of humanity both in this world and the next, the Messenger entered Makka, bowing on the back of his mule, as a victorious conqueror. He displayed no self-pride and had no thought of vengeance or retaliation. He proceeded toward the Ka'ba in complete modesty and absolute gratitude to God, who had made him victorious in his sacred mission. Stopping at the Ka'ba, he asked his enemies: "How do you expect me to treat you?" They replied: "You are a noble man, the son of a noble man." The Messenger stated: "This day there will be no reproach on you. God will forgive you; He is the Most Merciful of the Merciful. You can go away."[113]

---

[111] Ibn Kathir, *Al-Bidaya*, 4:330; Ibn Hisham, 6:41-45.

[112] Ibn Kathir, 4:331-32.

[113] Ibn Sa'd, 2:142; Ibn Hisham, 4:55; Tabari, 3:120; Baladhuri, *Futuh al-Buldan,* 1:47.

This marked the end of polytheism in Makka. While he was destroying the idols at the Ka'ba, he recited: *"Say: 'Truth has come and falsehood has disappeared. Indeed falsehood is subject to disappearance'"* (17:81).[114] Almost all Makkans now became Companions.

The Battle of Hunayn

The Arab tribes were waiting to see who would win before accepting Islam, saying: "If Muhammad prevails over his people, he is a Prophet." Consequently, after the Muslims' victory they began to enter Islam in throngs. This shocked the pagans, who organized a great gathering near Ta'if to coordinate their plans of attack.

The Hawazin and the Thaqif, famous for courage and archery, took the lead and prepared a great expedition against Makka. Informed of their movements by 'Abd Allah ibn Hadrad, whom he had sent to them, the Messenger left Makka with 12,000 Muslims who were enthusiastic over the 2,000 new conversions. To protect Makka and consolidate the new Muslims' belief by healing their wounded feelings, the Messenger did not want to fight within Makka.

The battle was joined at Hunayn, a valley between Makka and Ta'if. The new Muslims had more enthusiasm than wisdom, more a spirit of elation than of faith and confidence in the righteousness of their cause. The enemy had the advantage of knowing the ground thoroughly. They laid an ambush in which the Muslims' advance guard was caught or intentionally pushed by the Messenger, who might have planned to draw the enemy in under the guise of retreat. However, the retreat was confused and took place under a shower of enemy arrows.

---

[114] Bukhari, 5:93; Muslim, 3:1408; Ibn Hisham, 4:59; Ibn Sa'd, 2:136.

The Prophet, calm as ever in his faith and wisdom in that hour of danger, spurred his horse forward. His uncle 'Abbas was on his right, and his uncle's son Fadl was on his left. While Abu Sufyan ibn al-Harith was trying to stop him, the Messenger was shouting: "Now war has been kindled. I am the Prophet, that is no lie. I am the descendant of 'Abd al-Muttalib."[115]

'Abbas shouted: "Companions who made the pledge of allegiance under the acacia tree!"[116] From all sides came the response: "*Labbayk*! (at your service!)," and they rallied to the Prophet. The enemy, now in the center of the Muslim army, was surrounded on all sides. The Messenger's courage, wisdom, and steadfastness changed a seeming defeat into a decisive victory. It was by God's help that the Muslims won the day. They completed the victory with an energetic pursuit of the enemy, capturing their camps, flocks and herds, and families, which they had boastfully brought with them in expectation of an easy victory.

The routed enemy took refuge in Ta'if. The Muslims' victory persuaded the desert tribes to accept Islam, and shortly thereafter the rebel tribes and Ta'if also surrendered and entered Islam.

The expedition to Tabuk

The outcome of the Muslim–Byzantine encounter in Mu'ta shocked Arabia and the Middle East, for the Byzantines had not won, even though they had outnumbered the Muslims by thirty-three to one. Ultimately, thousands of people from the semi-independent Arab tribes living in Syria and adjoining

---

[115] *Bukhari*, "Jihad," 52; *Muslim*, "Jihad," 78.

[116] Ibn Kathir, 4:373.

areas converted to Islam. To avenge himself for Mu'ta and prevent the advance of Islam, Heraclius (the Byzantine Emperor) ordered military preparations to invade Arabia.

The Messenger, always aware of developments bearing on his mission, promptly decided to challenge the Byzantines on the battlefield. Any show of Muslim weakness might have revived the dying forces of Arabian polytheism and hostility, which had received a crushing blow at Hunayn. Such a development also could encourage the Hypocrites in and around Madina to cause serious damage to Islam from within. They already were in touch with the Ghassanid Christian prince and with the Byzantine Emperor, and had built a mosque— which the Qur'an calls the Mosque of Dirar (Dissension) (9:107)—near Madina to serve as their operational base.

Realizing the gravity of the situation, the Messenger publicly appealed to the Muslims to prepare for war and, against his usual practice, declared that the Byzantines were his target.

It was mid-summer. The scorching heat was at its peak, the harvest season had just arrived, and there was a shortage of material resources. Moreover, the enemy was one of the two current local superpowers. Despite this, the Companions responded ardently to his call and commenced their war preparations, all contributing much more than their financial means warranted. Huge amounts of money were donated by such wealthy Companions as 'Uthman and 'Abd al-Rahman ibn al-'Awf.[117] Those who could not be included in the Muslim army, due to shortages of riding animals and other necessary supplies, wept so bitterly and lamented their exclu-

---

[117] *Bukhari*, "Tafsir," 18; Ibn Hisham, 4:161; Tabari, *Tarikh*, 3:143; "Tafsir," 10:161.

sion so pathetically that the Messenger was moved. God praised them in Qur'an 9:92. The occasion, in fact, served as a touchstone for distinguishing the sincere from the insincere, the believers from the Hypocrites.

In 631, the Messenger and 30,000 soldiers left Madina and marched to Tabuk, quite close to what was then Byzantine territory in Syria. The Byzantine Emperor, who had begun amassing a huge army, abandoned his plans and withdrew his army, for the Messenger arrived before he was expected and well before Byzantine troop concentrations were completed.[118]

The Messenger stayed in Tabuk for 20 days, and forced several buffer states under Byzantine hegemony to pay the poll tax (*jizya*) and live under his rule. Many Christian tribes embraced Islam willingly.[119] This bloodless victory enabled the Muslims to consolidate their position before launching a prolonged conflict with the Byzantines, and shattered the power of both unbelievers and Hypocrites in Arabia.

A general evaluation of his military achievements

A significant point concerning the Messenger is that he was the most eminent commander in human history. To understand this dimension of his sacred mission, consider these following points:

- No other Prophet carried his mission to decisive victory in all aspects of life. Moses, who most resembles the Messenger, died while his people were still in the desert and unable to conquer Palestine after several decades of

---

[118] Ibn Sa'd, 2:165-68; Tabari, *Tarikh*, 3:100-11.

[119] Ibn Kathir, *Al-Bidaya*, 5:13.

preaching. Jesus' mission sought mainly to infuse a spiritual and moral revival among the Jews, who were drowning in materialism. After his elevation to Heaven, his disciples conveyed his message to Rome, despite severe persecution. Unfortunately, the price to be paid was the degeneration of Jesus' original creed.

When Prophet Muhammad died, he left behind a Muslim Arabia and dedicated Companions ready to convey Islam throughout the world. He achieved this end with a handful of self-sacrificing people who previously had not heard of belief or Scripture, and who had known nothing of civilized social life, world politics, good morals, and self-discipline. He transformed desert tribes engaged in civil wars and unending feuds, and equipped them with belief, sincerity, knowledge, good morals, love of humanity, compassion, and activism. They dedicated themselves to a Divine cause, and the result was an army of light. Rabi' ibn Amir, Muslim envoy to the Persian commander during the War of Qadisiya, said the Prophet

> ...elevates people from the dark pits of worldly life to the high, boundless realm of the spirit; from the humiliation of worshipping false and human-made divinities to the honor and dignity of worshipping One God, the only Creator and Sustainer of the universe; and frees them from the oppression and depression brought about by false religions and human systems to the luminous and peaceful climate of Islam."

- The Messenger never sought a worldly kingdom; he was sent to guide humanity to salvation in both worlds. His goal was to revive people, not to kill them. To achieve this, however, he had to arrange military expeditions and sometimes command armies. He sent out about 80 such expeditions, and actually commanded 28 of them. Fighting took place in almost half of these campaigns, and only

around 1,000 people died: approximately 250 Muslims
were martyred, and 750 non-Muslims were killed. He
established Islam, brought absolute security to Arabia for
the first time, and opened the way to global security at the
cost of only 1,000 lives. This is, as so many of his other
achievements are, unequalled in world history.

- The Messenger was the first to legislate an international
  law. Although the concept was known before Islam, international law was very limited. For example, there were no
  recognized rules concerning prisoners of war. The
  Messenger established a set of rules to bring a "discipline" to fighting. For example, the following is the order
  given by him and all his true successors to departing
  armies, an order obeyed to the letter by Muslims in their
  wars as Muslims:

  > Always keep fear of God in your mind. Remember that
  > you can't afford to do anything without His grace.
  > Don't forget that Islam is a mission of peace and love.
  > Don't destroy fruit trees or fertile fields in your paths.
  > Be just, and spare the feelings of the vanquished.
  > Respect all religious persons who live in hermitages or
  > convents, and spare their edifices. Don't kill civilians,
  > or violate women's chastity and the conquered's
  > honor. Don't harm old people and children, or accept
  > gifts from the civilian population. Don't billet your sol-
  > diers or officers in civilians' homes.[120]

- The Messenger's preliminary precautions left nothing to
  chance. He always acted with great care, insight, and fore-
  thought, and so never met with any setbacks. He had no
  part in the reverse suffered at Uhud. Also, he was extraordinarily successful in getting information from the enemy
  without resorting to force or torture. For example, some

---

[120] Andrew Miller, *Church History*, 285; Bukhari, "Manaqib," 9.

Muslim soldiers who had captured an enemy soldier tried to force military information out of him. The Messenger ordered his release and asked him how many camels his army slaughtered every day. Calculating how many camels are eaten by how many people in a day, he tried to work out how many soldiers were coming toward him.[121]

- The Messenger established a military intelligence service to provide him with all necessary information about the enemy. No news of his own movements, however, was ever leaked. Before setting out to conquer Makka, Khatib ibn Abi Balta'a secretly sent a letter with a woman to his relatives in Makka about the preparations. However, the Prophet was informed of this and sent 'Ali and Zubayr to intercept her, which they did.

Also, the Messenger kept his military preparations and ultimate destination a secret. He tended to march in one direction, and then turn toward his real destination later on. His tactics were characterized by speed, surprise attack, and flexibility. In most of his campaigns, he caught the enemy unprepared and overcame them relatively easily. For example, in the Battle of Khaybar, the Jews learned of his approach only because their farmers were abandoning their fields after seeing him in the early morning. They only had time to shelter in their citadels. When he marched upon Makka, his advance planning was so perfect that the Makkan polytheists surrendered unconditionally.

- In his position as a Prophet with a universal religion from God, he taught it so effectively that his Companions were always ready to sacrifice themselves. This was a main factors lying behind his victories. His Companions placed all

---

[121] Ibn Hisham, 2:269.

of their reliance and confidence in him. Therefore, he inculcated fear in enemies' hearts, as he himself said: "I am supported by God through implanting fear in the hearts of my enemies from a distance of a month's walk."[122]

He used psychology to demoralize his enemies. Poets like Hassan ibn Thabit and 'Abd Allah ibn Rawaha wrote or recited verses to demoralize the enemy. While performing the minor pilgrimage one year after the treaty of Hudaybiya, he ordered his Companions to run around the Ka'ba to demonstrate their strength to the Makkans watching from the neighboring hills. While running, 'Abd Allah ibn Rawaha recited:

> I start with the name of God,
> Apart from Whom there is no other god,
> And Muhammad is the Messenger of God.
> O unbelievers, and sons of unbelievers,
> clear out of his way.

Pleased with his recitation, he said: "His words are more penetrating to the Quraysh than arrows."[123]

- The Messenger introduced new strategies and shattered the unity of allied enemy tribes. During the Battle of the Trench, the Jewish Banu Qurayza broke their treaty with the Muslims at a most critical moment and joined the Qurayshi siege. Left between two hostile camps, he offered peace to the Banu Ghatafan, a Qurayshi ally. This discouraged the Banu Ghatafan from continuing the war. He also engendered disagreement and mutual mistrust between the Quraysh and the Banu Qurayza. During the campaign of Khaybar, he pretended to march upon the

---

[122] Bukhari, "Tayammum," 1, "Salat," 56.

[123] Nasa'i, *Sunan*, 5:212; Ibn Hisham, 4:13; Ibn Sa'd, 2:121.

Banu Ghatafan, allies of the Jews of Khaybar. Thus this tribe remained inactive and did not help the Jews.

- The Messenger did what he had to do, without hesitation or irresolution, at each step of his life. He never retreated or gave up hope during a battle. He stood steadfast during the critical moments of Uhud and Hunayn. He called to his scattering Companions: "Do not scatter! I am Muhammad, the Messenger of God. That is no lie!" When the Jewish tribes in and around Madina refused to honor their agreements, the Messenger marched upon them immediately. He did the same thing against the Banu Qurayza after the Battle of the Trench, without even stopping to take off his coat of mail, and against the Qurayshi army a day after the setback at Uhud. Such incidents are very significant in showing his resolution and invincibility.

- In almost every campaign, the Messenger took the initiative to attack and direct the battle. He did this even in set battles (e.g., Badr, Uhud, and the Trench). His use of surprise strategies and effective tactics defeated the enemy. He also used time and any opportunity most effectively.

- The Messenger usually changed his battle tactics and strategy. For example, during Badr he launched an overall attack after demoralizing the enemy in single combat. In Uhud's first stage, he rendered the enemy cavalry inactive through archers placed in the Aynayn mountain pass. Using such eminent warriors as Hamza, 'Ali, Abu Dujana, and Zubayr, he won the victory in the first stage. As for the Trench, he faced the enemy with a long, deep trench around Madina. Remaining within the city's confines, he forced the enemy to retreat after a 4-week siege.

- The Messenger was never short of necessary reinforcements or logistics, and always kept his lines of communication open. He brought up, along with such extraordinary statesmen as Abu Bakr and 'Umar and people of profound scholarship and spirituality, great soldiers and invincible commanders. His education featured three basic elements:

- Continuous physical training. He urged his Companions to train in archery, wrestling, swimming, and riding horses. Sometimes he arranged and occasionally participated in competitions and footraces. He also stressed the need to preserve one's health and strength.

- Good morals and being well-mannered.

- Devotion to God with unshakable belief, submission, and reliance, and obedience to God, himself, and others in authority.

The Muslim army conveyed peace and security to the lands it conquered. Each soldier was absolutely dedicated to Islam. The only criterion for them to judge between people was belief in God. They did not feel true love for anybody who opposed God and His Messenger, even if they were their parents, children, or siblings (58:22). As a result, sometimes family members faced each other on the battlefield.

Belief and submission made the Muslim soldiers so powerful and fearless that neither the numerical strength of the enemy nor fear of death could prevent them from conveying the Divine Message. 'Abd Allah ibn Hudafa al-Sahmi, captured by the Byzantines, was told by a Christian priest that his life would be spared if he converted. He was given 3 minutes to decide. 'Abd Allah replied: "Thank you, father. You have given me 3 minutes to tell you about Islam."

CHAPTER 4

A Universal Leader

His appointment of competent people

The Messenger appointed promising and competent Muslims to the work they could do best. He felt no need to change any appointment, for the person proved, through personal uprightness and competence, that he or she was the proper choice.

The Makkan period of Islam was inscribed in the Muslim community's memory as a time of unbearable persecution and torture. Abuse was not meted out only to the poor and unprotected Muslims (i.e., 'Ammar, Bilal, and Suhayb), but also to powerful Muslim members of the Qurayshi elite (i.e., Abu Bakr and 'Umar).[124] To protect his followers, the Messenger permitted those who were poor and unprotected to emigrate to Abyssinia. But he kept the powerful ones (i.e., 'Ali, Zubayr, Abu Bakr, 'Umar, and Sa'd ibn Abi Waqqas) in Makka, for Islam needed their support to spread and implant itself in Makka. These powerful Muslims went on to occupy the highest administrative positions of the Muslim state.

Abu Dharr was a poor, blunt, and upright bedouin who never restrained his faith or his feelings. When he heard Muhammad's declaration of Prophethood, he came to

---

[124] Ibn Kathir, *Al-Bidaya*, 3:40-1, 102-3; Ibn Hisham, *Sira*, 1:234.

Makka and converted. The Messenger used to preach Islam secretly in the earliest stage of his Prophethood. Abu Dharr was very pious and austere. However, since public administration requires special skills, the Messenger did not accept his request for an administrative post, saying: "You cannot manage the people's affairs. Don't apply for such jobs, for we don't assign such jobs to those who apply for them."[125]

The Messenger refused Abu Dharr, but implied the caliphates of Abu Bakr, 'Umar, and 'Uthman. Holding the hands of Abu Bakr and 'Umar, he said: "I have four viziers, two in the heavens and two in the world. Those in the heavens are Gabriel and Michael; as for those in the world, they are Abu Bakr and 'Umar."[126] Concerning the caliphate of 'Uthman, he declared: "It will be a trial for him."[127]

He knew his people

The Messenger knew his people more than they knew themselves. Like Abu Dharr, 'Amr ibn 'Abatha was a bedouin. He came to Makka and, meeting the Messenger, asked rudely: "What are you?" The Messenger replied very gently: "A Prophet of God." Such gentleness caused 'Amr to kneel down and declare: "I will follow you from now on, O Messenger." The Messenger did not want 'Amr to stay in Makka, for he would be unable to endure the torments inflicted upon the believers. So he told him: "Return to your tribe, and preach Islam among them. When you hear that I am victorious, come and join us."

---

[125] *Muslim*, "'Imara," 16-17.

[126] Muttaqi al-Hindi, *Kanz al-'Ummal*, 11:563, 13:15.

[127] *Bukhari*, "Fada'il al-Ashab," 5:7; *Muslim*, "Fada'il al-Sahaba," 29.

Years later, 'Amr came to Madina's mosque and asked: "Do you recognize me, O Messenger?" The Messenger, who had an extraordinarily strong and keen memory (another dimension of his Prophethood) answered promptly: "Aren't you the one who came to me in Makka? I sent you back to your tribe and told you to join us when you heard that I was victorious."[128]

I mentioned the case of Julaybib earlier.[129] After this moral lesson, Julaybib became an honest, chaste young man. Upon the Messenger's request, a noble family gave him their daughter in marriage. Shortly afterwards, Julaybib took part in a battle and, after killing 7 enemy soldiers, was martyred. When his corpse was brought to the Messenger, he put his head on Julaybib's knees and said: "O God, this one is of me, and I am of him."[130] He had discovered Julaybib's essential virtue and foreseen his future service for Islam.

---

[128] *Muslim*, "Musafirin," 294; Ibn Hanbal, *Musnad*, 4:112.

[129] His story, which appears in Volume 1, is as follows: One day, Julaybib asked the Messenger for permission to fornicate, since he could not restrain himself. Those who were present reacted in various ways. Some scoffed at him, others pulled his robe, and still others readied themselves to hit him. But the compassionate Prophet drew him near and began talking with him: "Would you let someone do this with your mother?" to which the young man replied: "My mother and father be your ransom, O Messenger, I don't agree with that." The Prophet said: "Naturally, no one agrees that his mother should be a party in such a disgraceful act."

He then continued asking Julaybib the same question, substituting *daughter, wife, sister*, and *aunt* for *mother*. Every time Julaybib replied that he would not agree to such an act. By the end of this conversation, Julaybib had lost all desire to fornicate. The Messenger concluded this "spiritual operation" by placing his hand on Julaybib's chest and praying: "O God, forgive him, purify his heart, and maintain his chastity."

[130] *Muslim*, "Fada'il al-Sahaba," 131.

The conquest of Khaybar allowed the Messenger to demonstrate his unique ability to recognize each Muslim's potential, skills, and shortcomings. When the siege was prolonged, he declared: "Tomorrow I will hand the standard to one who loves God and His Messenger and is loved by them."[131] This was a great honor, and all Companions earnestly hoped for it. He gave it to 'Ali, despite his youth, because of his great military and leadership skills. He took the standard and conquered the formidable stronghold of Khaybar.

Whoever the Messenger gave a job to performed it successfully. For example, he described Khalid ibn Walid as "a sword of God"[132]; Khalid was never defeated. Besides such great soldiers and invincible commanders as Qa'qa'a, Hamza, and Sa'd, the Messenger made 'Usama ibn Zayd commander over a great army containing such leading Muslims as Abu Bakr, 'Umar, 'Uthman, Talha, and Sa'd ibn Abi Waqqas. 'Usama was the approximately 17-year-old son of Zayd, the Messenger's black emancipated slave. His father had commanded the Muslim army at Mu'ta against the Byzantines, and was martyred.

The Messenger was 25 when he married Khadija bint Khuwaylid, a widow 15 years his senior. He did not marry another woman until her death in the tenth year of his Prophethood. All of his subsequent marriages, after the age of 53, were directly related to his mission. One important reason for this was that each wife had a different character and temperament, and so could convey to other Muslim women Islam's rules for women. Each one served as a guide and teacher for womanhood. Even such leading figures in subse-

---

[131] *Bukhari*, "Fada'il al-Ashab," 9; *Muslim*, "Fada'il al-Sahaba," 34.

[132] *Bukhari*, "Fada'il al-Ashab," 25.

quent generations as Masruq, Tawus ibn Kaysan, and 'Ata' ibn Rabah benefited considerably from them. The science of hadith is especially indebted to 'A'isha, who related more than 5,000 Traditions from the Messenger and was a great jurist.

Subsequent events proved how wise and apt were the Messenger's the choices, not least in the matter of marriage.

His wisdom

Leaders gain the love and trust of their people and are followed by them in proportion to their ability to solve their problems. These can be personal or public, or related to individual's private life, or the community's social, economic, and political affairs.

Some leaders resort to force and terror, or sanctions or punishments (i.e., exile, imprisonment, loss of citizenship rights), torture, or spy into private affairs to solve their problems. But such solutions have only short-term benefits. In addition, they create a vicious circle in which the more people struggle to solve problems by such means, the more they entangle themselves in them.

The Messenger solved all problems so skillfully and easily that no one challenged him. Although his people were by nature quarrelsome, ignorant, wild, and rebellious, he delivered a Message to them that was so grave that *If We had sent down this Qur'an onto a mountain, you would have seen it humbled and rent asunder out of fear of God* (59:21). He transformed them into a harmonious community of peace, happiness, knowledge, and good morals. Reflect closely upon the utopias imagined in the West, such as *The Republic* (Plato), *Utopia* (Thomas Moore), and *Civitas Solis* (T. Campanella), and you will see that, in essence, they dreamed of Madina during the time of Prophet Muhammad. Humanity has never witnessed the equal of that society.

In the first volume, we described how he prevented an imminent clan war among the Quraysh while repairing the Ka'ba,[133] and how he prevented a possible disaster after the Battle of Hunayn.[134] In addition, he skillfully solved an impending Emigrant–Ansar conflict while returning from fighting the Banu Mustaliq. When an internal clash nearly broke out when the army halted by a well, the Messenger immediately gave the order to march.

Merging two different communities

The emigration to Madina marks a turning point for Prophet Muhammad and for Islam. Belief, emigration, and holy struggle are three pillars of a single, sacred truth; three spouts of a fountain from which the water of life flows for the soldiers of truth. After drinking, they convey their message without becoming wearied and, when the opposition cannot be overcome, set out for a new land without regard

---

[133] Each clan claimed the honor of reinserting the sacred Black Stone in its place. Requested by the tribe to solve this problem, the future Prophet of Islam spread his mantle on a piece of cloth on the ground and, putting the Black Stone on it, invited the chiefs of the four major clans entrusted with repairing the Ka'ba to each take one corner of the cloth. When they raised the Black Stone to the spot where it was to be inserted, he took it and inserted it firmly in itsposition.

[134] Some Ansar were not happy with the way the Prophet divided the spoils after this battle, which occurred soon after Makka was conquered. The Prophet gave large amounts of booty to the new Makkan Muslims to strengthen their faith. To avoid a communal split, he called the Ansar together and reminded them of what he had bought them, how they had received him, and that he would always be with them. When he asked them if they still wanted the booty, they answered in unison that all they wanted was for him to stay with them.

for home, property, and family. The Prophet's emigration is so significant and sanctified that the virtuous people around him were praised by God as remain known as the Emigrants (Muhajirun). Those who welcomed them so warmly to Madina are known as the Helpers (Ansar). The Islamic calendar begins with this event.

Despite its significance, emigration is a difficult undertaking. When the Muslims resettle in Madina after years of persecution, they were destitute. Moreover, some were extremely poor, and others, who had earned their lives by trade, had no capital. The Muslims of Madina were mostly farmers, and the city's commercial life was controlled by Jews.

Another serious problem was that just before the Messenger's arrival, the Madinans had decided to make 'Abd Allah ibn Ubayy ibn Salul their chief. This plan naturally was abandoned, which made him a bitter enemy of the Messenger and an important foe. The Makkan polytheists still wanted to defeat the Prophet, and worked with him to achieve their goal. He told them: "Don't worry if he spreads Islam here. The main danger is that he might ally with the Christians and Jews against paganism. That is the real threat."

After he settled in Madina, the Messenger helped his people build a mosque. The importance of the mosque for the Muslim community's collective life is unquestionable. They meet there five times a day and, in the Presence of God, their Master, Creator, and Sustainer, increase in belief and submission to Him, the Prophet and Islam, and strengthen their solidarity. Especially in the first centuries of Islam, mosques functioned as places of worship and as centers of learning. The Prophet's Mosque in Madina was, in the time of the

Prophet himself and his immediate political successors, also the center of government.

Immediately after settling in Madina, the Messenger established brotherhood between Muslims, particularly between the Emigrants and the Helpers. They became very close to each other. For example, Sa'd ibn Rabi' took his Emigrant "brother" 'Abd al-Rahman ibn 'Awf home and said: "Brother, you have left everything in Makka. This house, with everything in it, belongs to both of us. You don't have a wife here; I have two. Whichever of them you like, I'll divorce her so that you may marry her." 'Abd al-Rahman answered him in tears: "Brother, may God bless you with your wife! Please show me to the city bazaar so that I may do some business."[135]

This brotherhood was so deep, sincere, and strong that the Helpers shared everything with the Emigrants. This lasted for some time. When the Emigrants had become accustomed to their new environment, they asked the Messenger:

> O Messenger of God. We emigrated here purely for the sake of God. But our Helper brothers are so good to us that we fear we will consume in this world the reward of our good deeds, which we expect to get in the Hereafter. Also, we feel very indebted to them. Please ask them to let us earn our own living.

The Messenger sent for the Helpers and told them of the situation. The Helpers unanimously objected, finding it unbearable to be separated from their brothers. To spare the Emigrants' feeling of indebtedness, the Helpers agreed that the Emigrants would work in their fields and gardens in return for wages until they could build their own houses.[136]

---

[135] *Bukhari*, "Manaqib al-Ansar," 3; Ibn Kathir, 3:279.

[136] *Bukhari*, "Hiba," 35; *Muslim*, "Jihad," 70.

As a second step in solving immediate problems, the Messenger signed a pact with the Jewish community in Madina. This document, which some scholars describe as Madina's first constitution, confederated the Muslims and Jews as two separate, independent communities.[137] Since the Messenger took the initiative in making this pact and acted as the final arbiter in all disputes, Madina came under Muslim control.

To guarantee Muslims' security within this city-state, the Messenger ordered the establishment of a new bazaar. Until then, Madina's economic life had been controlled by the Jewish community. After this, Jewish economic domination began to decline, for they no longer monopolized Madina's commerce.

While the Muslim community was establishing itself and growing in strength, it was forced to respond to internal and external attacks. After their victory of Badr, the Muslims fought the Makkans again at the foot of Mount Uhud. Their easy victory during the battle's first part was followed, unfortunately, by a reverse when the archers' disregarded the Prophet's instructions. Seventy Muslims were martyred, and the Messenger was wounded.

The Muslim army took shelter on the mountain and prepared to fight back. Lacking enough courage for a further attack, the Makkan forces left. Nevertheless, they changed their mind halfway and decided to march upon Madina. Informed of this, the Messenger mobilized his troops. One of his orders was enough, even though they were ill or wounded. His every call was a breath of life for their souls, a breath that could revive old, rotten bones. Busiri says:

---

[137] Ibn Hisham, 2:147.

> Were his value and greatness
> to be demonstrated by miracles,
> The bones that have rotted away
> were revived by calling his name.

The half-crushed army set out to counter the enemy. Almost everyone was wounded, but no one wanted to stay behind. In describing the situation, one Companion said: "Some Companions couldn't walk. They said: 'We want to be present at the front where the Messenger has ordered us to go. Even if we cannot fight, we will stand there with spears in our hands.' They were carried on other people's shoulders or backs." Seeing the Muslim army marching toward them, Abu Sufyan ordered his troops to return to Makka.

In praising those heroes of Islam, the Qur'an says:

> Those to whom the people said: "The people have gathered against you, therefore fear them"; but it increased them in faith, and they said: "God is suffi-cient for us; an excellent Guardian is He." (3:173)[138]

Consultation

The Messenger's wisdom was demonstrated when he consulted his Companions. This practice is so important in Islam that he never reached a decision, especially in public affairs, without it. Sometimes he even held counsel about his personal affairs. To cite only a few examples:

- 'A'isha accompanied the Prophet on the Banu Mustaliq campaign. At one halt, she lost her necklace and set out to find it. She returned to find that the army had left without her, as the camel drivers thought she was in her litter. Safwan, charged with collecting what was lost or left behind caravans, found her and brought her back to the

---

[138] *Bukhari*, "Maghazi," 25; Ibn Sa'd, 2:42-49; Ibn Hisham, 3:99-111, 128.

army. In the ensuing scandal, her fidelity was questioned, mainly by the Hypocrites.

The Messenger knew she was innocent. However, since the Hypocrites used this incident to slander him, he consulted some of his Companions like 'Umar and 'Ali. 'Umar said that 'A'isha was undoubtedly chaste and pure, and that she had been slandered. When asked how he knew, he replied:

> "O The Messenger, once you were praying. You stopped and explained that Archangel Gabriel had come and informed you that there was some dirt in your slippers. If there were some impurity in 'A'isha, God certainly would have informed you."[139]

The Messenger, who once said: "Whoever takes counsel, does not regret it in the end,"[140] always consulted those who could give informed advice on a particular matter.

- He consulted with his Companions before Badr, the first major post-Emigration military encounter, about whether the Muslims should fight the approaching Makkan army. The Muslim forces numbered 305 or 313, while the Makkans numbered around 1,000 men. One spokesman each for the Emigrants and the Helpers stood up and proclaimed their readiness to follow him wherever he might lead them.[141] During his life, all Companions continually promised to follow him in every step he took, and to carry out all of his orders. Despite this, the Messenger consulted with them about almost every community-wide matter so that this practice would become second nature.

---

[139] Halabi, *Insan al-'Uyun*, 2:613.

[140] Haythami, *Majma' al-Zawa'id*, 2:280.

[141] Ibn Sa'd, Tabaqat, 3:162; Muslim, "Jihad," 83 ; Ibn Hisham, 2:266-67.

- During Badr, the Muslim army was positioned somewhere on the battlefield. Hubab ibn Mundhir, who was not a leading Companion, stood up and said:

  > O Messenger, if God has not ordered you to assume this place, let's arrange ourselves around the wells and then seal all but one to deny water to the enemy. Set up your camp at the side of that open well (from which we will take water), and we will encircle you.

The Messenger adopted this view.[142]

- In 627, the Quraysh allied themselves with certain desert tribes and the Jewish Banu Nadir, who had emigrated from Madina to Khaybar. Forewarned of their plans, the Prophet asked for ideas about how to defeat the enemy offensive. Salman al-Farisi suggested digging a defensive trench around Madina, a stratagem unknown to the Arabs. The Messenger ordered it to be done. This war was forever after known as the Battle of the Trench (or Ditch).[143]

- The Muslims found the Treaty of Hudaybiya unpalatable, and were reluctant to obey the Prophet's order to sacrifice their sacrificial animals without making the pilgrimage. (One condition of the treaty was that they could not enter Makka that year.) The Messenger consulted with his wife Umm Salama. She replied: "O Messenger, don't repeat your order lest they disobey you and perish. Sacrifice your own animals and take off your pilgrim dress (*ihram*). When they understand the order is decisive, they'll obey you without hesitation." The Messenger did as she suggested.[144]

---

[142] Ibn Hisham, 2:272.

[143] Ibid., 3:235; Ibn Sa'd, 2:66.

[144] *Bukhari*, "Shurut," 15.

A manifest victory: The Treaty of Hudaybiya

The Messenger was a man of action. He never hesitated about putting his plans or decisions into action, for that would confuse and demoralize his followers. The Messenger always acted with deliberation and consulted others. But once he had decided or planned something, he carried it out immediately and had no second thoughts or a reason to regret his decision. Before acting, he took the necessary precautions, considered the probabilities, and consulted available experts. The ensuing finality of his decisions was an important reason for his victories and why his Companions followed him so completely.

One event worthy of further elaboration is the Treaty of Hudaybiya. The Messenger told his Companions that he had dreamed they would shortly enter the Holy Mosque in Makka in security, with their heads shaved or their hair cut short. His Companions, especially the Emigrants, were delighted. During that year, the Prophet set out for Makka with 1,500 unarmed men in pilgrim dress.

Informed of this event, the Quraysh armed themselves and the neighboring tribes to keep the Muslims out of Makka. They sent some 200 soldiers, led by Khalid ibn Walid and Ikrima ibn Abu Jahl, as far as Qura' al-Ghamim. Seeing the Muslims approaching, they returned to Makka to spread the news. When the Muslims reached Hudaybiya, about 12 miles from Makka, the Messenger told them to halt. Learning that there was a shortage of water, he threw an arrow down Hudaybiya's only well. Water began to gush and fill the well. Everyone drank some, performed *wudu'*, and filled their waterskins.[145]

---

[145] Muslim, Hadith No.1834; Bukhari, 4:256.

As the Makkans refused to let the Muslims enter Makka, the Messenger sent Budayl ibn Warqa, a man from the Khuda'a tribe (the Muslims' ally), to announce that the Muslims had come for pilgrimage and thus were unarmed. The Quraysh, in reply, sent 'Urwa ibn Mas'ud al-Thaqafi. While talking to the Messenger 'Urwa tried to grasp his beard, a sign of jesting. Mughira ibn Shu'ba struck his hand, saying he would cut it off if 'Urwa tried such a thing again, for his hand was impure.

Mughira was 'Urwa's cousin, and had accepted Islam about 2 months earlier. In fact, only a few months ago 'Urwa had paid the blood money for a crime Mughira had committed. How Islam had changed Mughira! The Companions' commitment to their cause and devotion to the Messenger shocked 'Urwa, who returned to the Quraysh and said: "I have visited Chosroes, Caesar, and the Negus. None of their subjects are so devoted to their rulers as his Companions are to Muhammad. I advise you not to struggle with him."[146]

The Quraysh did not heed his advice or give a warm welcome to Kharash ibn Umayya, whom the Messenger sent after 'Urwa. Kharash was followed by 'Uthman ibn al-'Affan, who had powerful relatives among the Quraysh. Although 'Uthman came to negotiate, the Makkans imprisoned him. When he did not return at the expected time, rumors circulated that he had been killed. At this point, the Prophet, sitting under a tree, took an oath from his Companions that they would hold together and fight to the death. He represented the absent 'Uthman by proxy in this oath.[147] Only Jadd ibn Qays, who hid behind a camel, did not take it.

---

[146] Bukhari, 3:180; Ibn Hanbal, 4:324; Tabari, 3:75.

[147] Ibn Hisham, 3:330.

The revelation that came on this occasion reads:

> God was well pleased with the believers when they were swearing allegiance to you under the tree, and He knew what was in their hearts, so He sent down peace of reassurance on them, and has rewarded them with a near victory. (48:18)

In that moment of tension, a cloud of dust appeared in the distance. This turned out to be a Makkan delegation led by Suhayl ibn 'Amr. When the Messenger learned this, he took his name (easiness) as a good omen and told his Companions: "The situation has eased." Eventually, the Quraysh agreed to a truce and the Treaty of Hudaybiya was concluded.

Under this treaty, the Prophet and his followers could make pilgrimage the following year, not this one, at which time the Makkans would vacate the city for 3 days The treaty also stipulated a 10-year truce, that people or tribes could join or ally themselves with whoever they wished, and that Qurayshi subjects or dependents who defected to Madina would be returned. This last condition was not reciprocal, and thus was opposed in the Muslim camp. It shocked people like 'Umar, who questioned the Messenger about it. However, it really was of little importance. Muslims sent back to Makka were not likely to renounce Islam; on the contrary, they would be agents of change within Makka.

Just before the treaty was signed, Abu Jandal, Suhayl's son, arrived in chains and asked to join the Muslims. The Messenger had to return him to his father in tears. However, he whispered to him: "God will shortly save you and those of your like."[148]

---

[148] Ibn Hisham, 3:321-33; Ibn Kathir, 4:188-93.

Shortly after the treaty was signed, 'Utba ibn Asid (also known as Abu Basir) defected to Madina. The Quraysh sent two men to demand his return. On their way back to Makka, Abu Basir escaped, killed one man and wounded the other. The Messenger, citing the treaty's terms, did not allow him to stay in Madina. So he settled at Iyss, a place on the road from Makka to Syria. The Muslims held in Makka began to join Abu Basir. As this settlement grew, the Makkans perceived a potential threat to their trade route. This forced them to ask the Messenger to annul the relevant term and admit defecting Makkans to Madina.[149]

The Qur'an called the Treaty of Hudaybiya "a manifest victory": *We have given you a manifest victory* (48:1). This proved true for several reasons, among them:

- By signing this treaty after years of conflict, the Quraysh admitted that the Muslims were their equals. In effect, they gave up their struggle but did not admit it to themselves. Seeing the Makkans deal with the Prophet as an equal and a ruler, a rising tide of converts flowed toward Madina from all over Arabia.

- Many Qurayshis would benefit from the resulting peace by finally reflecting on what was going on. Such leading Qurayshis as Khalid ibn Walid, 'Amr ibn al-'As, and 'Uthman ibn Talha, all famous for their military and political skills, accepted Islam. 'Uthman was the person entrusted with the Ka'ba's keys, and after the conquest of Makka the Messenger honored him with the same task.

- The Quraysh used to regard the Ka'ba as their exclusive property, and made its visitors pay them a tribute. By not subjecting the Muslims' deferred pilgrimage to this con-

---

[149] Ibn Hisham, 3:337-38.

dition, the Quraysh unwittingly ended their monopoly. The bedouin tribes now realized that the Quraysh had no right to claim exclusive ownership.

• At the time, there were Muslim men and women living in Makka. Not everyone in Madina knew who they were. Some were serving the Messenger as spies. Had a fight taken place in Makka, the victorious Muslim army might have killed some of them. This would have caused great personal anguish, as well as the martyrdom or identification of the Prophet's spies. The treaty prevented such a disaster.

The Qur'an points to this fact:

> He restrained their hands from you, and your hands from them, in the hollow of Makka, after He made you victors over them. God sees the things you do. They are the ones who disbelieved, and banned you from the Holy Mosque, and hindered the sacrificial animals from reaching their place of sacrifice. If it had not been for certain believing men and believing women (in Makka) whom you knew not—lest you should trample them and thus incur guilt for them unknowingly; that God may admit into His Mercy whom He will—(the believers and unbelievers) had been clearly separated, then We would have chastised the unbelievers among them with a painful chastisement. (48:24-25)

• The Prophet performed the minor pilgrimage the following year. The assertion: "There is no god but God, and Muhammad is the Messenger of God," rang throughout Makka. The Quraysh, camped on Abu Qubays hill, heard this portent of Islam's coming triumph. This was, in fact, God's fulfilling the vision He had given to His Messenger:

> God has indeed fulfilled the vision He vouchsafed to His Messenger: You shall enter the Holy Mosque, if

> God wills, in security, your heads shaved, your hair cut
> short, not fearing. He knew what you knew not, and,
> granted, besides this, a nigh victory. (48:27)

- The treaty allowed the Messenger to deal with others. In the post-treaty expeditions, the Muslims conquered the formidable Jewish citadels of Khaybar, telling them either to convert or accept Muslim rule by paying tribute in lieu of protection (*jizya*). Their neighbors, as well as other Arab tribes, were impressed with the Islamic state's growing strength.

The Muslims faithfully observed the treaty's terms; however, a tribe allied to the Makkans did not. The Banu Bakr attacked the Banu Khuda'a, who were allied with the Prophet. So in December 629, the Messenger marched a 10,000-man army against Makka, and captured it with almost no resistance on the first day of the new year. The Ka'ba was purified of idols and, over the next couple of days, the Makkans accepted Islam. This was due to happen because:

> He has sent His Messenger with the guidance and
> the religion of truth, that He may uplift it above
> every religion. God suffices as a witness.
> Muhammad is the Messenger of God, and those who
> are with him are hard against the unbelievers, mer-
> ciful to one another. You see them bowing, prostrat-
> ing, seeking grace from God and (His) good plea-
> sure. Their mark is on their faces, the trace of pros-
> tration. That is their likeness in the Torah, and their
> likeness in the Gospel is: as a seed that puts forth its
> shoot, and strengthens it, and it grows stout and rises
> straight upon its stalk, pleasing the sowers, that
> through them He may enrage the unbelievers. God
> has promised those of them who believe and do
> deeds of righteousness forgiveness and a mighty
> wage. (48:28-29)

Ending racism

Racism is one of our age's severest problems. Everyone has heard of how black Africans were transported across the Atlantic Ocean in specially designed ships, thought of and treated exactly like livestock. They were enslaved, forced to change their names and religion and language, were never entitled even to hope for true freedom, and were denied all human rights. The West's attitude toward non-Westerners remained unchanged until recent times. As a result, the political and social condition of Africans, even in the case of their descendents who lived in the West amidst non-black Americans or Europeans as theoretically equal fellow citizens, remained second-class (or even lower) citizens.

When the Messenger was raised as a Prophet, such racism was prevalent in Makka in the guise of tribalism. The Quraysh considered themselves (in particular) and Arabs (in general) superior to all other people. The Messenger came with the Divine Message and proclaimed that: "No Arab is superior to a non-Arab, and no white person is superior to a black person"[150]; Superiority is by righteousness and devotion to God alone (49:13); and: "Even if a black Abyssinian Muslim were to rule over Muslims, he should be obeyed."[151]

The Messenger eradicated color-based racism and discrimination so successfully that, for example, 'Umar once said of Bilal, who was black: "Bilal is our master, and was emancipated by our master Abu Bakr."[152] Zayd ibn Haritha,

---

[150] Ibn Hanbal, 5:441.

[151] Muslim, "'Imara," 37.

[152] Ibn Hajar, *Al-Isaba*, 1:165.

a black slave emancipated by the Messenger, was his adopted son before the Revelation banned such adoption. The Prophet married him to Zaynab bint Jahsh, one of the noblest (and non-black) Arab and Muslim women. In addition, he appointed Zayd commander of the Muslim army sent against the Byzantine Empire, even though it included such leading Companions as Abu Bakr, 'Umar, Ja'far ibn Abu Talib (the Messenger's cousin), and Khalid ibn Walid (the invincible general of the age).[153]

He appointed Zayd's son Usama to command the army he formed just before his death. Included therein were such leading Companions as Abu Bakr, 'Umar, Khalid, Abu 'Ubayda, Talha, and Zubayr. This established in the Muslims' hearts and minds that superiority is not by birth or color or blood, but by righteousness and devotion to God.

During his caliphate, 'Umar paid Usama a higher salary than his own son, 'Abd Allah. When his son asked why, 'Umar replied: "I do so because I know that the Messenger loved his father more than me, and that he loved Usama more than you."[154]

The last word

Prophet Muhammad had all the necessary leadership qualities for success in every aspect of life. But, more importantly, he was able to lead his community to success in every field. He is the source from which flowed all later developments related to command, statecraft, religion, spiritual development, and so on in the Muslim world.

---

[153] Muslim, "Fada'il al-Sahaba," 63.

[154] Ibn Sa'd, *Tabaqat*, 4:70; Ibn Hajar, 1:564.

In general, leaders should have the following qualities:

- *Realism.* Their messages and demands should not contradict reality. They should understand prevailing conditions as they actually are, and be aware of any advantages and disadvantages.

- *Absolute belief in their message.* Their conviction should never falter, and they should never renounce their mission.

- *Personal courage.* Even if left alone, they should have enough courage to persevere. When some of his pursuers reached the mouth of the cave in which they were hiding, Abu Bakr was afraid something would happen to the Messenger. However, the Prophet only said: *Don't worry, for God is with us.* (9:40)

- *Strong willpower and resolve.* They should never experience even one moment of hopelessness.

- *Awareness of personal responsibility.* Everything should be directed toward fulfilling this responsibility. In no way should they be seduced by the world's charms and life's attractions.

- *Farsighted and goal-centered.* Leaders should be able to discern and plan for potential developments. They should know how to evaluate the past, present, and future to reach a new synthesis. Those who frequently change their opinions only spread chaos in the community.

- *Personal knowledge of each follower.* Leaders should be fully aware of each follower's disposition, character, abilities, shortcomings, ambitions, and weak points. If they lack this knowledge, how can they fill vacant posts with the appropriate people?

- *Strong character and praiseworthy virtues.* Leaders should be determined but flexible while carrying out decisions, and know when to be unyielding and implacable or relenting and compassionate. They should know when to be earnest and dignified, when to be modest, and always be upright, truthful, trustworthy, and just.

- *No worldly ambitions or abuse of authority.* Leaders should live like the poorest members of their community. They should never discriminate among their subjects; rather, they should strive to love them, prefer them over themselves, and act so that their people will love them sincerely. They should be faithful to their community, and secure their community's loyalty and devotion in return.

The Messenger possessed all of these qualities, and many more as well. To cite only a few examples, he never even thought of abandoning his mission when confronted with great hostility and tempting bribes. Instead, he would tell them: "Say: 'There is no god but God,' and prosper in both worlds."[155] When his Companions complained about the harsh conditions and persecution in Makka, he answered:

> "You show haste. A day will come and a woman will travel from Hira [a town in southern Iraq] to Makka alone on her camel (in security) and circumambulate the Ka'ba as an act of worship, and the treasuries of the Sassanid Emperor will be captured by my community.[156]

Once the Makkan leaders came to him and said: "If you meet with us on a day when others, especially those poor ones,

---

[155] *Bukhari*, "Tafsir," 1; *Muslim*, "Iman," 355.

[156] Bukhari, "Manaqib," 25.

are not present, we may talk to you about accepting your religion." They despised poor Muslims like Bilal, 'Ammar, and
Habbab, and desired special treatment. The Messenger rejected such proposals without a second thought. The verses
revealed addressed him as follows:

> Send not away those who call on their Master morning
> and evening, seeking His Face (6:52), and Persevere
> together with those who call on their Master morning
> and evening, seeking His Face. (18:28)

CHAPTER 5

Other Dimensions of
His Prophethood

His prayers and supplications

The Messenger always prayed to God before any action. The books of Tradition (*hadith*) record no case in which he did not pray. As mentioned earlier, prayer is a mystery of servanthood to God, and the Messenger is the foremost in servanthood. This is made clear with every repetition of the declaration of faith: "I bear witness there is no god but God; I also bear witness that Muhammad is His servant and Messenger." Note that he is called *servant* before *Messenger.* Whatever he intended to do, he referred it to God through prayer.

God is the Creator of us and whatever we do. Although we should take necessary precautions and follow precedents to accomplish things in this material world, where cause and effect has a special place, we should never forget that everything ultimately depends on God for its existence. Therefore, we must combine action and prayer. This is also required by our belief in God's Unity.

The Messenger's knowledge of God can never be equaled. As a result, he was the foremost in love of, and paradoxically, in fear of Him. He was perfectly conscious that everything depends on God for its existence and subsistence. Whatever God wills, happens: *When He wills a thing, His command is to say to it "Be," and it is* (36:82). Things exist and the universe operates according to the laws established by God and the fulfillment of prerequisites. Fully aware of this, the Messenger did what he had to and then, combining action with prayer, left the result to God with absolute confidence.

His supplications have been transmitted to us. When we read them, we see that they have deep meaning and accord exactly with the surrounding circumstances. They reflect profound belief, deep sincerity, absolute submission and complete confidence. Some examples are given below:

- When you go to bed, perform *wudu'* as you do before daily prayers and pray:

> O God, hoping for (Your Mercy) and fearing (Your wrath), I submit myself to You, refer my affairs to You, and take refuge in You. There is no refuge or source of safety from Your wrath except You. I believe in the Book You sent down, and the Prophet you raised.[157]

- Without sins, a soul is like a polished mirror or a white cloth. Sins dirty the soul, and can be expunged only by repentance and asking His forgiveness. The Prophet used to pray the following, even though he was sinless: "O God, put between me and errors a distance as great as that which you have put between East and West. O God, cleanse me of my errors as a white garment is cleansed of dirt."[158] A whole volume could be written about the meaningful words used and the comparisons made here.

In addition to these supplications for specific cases, the Prophet also left behind comprehensive supplications of various lengths. We present some of them here:

---

[157] *Bukhari*, "Da'awat," 6; *Muslim*, "Dhikr," 56.

[158] *Bukhari*, "Adhan," 89; *Muslim*, "Masajid," 147.

- God, I ask You for all good, including what is at hand and what is deferred, what I already know and what I don't know. I take refuge in You from every evil, including what is at hand and what is deferred, what I already know and what I don't know.[159]

- God, nothing hinders what You grant, nor is anything granted that You hinder. No wealthy one can do us good, as wealth belongs to You.[160]

- God, I have not told anything, taken an oath, made a vow, or done anything that You did not previously will. Whatever You willed is, and whatever You didn't will is not. There is no strength or power save with You, and You are indeed All-Powerful over everything.[161]

- God, whatever prayer I have said, let it be for whomever You have mercy, and whatever curse I have called down, let it be for whomever You have cursed. Surely You are my Guardian in this world and the Hereafter. Make me die as a Muslim, and include me among the righteous.[162]

- God, I ask You for contentment after misfortune, a peaceful life after death, the pleasure of observing Your Face, and a desire to meet You. I take refuge in You from wronging others and from being wronged, from showing animosity and being subject to animosity, and from erring or committing unforgivable sins. If You leave me to myself, you leave me in weakness, need, sinfulness and error. I depend only on Your Mercy, so forgive all my

---

[159] Ibn Hanbal, *Musnad*, 6:147.

[160] *Bukhari*, "Adhan," 155; *Muslim*, "Salat," 205; *Abu Dawud*, "Salat," 139.

[161] Ibn Hanbal, *Musnad*, 5:191.

[162] Nasa'i, "Sahw," 62; Ibn Hanbal, 5:191.

sins, for only You can do so. Accept my repentance, for You are the Oft-Relenting, All-Compassionate.[163]

- God, You deserve most to be mentioned, and none but You deserve to be worshipped. You are more helpful than anyone whose help may be sought, more affectionate than every ruler, more generous than anyone who may be asked for something, and more generous than anyone who gives. You are the Monarch without partners, and the Unique One without like. Everything is perishable except You.

  You are never obeyed but by Your permission, and never disobeyed but within Your knowledge. When somebody obeys You, You reward them; when someone disobeys You, You forgive them. You witness everything, being nearer to it than any other witness; and protect everything, being nearer to it than any other protector. You ordained the acts of all people and determined their time of death. You know what is in every mind, and all secrets are manifest to You.

  The lawful is what You have made lawful; the forbidden is what You have forbidden. Religion is what You have laid down; the commandment is what You have decreed. The creation is Your creation, and the servants are Your servants. You are God, the All-Clement, All-Compassionate. I ask You, for the sake of the light of Your Face, by which the Heavens and Earth were illuminated, for the sake of every right belonging to You, and for the sake of those who ask of You, to forgive me just in this morning and just in this evening, and to protect me, by Your Power, from Hellfire.[164]

---

[163] Ibn Hanbal, 5:191.

[164] Haythami, *Majma' al-Zawa'id*, 10:117.

- God, I seek refuge in You from all knowledge that gives no benefit, from a heart that does not fear You, from an unsatisfied soul, and from prayer that cannot be answered.[165]

- God, I ask You for steadfastness in my affairs, resolution in guidance, gratitude for Your bounties and acceptable service to You, and a truthful tongue and a sound heart. I seek refuge in You from the evil of what You know. I ask You for the good of what You know, and Your forgiveness for what You already know. Surely You are the Knower of the Unseen.[166]

- God, I ask You to enable me to do good, to refrain from vice, to love the poor, and to forgive me and have mercy on me. When You will people's deviation and dissension and disorder in public life, make me die before taking part in that disorder. I ask You for Your love and for the love of whom You love, and the love of the acts that will make me nearer to Your love.[167]

- God, I ask You for the good in the beginning and in the end, in its most comprehensive form with its beginning and result, its manifest and secret kinds, and for the highest rank in Paradise.[168]

- God, help me remember and mention You, thank You, and worship You most properly.[169]

---

[165] *Muslim*, "Dhikr," 73; *Abu Dawud*, "Witr," 32.

[166] *Tirmidhi*, "Da'awat," 23; *Nasa'i,* "Sahw," 61.

[167] *Tirmidhi*, "Tafsir al-Qur'an," 39; Imam Malik, *Muwatta'*, "Qur'an," 73.

[168] Hakim, *Mustadrak*, 1:520.

[169] Ibid., 1:499.

- God, I ask You for guidance, fear of You, chastity, and independence of others.[170]

- God, bring all of our affairs to a good conclusion, protect us from disgrace and ignominy in the world, and from being tormented in the Hereafter.[171]

- God, we ask You for all of the good for which Your Prophet Muhammad asked You, and seek refuge in You from every evil from which Your Prophet Muhammad sought refuge in You.[172]

Prayer was a fundamental part of the Prophet's life. All the supplications quoted, together with many, have become keys in the hands of such great saints as Abu Hasan al-Shadhili, Ahmad al-Badawi, Ahmad al-Rifaʿi, and ʿAbd al-Qadir al-Jilani, who used them to knock on the door of God's Mercy.

The Prophet of universal mercy

The beginning of existence was an act of mercy and compassion without which the universe would be in chaos. Everything came into existence through compassion, and by compassion it continues to exist in harmony.

Muslim sages say that the universe is the All-Compassionate One's breath. In other words, the universe was created to manifest the Divine Name the All-Compassionate. Its subsistence depends on the same Name. This Name manifests itself first as the All-Provider, so that all living creatures can receive the food or nourishment they need to survive.

---

[170] *Ibn Maja*, "Duʿa," 2; *Muslim*, "Dhikr," 72; *Tirmidhi*, "Daʿawat," 73.

[171] Ibn Hanbal, 4:181; Hakim, 3:591.

[172] *Tirmidhi*, "Daʿawat," 89.

Life is God Almighty's foremost and most manifest blessing, and the true and everlasting life is that of the Hereafter. Since we can deserve this life by pleasing God, He sent Prophets and revealed Scriptures out of His compassion for humanity. For this reason, while mentioning His blessings upon humanity in *Surat al-Rahman* (the All-Merciful), He begins: *Al-Rahman. He taught the Qur'an, created humanity, and taught it speech* (55:1-4).

All aspects of this life are a rehearsal for the afterlife, and every creature is engaged in action toward this end. Order is evident in every effort, and compassion resides in every achievement. Some "natural" events or social convulsions may seem disagreeable at first, but we should not regard them as incompatible with compassion. They are like dark clouds or lightning and thunder that, although frightening, nevertheless bring us good tidings of rain. Thus the whole universe praises the All-Compassionate.

Muslim sages consider the Qur'an a "created book" issuing from His Attribute of Will. To write a book that people could not understand would be pointless. Therefore, He created Muhammad to tell people what the universe really means, and to relay His Commandments in the Qur'an through Muhammad so that we can know what is expected of us. Only by following these Commandments can we attain an eternal life of happiness. The Qur'an is the ultimate and most comprehensive Divine Revelation; Islam is the last, perfected, and universal form of Divine Religion; and Prophet Muhammad is the embodiment of Divine Compassion, one sent by God as a mercy for all worlds.

Prophet Muhammad is like a spring of pure water in the heart of a desert, a source of light in an all-enveloping darkness. Whoever appeals to this spring can take as much water as needed to quench their thirst, to become purified of all their sins, and to become illumined with the light of belief. Mercy was like a magic key in his hands, for with it he opened hearts that were so hardened and rusty that no one thought they could be opened. But he did even more: he lit a torch of belief in them.

The Messenger preached Islam, the religion of universal mercy. However, some self-proclaimed humanists say that Islam is "a religion of the sword." This is completely wrong. They make a great deal of noise when animals are killed or when one of their own is harmed, but are silent when Muslims are massacred. Their world is built on personal interest. It should be pointed out that abusing the feeling of compassion is just as harmful—sometimes even more harmful—than having no compassion at all.

Amputating a gangrenous limb is an act of compassion for the whole body. Likewise oxygen and hydrogen, when mixed in the proper ratios, form water, a most vital substance. When this ratio changes, however, each element resumes its original combustible identity.

Similarly, it is quite important to apportion compassion and to identify who deserves it, for "compassion for a wolf sharpens its appetite, and not being content with what it receives, it demands even more." Compassion for wrong-doers makes them more aggressive and encourages them to work against others. In fact, true compassion requires that such people be prevented from doing wrong. When the Messenger told his Companions to help people when they were just and unjust, they asked him to explain this seeming paradox. He replied: "You help such people by preventing them from engaging in injustice." So, compassion requires that those who cause trouble either be deprived of their means for, or prevented from, doing so. Otherwise, they eventually will take control and do as they please.

The Messenger's compassion encompassed every creature. In his role as an invincible commander and able statesman, he knew allowing blood-stained, blood-thirsty people to control others would be the most terrible form of tyranny imaginable. Therefore, out of compassion, he required that lambs should be able to live in security against wolves' attacks. He desired, of course, that everyone be guided. In fact, this was his greatest concern: *Yet it may be, if they believe not in this Message, you will consume yourself, following after them, with grief* (18:6).

But how should he deal with those who persisted in unbelief and fought him to destroy both him and his Message? He had to fight such people, for universal compassion encompasses every creature. This is why, when he was wounded severely at Uhud, he raised his hands and prayed: "O God, forgive my people, for they don't know."[173]

The Makkans, his own people, inflicted so much suffering on him that he finally emigrated to Madina. Even after that, the next 5 years were far from peaceful. However, when he conquered Makka without bloodshed in the twenty-first year of his Prophethood, he asked the Makkan unbelievers: "How do you expect me to treat you?" They responded unanimously: "You are a noble one, the son of a noble one." He then told them his decision: "You may leave, for no reproach this day shall be on you. May God forgive you. He is the Most Compassionate of the Compassionate."[174]

---

[173] *Bukhari*, "Anbiya'," 54; *Muslim*, "Jihad," 104.

[174] Ibn Hisham, *Sira*, 4:55; Ibn Kathir, *Al-Bidaya*, 4:344.

Sultan Mehmed the Conqueror said the same thing to the defeated Byzantines after conquering Istanbul 825 years later. Such is the universal compassion of Islam.

The Messenger displayed the highest degree of compassion toward the believers:

> There has come to you a Messenger from among yourselves; grievous to him is your suffering; anxious is he over you, full of concern for you, for the believers full of pity, compassionate. (9:128)

He lowered unto believers his wing of tenderness through mercy (15:88), and was the guardian of believers and nearer to them than their selves (33:6). When a Companions died, he asked those at the funeral if the deceased had left any debts. On learning that he had, the Prophet mentioned the above verse and announced that the creditors should come to him for repayment.[175]

His compassion even encompassed the Hypocrites and unbelievers. He knew who the Hypocrites were, but never identified them, for this would have deprived them of the rights of full citizenship they had gained by their outward confession of faith and practice. Since they lived among Muslims, their unbelief in eternal life may have been reduced or changed to doubt, thus diminishing their fear of death and the pain caused by the assertion of eternal non-existence after death.

God did not send a collective destruction upon the unbelievers, although He had eradicated many such people in the past: *But God would never chastise them while you were among them; God would never chastise them as they begged*

---

[175] *Muslim*, "Fara'iz,' 14; *Bukhari*, "Istiqraz," 11.

forgiveness (8:33). This verse refers to unbelievers of whatever time. God will not destroy peoples altogether as long as those who follow the Messenger are alive. Besides, He has left the door of repentance open until the Last Day. Anyone can accept Islam or ask God's forgiveness, regardless of how sinful they consider themselves to be.

For this reason, a Muslim's enmity toward unbelievers is a form of pity. When 'Umar saw an 80-year-old priest, he sat down and sobbed. When asked why he did so, he replied: "God assigned him so long a life span, but he has not been able to find the true path." 'Umar was a disciple of the Messenger, who said: "I was not sent to call down curses on people, but as a mercy"[176] and

> I am Muhammad, and Ahmad (praised one), and Muqaffi (the Last Prophet); I am Hashir (the final Prophet in whose presence the dead will be resurrected); the Prophet of repentance (the Prophet for whom the door of repentance will always remain open), and the Prophet of mercy.[177]

Archangel Gabriel also benefited from the mercy of the Qur'an. Once the Prophet asked Gabriel whether he had any share in the mercy contained in the Qur'an. Gabriel replied that he did, and explained: "I was not certain about my end. However, when the verse: *(One) obeyed, and moreover, trustworthy and secured* (81:21) was revealed, I felt secure about it."[178] When Ma'iz was punished for fornication, a Companion verbally abused him. The Messenger frowned at him and said: "You have backbitten your friend. His repen-

---

[176] *Muslim*, "Birr," 87.

[177] *Ibn Hanbal*, 4:395; *Muslim*, "Fada'il," 126.

[178] Qadi 'Iyad, *Al-Shifa'*, 1:17.

tance and asking God's pardon for his sin would be enough to forgive all the sinners in the world."[179]

The Messenger was particularly compassionate toward children. Whenever he saw a child crying, he sat beside him or her and shared his or her feelings. He felt a mother's pain for her child more than the mother herself. Once he said: "I stand in prayer and wish to prolong it. However, I hear a child cry and shorten the prayer to lessen the mother's anxiety."[180]

He took children in his arms and hugged them. Once when hugging his beloved grandsons Hasan and Husayn, Aqra ibn Habis told him: "I have 10 children, and have never kissed any of them." The Messenger responded: "One without pity for others is not pitied."[181] According to another version, he said or added: "What can I do for you if God has removed compassion from you?"[182]

He said: "Pity those on Earth so that those in the Heavens will pity you."[183] When Sa'd ibn 'Ubada became ill, the Messenger visited him at home and, seeing his faithful Companion in a pitiful state, began to cry. He said: "God does not punish because of tears or grief, but He punishes because of this," and he pointed to his tongue.[184] When 'Uthman ibn Mad'un died, he wept profusely. During the funeral, a woman remarked: "'Uthman flew like a bird to Paradise." Even in that mournful state, the Prophet did not lose his balance and cor-

---

[179] *Muslim*, "Hudud," 17-23; *Bukhari*, "Hudud," 28.

[180] *Bukhari*, "Adhan," 65; *Muslim*, "Salat," 192.

[181] *Bukhari*, "Adab," 18.

[182] *Bukhari*, "Adab," 18; *Muslim*, "Fada'il," 64; *Ibn Maja*, "Adab," 3.

[183] *Tirmidhi*, "Birr," 16.

[184] *Bukhari*, "Jana'iz," 45; *Muslim*, "Jana'iz," 12.

rected the woman: "How do you know this? Even I don't know this, and I am a Prophet."[185]

A member of the Banu Muqarrin clan once beat his maid-servant. She informed the Messenger, who sent for the master. He said: "You have beaten her without any justifiable right. Free her."[186] Freeing a slave free was far better for the master than being punished in the Hereafter because of that act. The Messenger always protected and supported widows, orphans, the poor and disabled even before announcing his Prophethood. When he returned home in excitement from Mount Hira after the first Revelation, his wife Khadija told him: "I hope you will be the Prophet of this Umma, for you always tell the truth, fulfill your trust, support your relatives, help the poor and weak, and feed guests."[187]

His compassion even encompassed animals. We hear from him: "A prostitute was guided to truth by God and ultimately went to Paradise because she gave water to a dog dying of thirst. Another woman was sent to Hell because she left a cat to die of hunger."[188] While returning from a military campaign, a few Companions removed some young birds from their nest to stroke them. The mother bird came back and, not finding its babies, began to fly around screeching. When told of this, the Messenger became angry and ordered the birds to be put back in the nest.[189]

---

[185] *Bukhari*, "Jana'iz," 3.

[186] Muslim, "Ayman," 31, 33; Ibn Hanbal, 3:447.

[187] Ibn Sa'd, *Tabaqat*, 1:195.

[188] *Bukhari*, "Anbiya'," 54; "Musaqat," 9; *Muslim*, "Salam," 153; Ibn Hanbal, 2:507.

[189] *Abu Dawud*, "Adab," 164; "Jihad," 112; Ibn Hanbal, 1:404.

Once he told his Companions that God reproached an earlier Prophet for setting fire to a nest of ants.[190] While in Mina, some of his Companions attacked a snake in order to kill it. However, it managed to escape. Watching this from afar, the Messenger remarked: "It was saved from your evil, as you were from its evil."[191] Ibn 'Abbas reported that when the Messenger saw a man sharpening his knife directly before the sheep to be slaughtered, he asked: "Do you want to kill it many times?"[192]

'Abd Allah ibn Ja'far narrates:

> The Messenger went to a garden in Madina with a few Companions. A very scrawny camel was in a corner. Seeing the Messenger, it began to cry. The Messenger went to it and, after staying beside it for a while, severely warned the owner to feed it properly.[193]

His love and compassion for creatures differed from that of today's self-proclaimed humanists, for he was sincere and balanced in this regard—a Prophet raised by God, the Creator and Sustainer of all beings, for the guidance and happiness humanity and jinn, and the harmony of existence. As such, he lived for others, and was a mercy for all the worlds, a manifestation of Compassion.

His mildness and forbearance

Mildness is another dimension of his character. He was a bright mirror in which God reflected His Mercy. Mildness is a reflection of compassion. God made His Messenger mild

---

[190] *Bukhari*, "Jihad," 153; *Muslim*, "Salam," 147.

[191] *Nasa'i*, "Hajj," 114; Ibn Hanbal, 1:385.

[192] Hakim, *Mustadrak*, 4:231, 233.

[193] Suyuti, *Al-Khasa'is al-Kubra'*, 2:95; Haythami, *Majma'*, 9:9.

and gentle, thereby allowing him to gain many converts to Islam and overcome numerous obstacles.

After the victory of Badr, the Battle of Uhud was a severe trial for the young Muslim community. Although the Messenger wanted to fight on the outskirts of Madina, most Muslims desired to fight on an open battlefield. When the two armies met at the foot of Mount Uhud, the Messenger positioned 50 archers in 'Aynayn pass and ordered them not to move without his permission, even if they saw that the Muslims had won a decisive victory.

The Muslim army, having only one-third of the men and equipment of the enemy, almost defeated the Makkan polytheists in the initial stage. Seeing the enemy fleeing, these archers forgot the Prophet's command and left their post. Khalid ibn Walid, the Makkan cavalry's commander, saw this and, riding round the mountain, attacked the Muslims from behind. The fleeing enemy soldiers turned back, and caught the Muslims in a crossfire. They began to lose, more than 70 were martyred, and the Messenger was wounded.

He might have reproached those who had urged him to pursue their desires as well as the archers who had abandoned their post, but he did not. Instead, he showed leniency:

> It was by the mercy of God that you were gentle to them; if you had been harsh and hard of heart, they would have dispersed from about you. So pardon them and ask forgiveness for them and consult with them in the affair. And when you are resolved, then put your trust in God; surely God loves those who put their trust (in Him). (3:159)

This verse shows two prerequisite for leadership: mildness and leniency toward those who make well-intentioned mistakes, and the importance of consultation in public administration.

This mildness and forgiveness was a reflection of God's Names the All-Mild, All-Clement, and All-Forgiving. God does not stop providing for people despite their rebellion or unbelief. While most people disobey Him by indulging in unbelief, by explicitly or implicitly associating partners with Him, or transgressing His Commandments, the sun continues to send them its heat and light, clouds full of rain come to their aid, and the soil never stops feeding them with its fruits and plants. God's Clemency and Forgiveness are reflected through the Messenger's compassion, mildness, and forgiveness.

Like Abraham, whom he used to say that he resembled, the Messenger was mild, imploring, clement, and penitent (11:75), gentle to believers, and full of pity and compassion for them (9:128). Abraham was never angry with people, regardless of how much they tormented him. He wished good even for his enemies, and implored God and shed tears in His Presence. Since he was a man of peace and salvation, God made the fire into which he was thrown cool and safe (21:69).

Like him, the Messenger was never angry with anybody because of what they did to him. When his wife 'A'isha was slandered, he did not consider punishing the slanderers even after she was cleared by the Qur'an. Bedouins often behaved impolitely with him, but he did not even frown at them. Although extremely sensitive, he always showed forbearance toward both friend and foe.

For example, while he was distributing the spoils of war after the Battle of Hunayn, Dhu al-Huwaysira objected: "Be just, O Muhammad." This was an unforgivable insult, for the Prophet had been sent to establish justice. Unable to endure such offences, 'Umar demanded permission to kill "that hypocrite" on the spot. But the Messenger only replied: "Who else will show justice if I am not just? If I don't show justice, then I am lost and brought to naught."[194] According to another possible meaning of this expression, he said: "If I am not just, then, by following me, you people have been lost and brought to naught."[195] In addition, he implied that this man would later take part in a seditious movement. This came true during the caliphate of 'Ali: Dhu al-Huwaysira was found dead among the Kharijites after the Battle of Nahrawan.

Anas ibn Malik related that a Jewess offered a roasted sheep to the Messenger after the conquest of Khaybar. Just before he took the first bite, he stopped and told the others not to eat, saying: "This sheep tells me it has been poisoned." Nevertheless, a Companion named Bishr died immediately after his first bite (taken before the Messenger had spoken). The Messenger sent for the woman and asked her why she had poisoned the meat. She replied: "If you're really a Prophet, the poison won't affect you. If you're not, I wanted to save people from your evil." The Messenger forgave her for her conspiracy to kill him.[196] According to some reports, however, Bishr's relatives demanded that she be punished, and she subsequently was.

Once when the Prophet was going home after talking to his Companions in the mosque, a bedouin pulled him by the collar and said rudely: "O Muhammad! Give me my due! Load up my two camels! For you will load them up with neither your own wealth nor that of your father!" Without showing any sign of being offended, he told others: "Give him what he wants."[197]

---

[194] *Muslim*, "Zakat," 142, 148; *Bukhari*, "Adab," 95; "Manaqib," 25.

[195] *Bukhari*, "Adab," 95; *Muslim*, "Zakat," 142.

[196] *Bukhari*, "Hiba," 28; *Abu Dawud*, "Diyat," 6.

[197] *Abu Dawud*, "Adab," 1; *Nasa'i*, "Qasama," 24.

Zayd ibn San'an narrates:

> Before I embraced Islam, the Messenger borrowed
> some money from me. I went to him to collect my debt
> before its due time, and insulted him: "O you children
> of 'Abd al-Muttalib, you are very reluctant to pay your
> debts!" 'Umar became very angry with me and shout-
> ed: "O enemy of God! Were it not for the treaty
> between us and the Jewish community, I would cut off
> your head! Speak to the Messenger politely!" However,
> the Messenger smiled at me and, turning to 'Umar, said:
> "Pay him, and add 20 gallons to it, because you fright-
> ened him."

'Umar relates the rest of the story:

> We went together. On the way, Zayd said unexpected-
> ly: "'Umar, you were angry with me. But I find in him
> all the features of the Last Prophet recorded in the
> Torah, the Old Testament. It contains this verse: His
> mildness surpasses his anger. The severity of impu-
> dence to him increases him only in mildness and for-
> bearance. To test his forbearance, I provoked him
> deliberately. Now I am convinced that he is the Prophet
> whose coming the Torah predicted. So, I believe and
> bear witness that he is the Last Prophet."[198]

This mildness and forbearance was enough for the conversion of Zayd ibn San'an, a Jewish scholar.

The Messenger was extremely meticulous in practicing
Islam. Nobody could match his supererogatory prayers.
Despite being sinless, he spent more than half the night praying and crying, and sometimes fasted two or three successive
days. Every moment he took another step toward the "praised
station" set for him by God. He was very tolerant toward others. Not wanting to burden his community, he did not perform

---

[198] Suyuti, *Al-Khasa'is*, 1:26; Ibn Hajar, *Al-Isaba*, 1:566.

the supererogatory prayers in the mosque. When people complained that an imam was prolonging the prayer, the Prophet mounted the pulpit and said: "O people! You cause people to dread the prayer. When you lead a prayer, don't prolong it, for others are sick or old or in urgent need."[199] Once his congregation complained about Mu'adh ibn Jabal, saying he prolonged the night prayer. The Prophet's love for Mu'adh did not stop him asking three times if he was a trouble-maker.[200]

The Messenger's mildness and forbearance captured hearts and preserved Muslim unity. As stated in the Qur'an, if he had been harsh and hard-hearted, people would have abandoned him. But those who saw him and listened to him were so endowed with Divine manifestations that they became saints. For example, Khalid ibn Walid was the Qurayshi general who caused the Muslims to experience a reverse at Uhud. However, when he was not included in the army that set out on the day after his conversion, he was so upset that he wept.

Like Khalid, Ikrima and 'Amr ibn al-'As were among those who did great harm to the Messenger and the Muslims. After their conversions, each became a sword of Islam drawn against unbelievers. Ibn Hisham, Abu Jahl's brother, converted to Islam shortly before the Messenger passed away. He was such a sincere Muslim that just before he was martyred at Yarmuk, he did not drink the water that Hudayfa al-'Adawi offered him. Rather, he asked that it be given to nearby wounded fellow Muslim groaning for water. He died, having preferred a fellow Muslim over himself.[201]

---

[199] *Bukhari*, "'Ilm," 28; "Adhan," 61.

[200] *Muslim*, "Salat," 179; *Nasa'i*, "Iftitah," 71; *Bukhari*, "Adab," 74.

[201] Hakim, *Mustadrak*, 3:242.

Such people attained high ranks in the enlightening atmosphere of the Messenger. They became his Companions, regarded and respected as the most virtuous people after the Prophets by almost all Muslims since the earliest days of Islam. Explaining their greatness, Said Nursi, the great twentieth-century Muslim revivalist, says:

> I wondered why even the greatest saints like Muhyi al-Din ibn al-'Arabi could not attain the rank of the Companions. One day God enabled me to perform in prayer a prostration that I could never repeat. I concluded that it is impossible to attain the Companions' ranks, for all of their prostrations were like that in meaning and merit.[202]

The Messenger brought up the Companions. Their greatness is shown in the fact that despite their small numbers, they successfully conveyed Islam to the furthest reaches of Asia and Africa within a few decades. In those areas, Islam became so deeply rooted that despite the concerted efforts by the superpowers of each era to extinguish Islam, it continues to gain new momentum and represents the only realistic alternative for human salvation. The Companions were transformed from their wretched pre-Islamic state to being guides and teachers of a considerable part of humanity until the Last Day, the vanguard of the most magnificent civilization in history.

In addition, the Messenger was absolutely balanced. His universal compassion did not prevent him from executing Divine justice, and his mildness and forbearance kept him from breaching any Islamic rule or humiliating himself. For example, during a military campaign Usama ibn Zayd threw an enemy soldier to the ground. When he was about to kill him, the man declared his belief in Islam. Judging this to be

---

[202] Said Nursi, *Sözler* (Istanbul: 1986), 459.

the result of a fear of imminent death, Usama killed him. When informed of the incident, the Messenger reprimanded Usama severely: "Did you cleave his heart open and see (if what you suspected is true)?" He repeated this so many times that Usama said later: "I wished I had not yet become a Muslim on the day I was scolded so severely."[203]

Likewise, once Abu Dharr got so angry with Bilal that he insulted him: "You son of a black woman!" Bilal came to the Messenger and reported the incident in tears. The Messenger reproached Abu Dharr: "Do you still have a sign of Jahiliya?" Full of repentance, Abu Dharr lay on the ground and said: "I won't raise my head (meaning he wouldn't get up) unless Bilal put his foot on it to pass over it." Bilal forgave him, and they were reconciled.[204] Such was the brotherhood and humanity Islam created between once-savage people.

His generosity

The Messenger is the most polished mirror in which God's Names and Attributes are reflected to the highest degree. As the perfect manifestation of these Names and Attributes, an embodiment of the Qur'an and Islam, he is the greatest and most decisive and comprehensive proof of God's Existence and Unity, and of the truth of Islam and the Qur'an. Those who saw him remembered God automatically. Each of his virtues reflected a Name or Attribute of God, and is a proof of his Prophethood. Like his mildness and forbearance, his generosity is another dimension of his excellent, matchless personality, a reflection and proof of his Prophethood.

The people of Arabia were renowned for their generosity even in pre-Islamic times. When we look at that era's poetry,

---

[203] *Muslim*, "Iman," 158; *Ibn Maja*, "Fitan," 1.

[204] *Bukhari*, "Iman," 22.

we see that the Arabs were proud of their generosity. However, their generosity was not for the sake of God or for an altruistic motive; rather, it was the cause of self-pride. But the Messenger's generosity was purely for God's sake. He never mentioned, and did not like to have mentioned, it. When a poet praised him for his generosity, he attributed whatever good he had or did to God. He never attributed his virtues and good deeds to himself.

The Messenger liked to distribute whatever he had. He engaged in trade until his Prophethood, and had considerable wealth. Afterwards, he and his wealthy wife Khadija spent everything in the way of God. When Khadija died, there was no money for her burial shroud. The Messenger had to borrow money to bury his own wife, the first person to embrace Islam and its first supporter.[205]

If the Messenger had desired, he could have been the richest man in Makka. But he rejected such offers without a second thought. Although God mandated that one-fifth of all war spoils should be at the Messenger's free disposal, he never spent it on himself or his family. He and his family lived austerely and survived on scanty provisions, for he always gave preference to others. For example, his share of the spoils of Hunayn was of 40,000 sheep, 24,000 camels, and 16 tons of silver.

Safwan ibn Umayya, from whom the Messenger had borrowed some weapons, gazed upon the spoils with greed and bewilderment. Aware of this, the Messenger gave him as many camels as he wanted. Astounded with such generosity, Safwan ran to his people and announced: "O my people! Accept Islam without hesitation, for Muhammad gives in

---

[205] Ibn Kathir, *Al-Bidaya*, 3:158-9.

such a way that only one who has no fear of poverty and relies fully on God can give!" Such generosity was enough to guide Safwan and his people, who had been among the bitterest enemies of Islam until just before that day, to the truth.[206]

The Messenger regarded himself a traveler in this world. Once he said: "What connection do I have with this world? I am like a traveler who takes shade under a tree and then continues on his way."[207] According to him, the world is like a tree under which people are shaded. No one can live forever, so people must prepare here for the second part of the journey, which will end either in Paradise or Hell.

The Messenger was sent to guide people to truth, and so spent his life and possessions to this end. Once 'Umar saw him lying on a rough mat and wept. When the Messenger asked him why he was weeping, 'Umar replied: "O Messenger of God, while kings sleep in soft feather beds, you lie on a rough mat. You are the Messenger of God, and as such deserve an easy life more than anyone else." He answered: "Don't you agree that the luxuries of the world should be theirs, and that those of the Hereafter should be ours?"[208]

Islam does not approve of monastic life. It came to secure justice and human well-being, but warns against overindulgence. Thus many Muslims have chosen an ascetic life. Although individual Muslims generally became rich after the Messenger passed away, others like Abu Bakr, 'Umar, and 'Ali preferred an austere life. This was partly because they felt

---

[206] Ibn Hisham, 4:135; Ibn Hajar, *Al-Isaba*, 2:187; *Muslim*, "Fada'il," 57.

[207] *Bukhari*, "Riqaq," 3.

[208] *Bukhari*, "Tafsir," 2; *Muslim*, "Talaq," 31.

the need to live as the poorest of their people, and partly because they strictly followed the Prophet's example. During his caliphate, Abu Bakr was offered a glass of cold water to break his fast during Ramadan. He brought the glass to his lips and suddenly began to weep. When asked why, he answered: "One day, the Messenger drank such a glass of cold water offered to him and wept. He said that God says: 'On that day, you will be questioned concerning every bounty.' We will be questioned about this water. I remembered that and wept."[209]

In the early days of his Caliphate, Abu Bakr earned his living by milking a woman's sheep. Some time later, he was given a small salary. While on his death-bed, he gave a pitcher to those around him and asked them to give it to the new caliph after his death. 'Umar succeeded him and, when he broke the pitcher, some coins came out, together with the following letter: "I lived according to the living standards of the poorest of Madina, and put in this pitcher the amount left of my salary. Therefore, these coins belong to the public treasury and must be returned there." On reading the letter, 'Umar wept and remarked: "O Abu Bakr, you have left an unbearable burden on your successors."[210]

The Messenger was, in the words of Anas, "the most comely and generous person."[211] Jabir ibn Samura reports:

> Once we were sitting in the mosque, and a full moon was shining above us. The Messenger entered. I looked first at the moon and then at his face. I swear by God that his face was brighter than the moon."[212]

---

[209] *Muslim*, "Ashriba," 140; *Abu Nu'aym*, "Hilya," 1:30.

[210] *Tabari*, "Tarikh," 4:252.

[211] *Muslim*, "Fada'il," 48; *Bukhari*, "Manaqib," 23.

[212] Suyuti, *Al-Khasa'is*, 1:123; Hindi, *Kanz al-'Ummal*, 7:168.

The Messenger never refused anyone and, as Farazdak said, only said the word "no" when reciting the profession of faith while praying. Once, a bedouin came and asked the Messenger for something. The Messenger complied with his request. The bedouin continued to ask, and the Messenger continued to give until he had nothing left. When the bedouin asked again, he promised that he would give it to him when he had it. Angered by such rudeness, 'Umar said to the Messenger: "You were asked and you gave. Again you were asked and you gave, until you were asked once more and you promised!" 'Umar meant that the Messenger should not make things so difficult for himself. The Messenger did not approve of 'Umar's words. 'Abd Allah ibn Hudafa al-Sahmi stood up and said: "O Messenger, give without fear that the Owner of the Seat of Honor will make you poor!' Pleased with such words, the Messenger declared: "I was command-ed to do so!"[213]

He never refused a request, for it was he who said: "The generous are near to God, Paradise, and people, but distant from the Fire. The miserly are distant from God, Paradise, and people, but near to the Fire,"[214] and: "O people! Surely God has chosen for you Islam as religion. Improve your prac-tice of it through generosity and good manners."[215] His mer-cifulness rose up as moisture into the sky, and then rained as generosity so that hardened hearts would be fertile enough to grow "good trees whose roots are firm and whose branches are in the Heavens, and which yield their fruits every season by the leave of their Master."

---

[213] Ibn Kathir, 6:63.

[214] *Tirmidhi*, "Birr," 40.

[215] Hindi, 6:571.

His modesty

In society, each person has a window (status) through which he or she looks out to see others and be seen. If the window is built higher than their real stature, people try to make themselves appear taller through vanity and assumed airs. If the window is set lower than their real stature, they must bow in humility in order to look out, see, and be seen. Humility is the measure of one's greatness, just as vanity or conceit is the measure of low character.[216]

The Messenger had a stature so high that it could be said to touch the "roof of the Heavens." Therefore, he had no need to be seen. Whoever travels in the realm of virtues sees him before every created being, including angels. In the words of Said Nursi, the Messenger is the noble aide-de-camp of God. He lowered himself to stay in the world for a while so that people might find the way to God. Since he is the greatest of humanity, he is the greatest in modesty. This follows the well-knowing adage: "The greater one is, the more modest one is."

He never regarded himself as greater than anybody else. Only his radiant face and attractive person distinguished him from his Companions. He lived and dressed like the poorest people and sat and ate with them, just as he did with slaves and servants. Once a woman saw him eating and remarked: "He eats like a slave." The Messenger replied: "Could there be a better slave than me? I am a slave of God."[217]

One time when he was serving his friends, a bedouin came in and shouted: "Who is the master of this people?" The Messenger answered in such a way that he introduced himself

---

[216] Said Nursi, *Letters,* 2:315.

[217] Haythami, *Majma',* 9:21.

while expressing a substantial principle of Islamic leadership and public administration: "The people's master is the one who serves them." Ali says that among people the Messenger was one of them. When he and Abu Bakr reached Quba while emigrating to Madina, some Madinese who did not know what the Prophet looked like tried to kiss Abu Bakr's hands. The only external sign distinguishing one man from the other was that Abu Bakr seemed older than the Messenger.[218]

While the Muslims were building their mosque in Madina, the Prophet carried two sun-dried bricks; everyone else carried one.[219] While digging the trench to defend Madina, the Companions bound a stone around their stomachs to quell their hunger; the Messenger bound two.[220] When a man seeing him for the first time began trembling out of fear, because he found the Prophet's appearance so awe-inspiring, the Messenger calmed him: "Brother, don't be afraid. I am a man, like you, whose mother used to eat dry bread."[221] Another time, an insane woman pulled him by the hand and said: "Come with me and do my housework." He complied with her request.[222] 'A'isha reported that the Messenger patched his clothes, repaired his shoes, and helped his wives with the housework.[223]

Although his modesty elevated him to the highest rank, he regarded himself as an ordinary servant of God: "No one

---

[218] Ibn Hisham, 2:137.

[219] Bukhari, 1:111; Muslim, 2:65; Semhudi, *Wafa'*, 1:237; Ibn Sa'd, 1: 240.

[220] Tirmidhi, "Zuhd," 39.

[221] Ibn Maja, "At'ima," 30; Haythami, 9:20.

[222] Qadi 'Iyad, *Al-Shifa'*, 1:131, 133.

[223] Tirmidhi, *Shama'il*, 78; Ibn Hanbal, 6:256.

enters Paradise because of his or her deeds." When asked if this was true for him as well, he replied that he could enter Paradise only through the Mercy of God.[224]

His Companions always asked for his advice or permission before any action. Once 'Umar asked his permission to go for the minor pilgrimage. The Messenger allowed this, and even asked 'Umar to include him in his supplications. 'Umar rejoiced so much that later he would say: "If the worlds had been granted to me that day, I wouldn't have felt the same happiness."[225]

Humility was one of the Prophet's greatest qualities. As he attained a higher rank each day, he increased in humility and servanthood to God. His servanthood is prior to his Messengership, as seen in the declaration of faith: "I bear witness that there is no god but God; I also bear witness that Muhammad is His servant and Messenger." He preferred being a Prophet–slave to being a Prophet–king.

One day, while sitting with Archangel Gabriel, the Messenger mentioned that he had not eaten for several days. As soon as he said this, another angel appeared and asked: "O Messenger of God, God greets you and asks if you wish to be a Prophet–king or a Prophet–slave?" Gabriel advised him to be humble toward his Master. As humility was a fundamental part of his character, the Messenger replied: "I wish to be a Prophet–slave."[226] God praises his servanthood and mentions him as a servant in several verses: *When the servant of*

---

[224] *Bukhari*, "Riqaq," 18.

[225] *Ibn Maja*, "Manasik," 5; *Tirmidhi*, "Da'awat," 109; *Abu Dawud*, "Witr," 23.

[226] Ibn Hanbal, 2:231; Haythami, 9:18.

God stood up in prayer to Him, they (the jinn) were well nigh upon him in swarms (to watch his prayer) (72:19), and:

> If you are in doubt concerning that which We have sent down on Our servant, then bring a sura of the like thereof, and call your witnesses beside God if you are truthful. (2:23)

After Khadija and Abu Talib died, the Messenger became convinced that he could no longer expect any victory or security in Makka. So before things became too critical, he sought a new base in Ta'if. As the townspeople were quite hostile, he felt that he had no support and protection. But then God manifested His Mercy and honored him with the Ascension to His Presence. While narrating this incident, God mentions him as His servant to show that he deserves Ascension through his servanthood:

> Glory be to him, Who carried His servant by night from the Holy Mosque to the Furthest Mosque, the precincts of which We have blessed, that We might show him some of Our signs. He is the All-Hearing, the All-Seeing. (17:1)

Humility is the most important aspect of the Messenger's servanthood. He declared: "God exalts the humble and abases the haughty."[227] 'Ali describes the Messenger as:

> He was the most generous person in giving, and the mildest and the foremost in patience and perseverance. He was the most truthful in speech, the most amiable and congenial in companionship, and the noblest of them in family. Whoever sees him first is stricken by awe, but whoever knows him closely is deeply attracted to him. Whoever attempts to describe him says: 'I have never seen the like of him.'[228]

---

[227] Hindi, *Kanz al-'Ummal,* 3:113; Haythami, 10:325.

[228] Tirmidhi, Hadith No. 3880.

The ethos created by the Messenger*

It is difficult for us to understand Prophet Muhammad fully. As we tend to compartmentalize the universe, life, and humanity itself, we have no unitary vision. However, Prophet Muhammad perfectly combined a philosopher's intellect, a commander valor, a scientist's genius, a sage's wisdom, a statesman's insight and administrative ability, a Sufi master's spiritual profundity, and a scholar's knowledge in his own person.

Philosophers produce students, not followers; social or revolutionary leaders make followers, not complete people; Sufi masters make "lords of submission," not active fighters or intellectuals. But in Prophet Muhammad we find the characteristics of a philosopher, a revolutionary leader, a warrior and statesman, and a Sufi master. His school is one of the intellect and thought, revolution, submission and discipline, and goodness, beauty, ecstasy, and movement.

Prophet Muhammad transformed crude, ignorant, savage, and obstinate desert Arabs into an army of skilled fighters, a community of sincere devotees of a sublime cause, a society of gentleness and compassion, an assembly of sainthood, and a host of intellectuals and scholars. Nowhere else do we see such fervor and ardor combined with gentleness, kindness, sincerity, and compassion. This is a characteristic unique to the Muslim community, one that has been visible since its earliest days.

The "Garden" of Muhammad. Islam, the school of Prophet Muhammad, has been a "garden" rich in every kind of "flower." Like cascading water, God has brought forth from it such majestic people as Abu Bakr, 'Umar, 'Uthman, 'Ali, 'Umar ibn Abd al-'Aziz, Mahdi al-'Abbasi, Harun al-Rashid, Alp Arslan, Mehmed the Conqueror, Selim, and

Sulayman. These were not only statesmen of the highest caliber and invincible commanders, but also men of profound spirituality, deep knowledge, oration, and literature.

The Messenger's blessed, pure climate produced invincible generals. Among the first generation we see such military geniuses as Khalid, Sa'd ibn Abi Waqqas, Abu 'Ubayda, Shurahbil ibn Hasana, and A'la al-Khadrami. They were succeeded by such brilliant generals as Tariq ibn Ziyad and 'Uqba ibn Nafi', both of whom combined military genius with human tenderness and religious conviction and devotion.

When 'Uqba, the conqueror of North Africa, reached the Atlantic Ocean, 2,000 miles away from Arabia, he cried out: "And now, God, take my soul! If this sea didn't stretch out before me, I would convey Your holy Name across it to other lands!" We can hardly imagine Alexander the "Great" thinking such thoughts as he set out for Persia. Yet as conquerors, the two men achieved comparable feats.

'Uqba's idealism and his "possibility" with respect to the Divine Will would be transmuted into irresistible action in this world. Alexander's empire crashed after his death; the lands 'Uqba conquered still retain Islam as their dominant worldview, creed, and lifestyle 14 centuries later, despite attempts to change this reality.

Tariq was a victorious commander, not only when he defeated the 90,000-man Spanish army with a handful of self-sacrificing, valiant men, but also when he stood before the king's treasure and said: "Be careful, Tariq! You were a slave yesterday. Today you are a victorious commander. And tomorrow you will be under the earth."

Yavuz Selim, an Ottoman Sultan who regarded the world as too small for two rulers, was truly victorious when he crowned some kings and dethroned others, and also when he silently entered Istanbul at bedtime, after conquering Syria and Egypt, to avoid the people's enthusiastic welcome. He also was victorious when he ordered that the robe soiled by his teacher's horse be placed over his coffin because of its sanctity—it had been "soiled" by the horse of a scholar.

During the rapid conquests after the Prophet, many conquered people were distributed among the Muslim families. Those emancipated slaves eventually became the foremost religious scholars: Hasan ibn Hasan al-Basri (Basra); 'Ata' ibn Rabah, Mujahid, Sa'id ibn Jubayr, and Sulayman ibn Yasar (Makka); Zayd ibn Aslam, Muhammad ibn al-Munkadir, and Nafi' ibn Abi Nujayh (Madina); 'Alqama ibn Qays al-Nakha'i, Aswad ibn Yazid, Hammad, and Abu Hanifa Nu'man ibn Thabit (Kufa); Tawus and ibn Munabbih (Yemen); 'Ata ibn 'Abd Allah al-Khorasani (Khorasan); and Maqhul (Damascus). They all opened as splendid, sweet-smelling flowers in the garden of Muhammad. They established the Islamic legal code and brought up thousands of jurists, who wrote and complied volumes that are still valued as legal references.

One of these jurists, Imam Abu Hanifa, founded the Hanafi legal school, which has hundreds of millions of followers today. He brought up such great scholars as Imam Abu Yusuf, Imam Zufar, and Imam Muhammad Hasan al-Shaybani, who taught Imam Muhammad Idris al-Shafi'i. The notes Abu Hanifa dictated to Imam al-Shaybani were expounded centuries later by Imam Sarakhsi (the "Sun of Imams") in the 30-volume work *Al-Mabsut*.

Imam Shafi'i, who established the methodological principles of Islamic law, is regarded as reviver or renewer of religious sciences. However, when his students told Imam

Sarakhsi that Imam Shafi'i had memorized 300 fascicles of the Prophetic Traditions, the latter answered: "He had the zakat (one-fortieth) of the Traditions in my memory." Imam Shafi'i, Abu Hanifa, Imam Malik, or Ahmad ibn Hanbal, and so many others, were brought up in the school of Prophet Muhammad.

And then there are such Qur'anic interpreters as Ibn Jarir al-Tabari, Fakhr al-Din al-Razi, Ibn Kathir, Imam Suyuti, Allama Hamdi Yazir, and Sayyid Qutb. In addition, there are such famous hadith collectors as Imam Bukhari, Muslim, Tirmidhi, Abu Dawud, Ibn Maja, Nasa'i, Ibn Hanbal, Bayhaqi, Darimi, Daraqutni, Sayf al-Din al-'Iraqi, Ibn Hajar al-Asqalani, and many others. They are all ever-shining stars in the luminous sky of Islamic sciences. All received their light from Prophet Muhammad.

According to Islam, God created humanity on the best pattern, as the most universal and all-embracing theater of Divine Names and Attributes. But people, because of their heedlessness, can fall to the lowest levels. Sufism, the inner dimension of Islam, leads people to perfection or enables them to reacquire their primordial angelic state. Islam has produced countless saints. As it never separated our metaphysical quest or gnosis from the study of nature, many practicing Sufis were also scientists. Such leading saints as 'Abd al Qadir al-Jilani, Shah Naqshband, Ma'ruf al-Karkhi, Hasan Shazili, Ahmad Badawi, Shaykh al-Harrani, Ja'far al-Sadiq, Junayd al-Baghdadi, Bayazid al-Bistami, Muhy al-Din al-'Arabi, and Mawlana Jalal al-Din al-Rumi have illumined the way to truth and trained others to purify their selves.

Being embodiments of sincerity, Divine love, and pure intention, Sufi masters became the motivating factor and the source of power behind the Islamic conquests and the subsequent Islamization of those lands. Figures like Imam Ghazali, Imam Rabbani, and Bediuzzaman Said Nursi are revivers or renewers of the highest degree, and combined in themselves the enlightenment of sages, the knowledge of religious scholars, and the spirituality of great saints.

Islam is the middle way. Its elaborate hierarchy of knowledge is integrated by the principle of Divine Unity. There are juridical, social and theological sciences, as well as metaphysical ones, all deriving their principles from the Qur'an. Over time, Muslims developed elaborate philosophical, natural, and mathematical sciences, each of which has its source in a Beautiful Name of God. For example, medicine depends on the Name All-Healing; geometry and engineering on the Names All-Just and All-Determiner, and All-Shaper and All-Harmonizing; philosophy reflects the Name All-Wise.

Each level of knowledge views nature in a particular light. Jurists and theologians see it as the background for human action; philosophers and scientists see it as a domain to be analyzed and understood; and metaphysicians consider it the object of contemplation and the mirror reflecting suprasensible realities. The Author of Nature has inscribed His Wisdom upon every leaf and stone, on every atom and particle, and has created the world of nature in such a way that every phenomenon is a sign singing the glory of His Oneness.

Islam has maintained an intimate connection between science and Islamic studies. Thus the traditional education of Islamic scientists, particularly in the early centuries, comprised most of contemporary sciences. In later life, each scientist's aptitude and interest would cause him or her to become an expert and specialist in one or more sciences.

Universities, libraries, observatories, and other scientific institutions played a major role in the continuing vitality of Islamic science. These, together with students who would travel hundreds of miles to study under acknowledged scholars, ensured that the whole corpus of knowledge was kept intact and transmitted from one place to another and from one generation to the next. This knowledge did not remain static; rather, it continued to expand and enrich itself. Today, there are hundreds of thousands of Islamic (mainly in Arabic) manuscripts in the world's libraries, a large number of which deal with scientific subjects.[229]

For example, Abu Yusuf Ya'qub al-Kindi (the "Philosopher of the Arabs") wrote on philosophy, mineralogy, metallurgy, geology, physics, and medicine, among other subjects, and was an accomplished physician. Ibn al-Haytham was a leading Muslim mathematician and, without doubt, the greatest physicist. We know the names of over 100 of his works. Some 19 of them, dealing with mathematics, astronomy, and physics, have been studied by modern scholars. His work exercised a profound influence on later scholars, both in the Muslim world and in the West, where he was known Alhazen. One of his works on optics was translated into Latin in 1572.

---

[229] George Sarton, in his monumental *Introduction to the History of Science*, divided his work into chronological chapters, naming each chapter after the most eminent scientist of that period. From the middle of the second century AH (eight century CE) to the middle of the fifth century AH (eleventh century CE), each 50-year period carries the name of a Muslim scientist. Thus we have the "Time of al-Kharizmi," the "Time of al-Biruni," and so on. These chapters also contain the names of many other important Islamic scientists and their main works. (Tr.)

Abu al-Rayhan al-Biruni was one of the greatest scholars of medieval Islam, and certainly the most original and profound. He was equally well-versed in mathematics, astronomy, the physical and natural sciences, and also distinguished himself as a geographer and historian, a chronologist and linguist, and as an impartial observer of customs and creeds. Such figures as al-Kharizmi (mathematics), Ibn Shatir (astronomy), al-Khazini (physics), Jabir ibn Hayyan (medicine) are remembered even today. Andalucia (Muslim Spain) was the main center from which the West acquired knowledge and enlightenment for centuries.

Islam founded a most brilliant civilization. This should not be considered surprising, for the Qur'an begins with the injunction: *Read: In the Name of Your Master Who creates* (96:1). The Qur'an told people to read when there was very little to read and most people were illiterate. What we understand from this apparent paradox is that humanity is to "read" the universe itself as the "Book of Creation."

Its counterpart is the Qur'an, a book of letters and words. We are to observe the universe, perceive its meaning and content, and through those activities gain a deeper perception of the beauty and splendor of the Creator's system and the infinitude of His Might. Thus we are obliged to penetrate into the universe's manifold meanings, discover the Divine laws of nature, and establish a world in which science and faith complement each other. All of this will enable us to attain true bliss in both worlds.

In obedience to the Qur'an's injunctions and the Prophet's example, Muslims studied the Book of Divine Revelation (the Qur'an) and the Book of Creation (the universe) and eventually erected a magnificent civilization. Scholars from all over Europe benefited from centers of higher learning located in Damascus, Bukhara, Baghdad, Cairo, Faz, Qairwan, Zeituna, Cordoba, Sicily, Isfahan, Delhi and other great Islamic cities. Historians liken the Muslim world of the medieval ages, dark for Europe but golden and luminous for Muslims, to a beehive. Roads were full of students, scientists, and scholars traveling from one center of learning to another.

For the first 5 centuries of its existence, the realm of Islam was a most civilized and progressive area. Studded with splendid cities, gracious mosques, and quiet universities, the Muslim East offered a striking contrast to the Christian West, which was sunk in the Dark Ages. Even after the disastrous Mongol invasions and Crusades of the thirteenth century CE and onwards, it displayed vigor and remained for ahead of the West.

Although Islam ruled two-thirds of the known civilized world for at least 11 centuries, laziness and negligence of what was going on beyond its borders caused it to decay. However, it must be pointed out clearly that only Islamic civilization decayed—not Islam. Military victories and superiority, which continued into the eighteenth century, encouraged Muslims to rest on their laurels and neglect further scientific research. They abandoned themselves to living their own lives, and recited the Qur'an without studying its deeper meanings. Meanwhile, Europe made great advances in sciences, which they had borrowed from the Muslims.

What we call "sciences" are, in reality, languages of the Divine Book of Creation (another aspect of Islam). Those who ignore this book are doomed to failure in this world.

When the Muslims began to ignore it, it was only a matter of time before they would be dominated by some external force. In this case, that external force was Europe. European cruelty, oppression, and imperialism also contributed greatly to this result.

The present modern civilization cannot last for long, for it is materialistic and cannot satisfy humanity's perennial needs. Such Western sociologists as Oswald Spengler have predicted its collapse on the grounds that it is against human nature and values. On the other hand, Islam has been around for 14 centuries. In addition, it is fully capable of establishing the bright world of the future on the firm foundation of its creed, ethics, spirituality, and morality, as well as its legal, social and economic structures.

Endnote

* This is the tribute of Lamartine, a French historian, to the Prophet of Islam: "Is there any man greater than Muhammad?"

Never a man set himself, voluntarily or involuntarily, a more sublime aim, since this aim was superhuman: To subvert superstitions which had been interposed between man and his Creator, to render God unto man and man unto God; to restore the rational and sacred idea of divinity amidst the chaos of the material and disfigured gods of idolatry then existing. Never has a man undertaken a work so far beyond human power with so feeble means, for he had in the conception as well as in the execution of such a great design no other instrument than himself, and no other aid except a handful of men living in a corner of desert. Finally, never has a man accomplished such a huge and lasting revolution in the world, because in less than two centuries after its appearance, Islam, in faith and arms, reigned over the whole of Arabia, and conquered in God's name Persia, Khorasan, Western India, Syria, Abyssinia, all the known continent of Northern Africa, numerous islands of Mediterranean, Spain, and a part of Gaul.

If greatness of purpose, smallness of means, and astounding results are the three criteria of human genius, who could dare to compare any great men to Muhammad? The most famous men created arms, laws, and empires only. They founded, if anything at all, no more than material powers which often crumbled away before their eyes. This man moved not only armies, legislation, empires, peoples, and dynasties, but millions of men in one-third of the then-inhabited world; and more than that, he moved the altars, the gods, the religions, the ideas, the beliefs, and the souls. On the basis of a Book, every letter of which has become law, he created a spiritual nationality which has blended together peoples of every tongue and of every race. He has left to us the indelible characteristic of this Muslim nationality, the hatred of false gods, and the passion for the One and immaterial God. This avenging patriotism against the profanation of Heaven formed the virtue of the followers of Muhammad: the conquest of one-third of the Earth to his creed was his miracle.

The idea of God's Unity proclaimed amidst the exhaustion of fabulous theogenies was in itself such a miracle that upon its utterance from his lips it destroyed all the ancient temples of idols and set on fire one-third of the world. His life, his meditations, his heroic reviling against the superstitions of his country, and his boldness in defying the furies of idolatry; his firmness in enduring them for thirteen years in Makka, his acceptance of the role of the public scorn and almost of being a victim of his fellow countrymen: all these and, finally his incessant preaching, his wars against odds, his faith in his success and his superhuman security in misfortune, his forbearance in victory, his ambition which was entirely devoted to one idea and in no manner striving for an empire; his endless prayer, his mystic conversations with God, his death and his triumph after death; all these attest not to an imposture but to a firm conviction. It was his conviction which gave him the power to restore a creed. This creed was twofold: God's Unity and the immateriality of God—the former telling what God is, the latter telling what God is not.

Philosopher, orator, apostle, legislator, warrior, conqueror of ideas, restorer of rational dogmas, of a cult without images; the founder of twenty terrestrial states and of one spiritual state, that is Muhammad. As regards all standards by which human greatness may be measured, we may well ask: Is there any man greater than he? (Tr.)

CHAPTER 6

The Sunna and Its Place
in Islamic Legislation

The science of *hadith* deals with Prophet Muhammad's life, especially his words and actions, and the actions he approved of in others. In this section, we will restrict ourselves to his own words and actions. These words and their meanings are his alone, for they were not included in the Qur'an, the Recited Revelation and whose meaning and wording belong to God exclusively. His actions include those whose rule and authority we are obliged to follow as laws, and his personal affairs, which are a source of spiritual reward and blessing if followed.

The science of *fiqh* (Islamic law) does not concern itself with the Prophet's personal affairs. The *fuqaha'* (jurists) consider that if those affairs touch upon the voluntary and purposed acts, they should be dealt with under the relevant law. However, if they are matters of the Prophet's personal likes and dislikes, which are not a basis for legislation, they are of no concern to the jurists. According to the *muhaddithun* (scholars of Hadith [Traditionists]), everything related to the Messenger is included in the meaning of Hadith (Tradition) and concerns them.

The Sunna is the record of the Messenger's every act, word, and confirmation, as well as the second source of Islamic legislation and life (the Qur'an is the first one). All scholars of religious sciences, and sometimes those of the natural scientists, use it to establish the principles of their disciplines and to solve difficulties. The Qur'an and authentic prophetic Traditions enjoin Muslims to follow the Sunna.

The Qur'an and the Sunna are inseparable. The Sunna clarifies the ambiguities in the Qur'an by expanding upon what is mentioned only briefly in it, specifies what is unconditional, enables generalizations from what is specifically stated, and particularizations from what is generally stated.

For example, how to pray, fast, give alms, and make pilgrimage was established and expounded in the Sunna. So were such principles or legislation that no one can inherit from the Prophet, killers cannot inherit from their victims, the meat of domestic donkeys and wild animals cannot be eaten, and men cannot marry a wife's female cousins if she is still living. Indeed, the Sunna is relevant to all aspects of Islam, and Muslims must design their lives according to it. For this reason, it has been studied and transmitted to each new generation with almost the same care as the Qur'an.

The Messenger ordered his Companions to obey his Sunna absolutely. He spoke distinctly, so they could understand and memorize his words, and encouraged them to convey his every word to future generations. Sometimes he even urged them to write his words down, for: "Whatever I say is true." The Companions were fully attentive to what his words and deeds and showed a great desire to mold their lives to his, even in the smallest details. They regarded his every word and deed as a Divine trust to which they must adhere and follow as closely as possible. Viewing his words as Divine gifts, they internalized, preserved, and transmitted them.

As truthfulness is the cornerstone of the Islamic character, the Companions did not lie. Just as they did not distort or alter the Qur'an, they did their best to preserve the Traditions and entrust them to future generations by either memorizing them or writing them down. Among the Hadith compilations made during the time of the Companions, three are very famous: *Al-Sahifa al-Sadiqa* by 'Abd Allah ibn 'Amr ibn al-'As, *Al-Sahifa al-Sahiha* by Hammam ibn Munabbih, and *Al-Majmu'* by Zayd ibn 'Ali ibn Husayn.

The Companions were extremely conscientious in relating the Traditions. For example, 'A'isha and 'Abd Allah ibn 'Umar would relate them word for word, not changing even one letter. Ibn Mas'ud and Abu al-Darda' would tremble, as if feverish, when asked to report a Tradition.

Caliph 'Umar ibn 'Abd al-'Aziz (ruled 717-20 CE) ordered that the orally preserved and circulated individual Tradition compilations be written down. Such illustrious figures as Sa'id ibn al-Musayyib, Sha'bi, 'Alqama, Sufyan al-Thawri, and Zuhri pioneered this sacred task. They were followed by the greatest specialists, who were entirely focused on the Traditions' accurate transmittal as well as studying their meaning, wording, and their narrators' careful critiques.

Thanks to these Traditionists, we have the second source of Islam in its original purity. Only through studying the Prophet's life and then conforming our own to it can we gain God's good pleasure and travel the way leading to Paradise. The greatest saints receive their light from this "sun" of guidance, Prophet Muhammad, and send it to those in darkness so that they may find their way.

The Sunna and its role

Sunna literally means "a conduct and a good or evil path to be followed." This is the meaning used in the following *hadith*:

> Those who establish a good path in Islam receive the
> reward of those who follow it, without any decrease in
> their reward. Those who establish an evil path in Islam
> are burdened with the sins of those who follow it, with-
> out any decrease in their burden.[230]

This term has different terminological connotations according to each group of Traditionists, methodologists, and jurists. Traditionists view it as including everything connected to the religious commandments reported from the Messenger and categorized, according to the Hanafi legal school (followers of Abu Hanifa), as obligations, necessities, practices particular to or encouraged by the Prophet as recommended and desirable.

Methodologists consider it to be every word, deed, and approval of the Messenger as related by his Companions. Jurists, who approach it as the opposite of innovation in religion, consider it a synonym for *hadith*. They use it for the Prophet's words, deeds, and approvals, all of which provide a basis for legislation and categorizing people's actions.

Derived from the word *haddatha* (to inform), *hadith* literally means "a tiding or information." Over time, it has assumed the meaning of every word, deed, and approval ascribed to the Messenger. Ibn Hajar says: "According to the Shari'a, the Hadith is everything related to the Messenger."

Another literal meaning is something that takes place within time. This is why some scholars of fine discernment write that *hadith* is that which is not Divine, eternal, or without beginning in time. This fine line separates Hadith from the Qur'an, as the latter is Divine, and eternal, and without beginning in time. The Messenger distinguished his

---

[230] *Muslim*, "Zakat," 69; *Ibn Maja*, "Muqaddima," 203.

words from the Qur'an: "It is two things only, nothing else: the Word and guidance. The best word is the Word of God, and the best guidance is the guidance of Muhammad."[231]

Categories of the Sunna

The Sunna is divided into three categories: verbal, practical, and based on approval.

The Verbal Sunna. This category consists of the Messenger's words, which provide a basis for many religious commandments. To cite a few examples:

- "No bequest to the heir."[232] In other words, people cannot bequeath any of their wealth to their heirs, since they will naturally inherit the bulk of the estate. A bequest can be made to the poor or some social service institutions.

- "Don't harm (others), and don't return harm for harm."[233] That is, do not engage in any negative and damaging behavior toward others, and do not retaliate against them by returning bad for bad.

- "A tenth will be given (out of crops grown in fields) watered by rain or rivers; but a twentieth (out of those grown in fields) watered by people (irrigation or watering)."[234] The Qur'an enjoins charity, but goes into no detail about how to do so correctly. All such regulations were established by the Sunna.

---

[231] *Ibn Maja*, "Muqaddima," 7.

[232] *Ibn Maja*, "Wasaya," 6; *Tirmidhi*, "Wasaya," 5.

[233] Ibn Hanbal, *Musnad*, 1:313.

[234] *Tirmidhi*, "Zakat," 14; *Bukhari*, "Zakat," 55.

- "A sea is that of which the water is clean and the dead animals are lawful to eat."[235] He gave this response when
  someone asked him if *wudu'* could be done with sea-
  water. This has provided a basis for many other rulings.

The Practical Sunna. The Qur'an usually lays down only
general rules and principles. For example, it enjoins prayer
and pilgrimage but does not describe in detail how to perform
them. The Messenger, taught by God through inspiration or
through Gabriel, provided this information through his
actions. His life was one long, unique example to be followed
by all Muslims. For example, he led the daily prayers before
his Companions five times a day and ordered them to pray as
he prayed.[236]

The Sunna based on approval. The Messenger corrected
his Companions' mistakes usually by ascending the pulpit
and asking: "Why has somebody done this?"[237] When he saw
something agreeable in them, he gave his approval either
explicitly or by keeping silent. For example:

- Two Companions traveling in the desert could not find
  enough water for *wudu'* before praying, and so used sand
  (tayammum). When they found water later on before the
  prayer's time had passed, one of them performed wudu'
  and repeated the prayer, and the other did not. When they
  asked The Messenger about it later, he told the one who

---

[235] Abu Dawud, "Tahara," 41; Tirmidhi, "Tahara," 52; Nasa'i, "Tahara,"
47. Generally, the Qur'an forbids eating animals that were not slaughtered according to Islamic rules. The Sunna, however restricts this general rule (commandment) by allowing the consumption of sea animals that
die in water.

[236] *Bukhari*, "Adhan," 18; Ibn Hanbal, 5:53.

[237] *Bukhari*, "Salat," 70; *Muslim*, "Nikah," 5.

had not repeated the prayer: "You acted in accordance with the Sunna." Then, he turned to the other one and said: "For you, there is double reward."[238]

- The Messenger ordered a march upon the Banu Qurayza immediately after the Battle of the Trench. He said: "Hurry up! We'll perform the afternoon prayer there." Some Companions, concluding that they should hasten and pray over there started out without delay. Others understood that they were to hasten to the Banu Qurayza's territory only, and that they could pray before departing. The Messenger approved of both interpretations.[239]

The Sunna in the Qur'an

The Sunna is the main source of our religious life. It is promoted and encouraged by the Qur'an: *He Who raised among the unlettered ones a Messenger from them, reciting to them His revelations, purifies them and instructs them in the Book and the Wisdom* (62:2). According to most Qur'anic interpreters and Traditionists, *the Wisdom* signifies the Sunna. The Qur'an, being a miraculous exposition, contains nothing superfluous and does not exceed the proper terms. As *Wisdom* comes after *Book,* it must be something different. *The Book* is the Qur'an, and *the Wisdom* is the Sunna showing how the Qur'an is to be applied to our daily lives.

The Qur'an commands absolute obedience to the Messengers, for they have been sent to guide people to truth in every sphere of their lives. Our loyalty is to God, Who has sent His Messenger and told us to obey him, and not to that man personally: *We have not sent a Messenger save to be*

---

[238] *Darimi,* "Tahara," 65; *Abu Dawud,* "Tahara," 126.

[239] *Darimi,* "Maghazi," 30; "Khawf," 5.

obeyed by God's leave (4:64), and: *O you who believe! Obey God and His Messenger, and do not turn away from him* (8:20).

Obedience to God means unconditional obedience to what has been revealed in the Qur'an. Obedience to the Messenger means following his way of life as closely as possible by obeying what is enjoined and prohibited in the Qur'an and by the Messenger. The Sunna is a comprehensively detailed account of his life. He told his community: "Take care! I have been given the Book and its like together with it."[240]

As stated in 8:20, Muslims must not turn away from the Messenger. Therefore, disobeying, belittling, or criticizing the Sunna amounts to heresy or even apostasy. Many other verses emphasize the necessity of following the Sunna, such as: *O you who believe! Obey God and obey the Messenger and those in authority from among you* (4:59). The verse stresses obedience to God and to the Messenger. The repetition of *obey* in the imperative mood indicates that the Messenger is authorized to command or forbid, and that Muslims must do what he says. Besides, where obedience to those Muslims in authority is ordered, the Prophet has a far greater right to be obeyed.

Another verse states: *Obey God and His Messenger and do not dispute with one another, lest you should be dissolved (dispersed) and your strength fade away; and be steadfast* (8:46). Muslim strength and unity lie in submission to God and His Messenger. The Messenger established the Sunna by living the Qur'an, which means that it is the only way his community can follow. Based on this, we can

---

[240] *Abu Dawud,* "Sunna," 5.

say that the Sunna is both more comprehensive than the Qur'an and indispensable for leading an upright life in Islamic terms.

Muslims can obey God and show their love for Him only by obeying the Messenger or by following his Sunna: *Say (O Muhammad): "If you love God, follow me so that God loves you"* (3:31); *Surely there is for you in the Messenger an excellent example for him who aspires to God and the Hereafter, and mentions God oft* (33:21); and many other verses. Those who claim to love God or that God loves them, despite their non-adherence to the Sunna, are seriously deluded and astray.

Muslims must cling to the Sunna if they want to remain on the Straight Path and avoid deviation. For example: One day a woman said to 'Abd Allah ibn Mas'ud: "I have heard that you call down God's curse upon women who tattoo their bodies, pluck their facial hair, force their teeth apart in order to look more beautiful, and who change the creation of God."[241] Ibn Mas'ud answered: "All of this is found in the Qur'an." The woman objected: "I swear by God that I have read the entire Qur'an, but I couldn't find anything related to this matter." Ibn Mas'ud told her: "Our Prophet called God's curse upon women who wear wigs, who join somebody's hair to theirs, and who have tattoos on their bodies. Haven't you read: *Whatever the Messenger brings you, adopt it; whatever he forbids you, refrain from it* (59:7)?"[242]

---

[241] This covers such cosmetic surgery procedures as changing the shape of the nose or lips, inserting breast implants, or somehow altering other bodily features through cosmetic surgery to look more beautiful. Such operations are allowed only when medically necessary, as in the case of severe burns or deformity.

[242] *Muslim,* "Libas," 120.

The Qur'an also declares:

> Nay, by your Master, they will never become believers
> until they choose you as judge to settle the matters in
> dispute between them. (4:65)

The Sunna in the Traditions

The way of the Prophet is the way of God. As the Sunna
is the way of the Prophet, those who reject it are, in essence,
rejecting (and disobeying) God. As the Prophet stated:
"Whoever obeys me, obeys God; whoever disobeys me, disobeys God."[243] Such disobedience is "rewarded" with Hell:
"My nation will enter Paradise, except those who rebel."
When asked who these rebels were, the Prophet answered:
"Whoever obeys me will enter Paradise; whoever disobeys
me rebels."[244]

The Sunna links all past, present, and future Muslims. It
also enables Muslims to maintain their unity, as it forms a
unique culture and system. Concerning this, the Messenger
declared: "Those who survive me will witness many disputes
and disagreements. Therefore, follow my way and the way of
my rightly-guided and rightly-guiding successors. Hold firm
to that way—cling to it with your teeth."[245]

Following the Sunna, on both the individual and the collective level, becomes vital when Islam is attacked and
Muslims lose their supremacy. The Messenger stated that "at
a time when the Muslim community breaks with Islam and
consequently disintegrates, the one who holds firm to the

---

[243] *Bukhari*, "Ahkam," 1; *Ibn Maja*, "Muqaddima," 1.

[244] *Bukhari,* "I'tisam," 2; *Ibn Hanbal*, 2:361.

[245] *Abu Dawud*, "Sunna," 5; *Tirmidhi*, "'Ilm," 16; *Ibn Maja*, "Muqaddima,"
6.

Sunna gains the reward of a martyr."[246] Given this, those who criticize it should be asked, as the Qur'an asks unbelievers: *Where are you headed?*

The Sunna's role

The Sunna has two main functions. First, it enjoins and prohibits, lays down the principles related to establishing all religious obligations and necessities, and determines what is lawful or unlawful. Second, it interprets the Qur'an.

In each daily prescribed prayer, we recite: *Guide us to the Straight Path, to the path of those you have blessed, not of those who incurred (Your) wrath, nor of the misguided* (1:5-7). The verses mention, but do not specify, two groups of people. According to the Prophet, those who incurred God's wrath are Jews who have gone astray, and the misguided are Christians who have gone astray.[247]

The Jews killed many of their Prophets and caused trouble in many places. Although they had once followed Divine guidance and guided others to the Straight Path (during the times of Moses, David, and Solomon), over time many of them went astray and incurred both God's wrath and public ignominy. Those who follow this way also are included in *those who incurred (Your) wrath.* Such Jews are condemned harshly in the Bible as well. In fact, the Bible is much harsher toward them than the Qur'an. In many verses, the Qur'an reproaches such Jews and Christians very mildly and compassionately.

At first, the Christians obeyed Jesus and followed his way despite severe persecution. They heroically resisted all forms

---

[246] Abu Nu'aym, *Hilya'*, 8:200; Daylami, *Musnad al-Firdaws*, 4:198.

[247] *Tirmidhi*, "Tafsir al-Qur'an," 2; *Tabari*, "Tafsir," 1:61, 64.

of hypocrisy and Roman oppression. But over time, many came under the influence of various Middle Eastern religions and philosophies as well as Roman paganism. By the time Christianity became the Roman Empire's official religion, it already was divided into many sects and had more than 300 Gospels in circulation. Although many remained devoted to the original creed of Jesus, many others contaminated these pure teachings with borrowed elements. The Qur'an therefore describes them as the misguided.

By making the above interpretation, the Prophet explained how people who had been blessed with Divine guidance could go astray and end up deserving God's wrath. Thus, he warned Muslims not to follow such Jews and Christians.

Out of many examples showing how the Sunna interprets the Qur'an, we also cite the following:

- When the verse: *Those who believed and did not mix their belief with wrongdoing: for them is security and they are those who are truly guided* (6:82) was revealed, the Companions, well aware what wrongdoing meant, asked the Messenger fearfully: "Is there one among us who has never done wrong?" The Messenger explained: "It's not as you think. It's as Luqman said to his son: *Don't associate any partners with God; surely, associating partners with God is a grave wrongdoing* (31:13).[248]

- 'A'isha and Ibn Mas'ud are of the opinion that the mid-time prayer in: *Attend the prayers without any omission and the mid-time prayer* (2:238) is the afternoon prayer. Once 'A'isha ordered her servant to write a copy of the Qur'an for her and reminded her: "When you come to the

---

[248] *Bukhari,* "Tafsir," 31/1.

verse: Attend the prayers without any omission, and the mid-time prayer, inform me." When this verse was to be copied out, 'A'isha dictated to her servant: "Attend the prayers without any omission, and the mid-time prayer, the afternoon prayer," and added: "This is what I heard from the Messenger."[249] Although there are some other interpretations, 'A'isha and Ibn Mas'ud were certain that it was the afternoon prayer.

In addition to interpreting the Qur'an's ambiguities, the Sunna fills in the details about those subjects that the Qur'an mentions only briefly. For example, the Qur'an orders Muslims to pray properly, but does not explain how they should pray. Although some leading interpreters deduce the prayer times from such verses such as: *Perform the prayer correctly at the two ends of the day and nigh of the night; surely the good deeds remove the evil deeds* (11:114), the exact prayer time was established by the Prophet as follows:

> On two occasions, Archangel Gabriel led me in the five daily prayers at the Ka'ba. On the first time, he prayed the noon prayer at noon, when an item's shadow was only as long as its base. When the shadow was as long as the actual item, he prayed the afternoon prayer. He prayed the evening prayer when it was time for a person to break the fast. He prayed the late evening (or night) prayer when dusk disappeared, and the dawn (or morning) prayer when those who intend to fast can no longer eat or drink. The second time, he prayed the noon prayer when an item's shadow was as long as the actual item, and prayed the afternoon prayer when it was twice as long as the actual item. He prayed the evening prayer at the same time he had prayed it previously. He prayed the night prayer after

---

[249] *Tirmidhi*, "Tafsir al-Qur'an," 3.

one-third of the night had passed, and the dawn prayer
when it was lighter and the sun had still not risen.
Then he turned to me and said: "O Muhammad, each
of the five daily prayers should be performed between
these two periods of time, as the Prophets before you
did it."[250]

The Messenger also taught his community everything
related to prayer: its conditions; all obligatory, necessary, and
commendable acts that validate and ennoble it; and all acts
that invalidate and damage it. He passed on, both through
words and actions, all that they needed to know about worship. This all-inclusive term is not limited to the actual
prayers, but also includes such areas as fasting, alms-giving,
pilgrimage, and many more. Just as he told his followers to
"pray as you see me pray," he told them to "learn from me the
rites and ceremonies of pilgrimage"[251] after he actually performed it with his Companions. If the Qur'an had gone into
such exhaustive detail on such matters, it would have been
many times its present size.

The Sunna also restricts general laws and commandments in the Qur'an. For example, it lays down general principles of inheritance. When the Prophet's daughter Fatima
went to Abu Bakr, the first Caliph, and asked for her inheritance, Abu Bakr replied: "I heard the Messenger say: 'The
community of the Prophets does not leave anything to be
inherited. What we leave is for charity.'"[252] This *hadith*
excludes the Prophets and their children from the laws of
inheritance. Likewise, the Messenger decreed that "the killer

---

[250] *Abu Dawud*, "Salat," 2; *Tirmidhi,* "Mawaqit," 1.

[251] *Nasa'i*, "Manasik," 220; *Ibn Hanbal*, 3:366.

[252] *Bukhari*, "I'tisam," 5; "Khums," 1; *Muslim*, "Jihad," 51; Ibn Hanbal,
2:463.

(of his testator) would be disinherited."[253] In other words, if someone kills his or her parents, brother (sister), or uncle (aunt), they cannot inherit from them.

The Qur'an commands: *And the thief, male and female, cut off the hands of both, as a recompense for what they have earned, and a punishment exemplary from God; God is All-Mighty, All-Wise* (5:38). Whether this punishment is to be applied to every thief, or only to those who steal goods of a certain value, is not clear.

Also, in: *O believers, when you stand up to pray wash your faces, and your hands up to elbows...* (5:6), the *hand* extends to the elbow. But the Qur'an does not mention specifically what part of the *hand* should be cut, nor in what circumstances this punishment should be applied. For example, during 'Umar's caliphate there was a period of famine, and he did not apply this punishment.

The Qur'an decrees: *O you who believe! Consume not your goods among yourselves in vanity [through theft, usury, bribery, hoarding, and so on], except it be trade by mutual agreement* (4:29). Islam encourages trade as a livelihood, as long as it is carried out according to Islamic law. One condition, as stated in the verse, is mutual agreement. However, the Messenger decreed: "Don't sell fruits until their amount is definite in the tree [so that the amount to be given as alms can be determined]"[254] and: "Don't go to meet peasants outside the market to buy their goods [Let them earn the market prices of their goods]."[255]

---

[253] *Tirmidhi*, "Fara'id," 17.

[254] *Bukhari*, "Buyu'," 82; *Muslim*, "Buyu'," 51.

[255] *Muslim*, "Buyu'," 5:14-17.

In sum, the Qur'an contains general principles that are explained by the Messenger and then applied by him to daily life. God allowed His Messenger to issue rulings, as necessary, and ordered the believers: *Whatever the Messenger brings you, adopt it; whatever he forbids you, refrain from it* (59:7).

Establishing the Sunna ·

The Sunna was memorized, recorded, and carefully preserved so that it could be passed down without distortion or alteration. The Sunna is included in the meaning of: *We have sent down the dhikr [the collection of Divine warnings and recitations, the Divine guidance] in parts, and We are its preserver* (15:9).

The Sunna, the unique example set by the Messenger for all Muslims to follow, shows us how to bring our lives into agreement with God's Commands. This being the case, the Messenger stood at the intersection of ignorance and knowledge, truth and falsehood, right and wrong, and this world and the other. He established, through his words as well as his actions and those of which he approved, the Divine way that all Muslims must follow.

The Sunna is the window opened on the Messenger of God, the sacred way leading to the blessings of Islam. Without it, Muslims cannot implement Islam in their daily lives, establish a connection with the Messenger, or receive his blessings. Those who ignore it run a grave danger of deviating and placing themselves outside Islam, for it is an unbreakable rope guaranteeing Muslim unity and elevating those who hold fast to it to Paradise.

There are several motives for establishing the Sunnah. Among them are the following:

- God commands Muslims to follow the Sunna:

  > Whatever the Messenger brings you, adopt it; whatev-
  > er he forbids you, refrain from it; fear God and seek
  > His protection, surely God is He Whose punishment is
  > severe. (59:7)

  Besides relaying the Qur'an, the Messenger expanded on
  it through the Sunna. The word *whatever* covers everything related to the Qur'an (the Revelation Recited) and
  the Hadith (the Revelation Unrecited). He only spoke what
  was revealed to him, or inspired in him, by God. Verse
  59:7 tells Muslims to obey the Messenger so that they can
  become deserving of God's protection. Aware of this, the
  Companions paid close attention to his every word and
  were very careful in carrying out his commands.

- A Muslim can obtain God's good pleasure and attain true
  bliss in both worlds only by following the Sunna, for its
  sole purpose is to lead humanity to safety and eternal happiness. The Qur'an declares:

  > Verily, there is for you a most excellent example in the
  > Messenger of God, for him who aspires to God and the
  > Last Day, and mentions God oft. (33:21)

- The Messenger encourages Muslims to learn his Sunna.
  The Companions knew what they needed to do to avoid
  eternal punishment and receive God's blessing, and so
  zealously memorized and recorded the Prophet's sayings.
  They heard him pray:

  > [On the day when some faces will be radiant and
  > some mournful], may God make radiant [with joy and
  > happiness] the face of the one who has heard a word
  > from me and, preserving (memorizing) it, conveys it
  > to others.[256]

---

[256] *Tirmidhi*, "'Ilm," 7.

According to another version, he prayed:

> May God make radiant the face of the servant who has
> heard my speech and, committing it to memory and
> observing it in daily life, conveys it to others.[257]

- The Companions knew the Prophet would intercede for
  them only if they followed the Sunna:

> On the Day of Judgment, I will put my head on the
> ground and ask God to forgive my nation. I will be
> told: "O Muhammad, raise your head and ask; you will
> be given whatever you ask. Intercede; your interces-
> sion will be accepted."[258]

The Messenger spoke distinctly and sometimes repeated
his words so his audience could memorize them.[259] He
taught them supplications and recitations that were not in
the Qur'an with the same care and emphasis as he taught
the Qur'an.[260] He continually urged his Companions to
spread his words and teach others what they knew. If they
did not, he warned them: "If you are asked about something you know and then conceal that knowledge, a bridle
of fire will be put on you on the Day of Judgment."[261] The
Qur'an also conveys this warning:

> Those who conceal what God has sent down of the
> Book and sell it for a little price, they do not eat in their
> bellies but the fire; God shall not speak to them on the
> Day of Resurrection, nor shall He purify them; for
> them is a painful torment. (2:174)

---

[257] *Ibn Maja*, "Muqaddima," 18.

[258] *Bukhari*, "Tafsir," 2:1; *Muslim*, "Iman," 322.

[259] *Bukhari*, "Manaqib," 23; *Muslim*, "Fada'il al-Sahaba," 160.

[260] *Muslim*, "Salat," 61; *Abu Dawud*, "Salat," 178.

[261] *Tirmidhi*, "'Ilm," 3; *Ibn Maja*, "Muqaddima," 24.

Keeping these words and warnings in mind, the Companions strove to memorize the Qur'an and the Sunna and to record the latter. They then lived their lives in accordance with Islamic principles and commands, and conveyed what they knew to others. They formed study and discussion groups to refine their understanding. The Messenger encouraged them to do this:

> If people come together in a house of God and recite from the Book of God and study it, peace and tranquillity descends upon them, (God's) Compassion envelops them, angels surround them, and God mentions them to those in His presence.[262]

Other motives

The Companions lived in an ethos that never lost its freshness. Like a growing embryo in the womb, the Muslim community grew and flourished, eventually including all areas of life. It was fed continuously with Revelation. Such factors, along with the Sunna and the Companions' devotion to the Prophet, drove them to record or memorize whatever The Messenger said or did.

For example, when 'Uthman ibn Mad'un died, the Messenger shed as many tears as he had over Hamza's corpse. He kissed his forehead and attended the funeral. Witnessing this, a woman said: "How happy you are, 'Uthman. You have become a bird to fly in Paradise." The Messenger turned to her and asked: "How do you know that, while I, a Prophet, do not know? Unless God informs, no one can know whether someone is pure enough to deserve Paradise and whether he will go to Paradise or Hell." The woman collected herself, and said that she would never make

---

[262] *Muslim*, "Dhikr," 38; *Ibn Maja*, "Muqaddima," 17.

such an assumption again.[263] Is it conceivable that she and the Companions present at the funeral should have forgotten that event? They did not forget it, as well as others that they witnessed during the Prophet's lifetime.

Another example: Quzman fought heroically at Uhud, and was finally killed. The Companions considered him a martyr. However, the Prophet told them that Quzman had gone to Hell. Someone later informed them that Quzman had committed suicide because of his wounds, and had said before he died: "I fought out of tribal solidarity, not for Islam." The Messenger concluded: "God strengthens this religion even through a sinful man."[264] Like others, that event and his final comment could never have been forgotten by the Companions, nor could they have failed to mention it whenever they talked about Uhud or martyrdom.

A similar incident took place during the conquest of Khaybar. 'Umar reports:

> On the day Khaybar was conquered, some Companions listed the martyrs. When they mentioned so-and-so as a martyr, the Messenger said: "I saw him in Hell, for he stole a robe from the spoils of war before it was distributed." He then told me to stand up and announce: "Only believers (who are true representatives or embodiments of absolute faith and trustworthiness) can enter Paradise."[265]

Each word and action of the Messenger refined the Companions' understanding and implementation of Islam. This motivated them to absorb his every word and action.

---

[263] *Ibn Athir*, "Usd al-Ghaba," 3:600.

[264] *Muslim*, "Iman," 178; *Bukhari*, "Iman," 178.

[265] *Muslim*, "Iman," 182.

When they settled in newly conquered lands, they conveyed their knowledge to the new Muslims, thereby ensuring that the Sunna would be transmitted from one generation to the next.

They were so well-behaved toward the Messenger that they would remain silent in his presence and let bedouins or others ask him questions. One day a bedouin named Dimam ibn Tha'laba came and asked rudely: "Which one of you is Muhammad?" They replied that he was the white-complexioned man sitting against the wall.

The bedouin turned to him and asked loudly: "O son of 'Abd al-Muttalib, I will ask you some questions! They may be injurious to you, so don't become annoyed with me." The Prophet told him to ask whatever was in his mind. He said: "Tell me, for the sake of God, your Master and the Master of those before you, did He send you to these people as a Prophet?" When the Prophet said that this was true, Dimam asked: "Tell me, for God's sake, is it God Who ordered you to pray five times a day?" When the Prophet said that this was true, Dimam continued questioning him in the same manner about fasting and alms-giving. Always receiving the same answer, Dimam announced: "I am Dimam ibn Tha'laba, from the tribe of Sa'd bin Bakr. They sent me to you as an envoy. I declare that I believe in whatever message you have brought from God."[266]

Like many others, this event too was not allowed to fall into oblivion; rather, it was handed down to succeeding generations until it was recorded in the books of Tradition.

Ubayy ibn Ka'b was one of the foremost reciters of the Qur'an. One day the Messenger sent for him and said: "God

---

[266] *Muslim*, "Fada'il al-Sahaba," 161.

ordered me to recite *Surat al-Bayyina to you*." Ubayy was so moved that he asked: "Did God mention my name?" The Messenger's answer moved him to tears.[267] This was so great an honor for Ubayy's family that his grandson would introduce himself as "the grandson of the man to whom God ordered His Messenger to recite *Surat al-Bayyina*."

This was the ethos in which the Companions lived. Every day a new "fruit of Paradise" and "gift" of God was presented to them, and every day brought new situations. Previously unaware of faith, Divine Scripture, and Prophethood, these desert Arabs, gifted with a keen memory and a talent for poetry, were brought up by the Messenger to educate future Muslim generations. God chose them as His Messenger's Companions, and willed them to convey His Message throughout the world.

After the Prophet's death, they conquered in the name of Islam all the lands from Spain to China, from Caucasia to India, with unprecedented speed. Conveying the Qur'an and the Sunna everywhere they went, many of the conquered people joined their households and embraced Islam. The Muslims instructed these new Muslims in the Qur'an and the Sunna, thereby preparing the ground for all the leading Muslim scholars and scientists to come.

The Companions considered memorizing and transmitting the Qur'an and the Sunna as acts of worship, for they had heard from the Messenger say: "Whoever comes to my mosque should come either to learn the good or to teach it. Such people have the same rank as those who fight in the way of God."[268]

---

[267] Bukhari, "Tafsir," 98:1-3; Muslim, "Fada'il al-Sahaba," 122.

[268] Ibn Maja, "Muqaddima," 17.

Anas reports that they frequently met to discuss what they heard from the Messenger.[269] Women also were taught by the Messenger, who set aside a specific day for them. His wives actively conveyed to other women whatever they learned from the Messenger. Their influence was great, for through them the Prophet established family ties with the people of Khaybar (through Safiyya), the Banu Amir ibn Sa'sa'a (through Maymuna), the Banu Makhzum (through Umm Salama), the Umayyads (through Umm Habiba), and the Banu Mustaliq (through Juwayriya). The women of these tribes would come to their "representative" among the Prophet's household ask her about religious matters.

In the last year of his Messengership, the Messenger went to Makka for what has become known as the Farewell Pilgrimage. In his Farewell Sermon at 'Arafat to more than 100,000 people, he summarized his mission and told his audience: "Those who are here should convey my speech to those who are not."[270] Some time later, the last verse to be revealed commanded the Muslim community to practice and support Islam: *Fear a day when you will be returned unto God and every soul shall be paid what it earned; they will not be wronged* (2:281).

The Companions and the Sunna

The Companions obeyed the Messenger in everything. They were so imbued with love for him that they strove to imitate him in every possible way. In fact, the Qur'an itself led them to do this, for it states that obeying the Messenger is directly related to belief:

---

[269] Muhammad 'Ajjaj al-Khatib, "Al-Sunna Qabl al-Tadwin," 160.

[270] *Bukhari*, "'Ilm," 9; Ibn Hanbal, 5:41.

> But no, by your Master! They will not believe till they
> make you the judge in disputes between them, then
> they shall find in themselves no impediment touching
> your verdict, but shall surrender in full submission.
> (4:65)

The following are only a few examples of their degree of submission.

- Shortly before his death, the Messenger raised an army, appointed Usama to command it, and told him to "advance only as far as the place where your father was martyred, and strengthen our rule there."[271] The Messenger took to his bed before the army departed. When Usama visited him, the Messenger prayed for him.

  The army was just about to set out when the Messenger died. Abu Bakr, his immediate political successor and the first caliph, dispatched the army without a second thought, despite uprisings in various parts of Arabia. He accompanied the soldiers to the outskirts of Madina and said: "By God, even if wolves attack us from all directions, I will not lower a flag hoisted by the Messenger."[272]

- The Messenger's death shocked and grieved Madina's Muslims. The subsequent election to choose the caliph caused some dissension among the Companions. Abu Bakr shouldered a very heavy task, for the army was waiting to be sent, reports of uprisings were coming in, and small groups were not satisfied with his election.

  Just at this juncture, Fatima (the Prophet's daughter) asked him for her share in the land of Fadak. Abu Bakr

---

[271] Ibn Sa'd, *Tabaqat*, 2:190.

[272] Suyuti, *Tarikh al-Khulafa'*, 74.

did not want to offend her, but also was determined to remain faithful to the Sunna. He used to say: "I can't forsake anything that the Messenger did."[273] He had heard something from the Messenger, which Fatima had not: "We, the community of the Prophets, do not bequeath anything. Whatever we leave is charity."[274]

- After the conquest of Makka, people from all over Arabia embraced Islam. Of course, many were not as devoted to Islam as the Companions. Some apostatized and, following Musaylima the Liar, revolted against Madina. Others showed signs of revolt by refusing to pay the prescribed alms-tax. Abu Bakr fought such people until peace and security reigned in Arabia once again.

- 'Umar was known as "the one who submits himself to truth." Unaware of the Prophet's decree, he put forward his own judgment about how much money should be paid to compensate someone for a cut finger. A Companion opposed him: "O Commander of the Faithful! I heard the Messenger say: 'The blood money for both hands together is the same as that paid for a life. This amount is shared out equally among the fingers, as ten camels for each.'"[275] 'Umar instantly withdrew his ruling and said to himself: "O son of Khattab! Do you dare to judge, through your own reasoning, on a matter the Messenger decreed?"

- Abu Musa al-Ash'ari went to visit 'Umar in his office. He knocked on the door three times and then left, for no

---

[273] *Bukhari*, "Fara'id," 3.

[274] *Bukhari*, "Khums," 1; *Muslim*, "Jihad," 52.

[275] Ibn Hanbal, 4:403; Hindi, *Kanz al-'Ummal*, 15:118.

one answered. After Abu Musa left, 'Umar opened the door and asked who had knocked. Learning that Abu Musa had knocked, 'Umar sent for him and asked why he had left. Abu Musa answered: "The Messenger said: 'When you visit someone, knock on the door. If you are not allowed to enter after you knock for the third time, go away,'" 'Umar asked him if he could verify this *hadith*, which was unknown to him. Abu Musa brought Abu Sa'id al-Khudri, who testified to its truth. 'Umar conceded.[276]

• When 'Umar was stabbed while prostrating in the mosque, he was asked if he wanted to designate his successor. 'Umar answered: "If I designate, one who is better than me (Abu Bakr) did so. If I do not designate, one who is better than me (the Messenger) did not do so."[277] 'Umar was certain to follow the latter action. However, to prevent any possible disagreement, he left the matter to a consultative committee that he formed for this very purpose.

• When 'Umar saw Zayd ibn Khalid al-Juhani perform a supererogatory prayer after the afternoon prayer, he reproached him for doing what the Messenger had not done. Zayd told him: "Even if you break my head into pieces, I shall never give up this two *rak'a* prayer, for I saw the Messenger perform it."[278]

Umm Salama, one of the Prophet's wives, reported that one day her husband could not perform the two *rak'a*

---

[276] *Muslim*, "Adab," 7:33; Ibn Hanbal, 3:19.

[277] *Bukhari*, "Ahkam," 51.

[278] Ibn Hajar, *Fath al-Bari'*, 3:83.

supererogatory prayer after the noon prayer because he was busy with a visiting delegation. So, he prayed that prayer after the afternoon prayer.[279] Zayd must have seen the Messenger perform it at that time.

- 'Ali once drank water while standing. Maysara ibn Ya'qub criticized him: "Why are you drinking while standing?" 'Ali answered: "If I do so, it's because I saw the Messenger do so. If I drink while sitting, it's because I saw the Messenger do so."[280]

- Instead of washing the feet during *wudu'*, Muslims can wipe the upper surface of light, thin-soled boots worn indoors (or inside overshoes[281]) with wet hands. Showing the Sunna's supremacy over personal reasoning, 'Ali said: "If I had not seen the Messenger wipe the upper surface of his light, thin-soled boots, I would deem it more proper to wipe their soles."[282]

- If a Muslim kills another by mistake, the killer's heirs must pay blood-money. 'Umar thought that a wife could not inherit any blood-money due her husband. However, Dahhak ibn Abi Sufyan informed him that when Ashyam ibn Dibabi had been killed, the Messenger had given some of the blood-money to his wife. 'Umar declared:

---

[279] *Bukhari*, "Mawaqit," 33.

[280] Ibn Hanbal, 1:134.

[281] It should be as strong as one can walk it for 3 miles, and both itself and whatever is worn with it (e.g., socks or shoes) should be clean. It is usually worn over socks.

[282] *Abu Dawud*, "Tahara," 63.

"From now on, wives will inherit from the blood-money of their husbands."[283]

- Abu 'Ubayda ibn Jarrah commanded the Muslim armies fighting in Syria. When 'Umar went to visit him in Amwas, pestilence had broken out already. Before 'Umar entered the city, 'Abd al-Rahman ibn al-'Awf told him: "I heard the Messenger say: 'If you hear that pestilence has broken out in a place, don't enter it. If you are in such a place already, don't leave it.'"[284] 'Umar, so obedient to the Sunna, returned home without seeing his faithful friend for the last time.

Further remarks on the Sunna's importance

The Qur'an declares:

> It is not for any believer, man or woman, when God and His Messenger have decreed a matter, to have the choice in the affair. Whosoever disobeys God and His Messenger has gone astray into manifest error. (33:36)

> ...Those who believe in Our signs, those who follow the Messenger, the unlettered Prophet, whom they find written down with them in the Torah and the Gospel, enjoining the good and forbidding the evil, making lawful the good things and making unlawful the corrupt things, and relieving them of their loads and the fetters that were upon them. Those who believe in him and succor him and help him, and follow the light that has been sent down with him—they are the ones who prosper. (7:156-57)

---

[283] *Abu Dawud*, "Fara'id," 18; *Ibn Maja*, "Diyat," 12; *Tirmidhi*, "Fara'id," 18.

[284] *Bukhari*, "Tib," 30; Ibn Athir, *Usd al-Ghaba*, 3:48.

The Traditions further declare:

- The best of words is the Book of God; the best way to follow is that of Muhammad. The worst affair is innovations (against my Sunna). Each innovation is a deviation.[285]

- "Everyone of my community will enter Paradise, except those who rebel." When they asked who these rebels were, he replied: "Whoever obeys me will enter Paradise; whoever disobeys me is a rebel."[286]

- In the case of my community, I am like someone who has lit a fire. Insects and butterflies flock to it. I hold you by the cloth [of your garments to keep you away from the fire], but you pull yourselves into it.[287]

- Don't let me find any of you seated in armchairs, who, when something I ordered or forbade is reported to them, respond: "We have no knowledge of it. So, we follow whatever we find in the Book of God."[288]

- Be careful! Surely I have been given the Book and its like together with it.[289]

- Those who outlive me will witness many controversies. Follow my way and that of the rightly guided successors (caliphs) who will guide to truth. Hold fast to it and

---

[285] *Muslim*, "Jumu'a," 43; *Nasa'i*, "'Idayn," 22; *Abu Dawud*, "Sunna," 5.

[286] *Bukhari*, "I'tisam," 2.

[287] *Muslim*, "Fada'il," 17,18; *Bukhari*, "Riqaq," 26.

[288] *Abu Dawud*, "Sunna," 5; *Ibn Maja*, "Muqaddima," 2; *Tirmidhi*, "'Ilm," 10.

[289] *Abu Dawud*, "Sunna," 5.

cling to it stubbornly with your teeth. Refrain from newly invented things (in religion), for each such thing is an innovation, and each innovation is a deviation.[290]

- I have left to you two precious things that, if you hold fast to them, will never lead you astray: The Qur'an and the Sunna.[291]

---

[290] *Tirmidhi*, "'Ilm," 16; *Abu Dawud*, "Sunna," 5; *Ibn Maja*, "Muqaddima," 6.

[291] Imam Malik, *Muwatta'*, "Qadar," 3.

CHAPTER 7

Relating the Traditions

The Companions and the immediately following generations were meticulous in narrating or transmitting these
Traditions.[292] They strove to separate sound Traditions from
those that had been fabricated (to meet personal or sectarian
needs). After memorizing them word for word, they transmitted the sound ones to the following generations.

The Messenger's warning and the
Companions' self-control

Islam is distinguished from unbelief by its firm rooting in
truthfulness. True Muslims do not lie. The Companions and
their successors proved their attachment to Islam though their
personal sacrifice. They also feared God, lived austerely, and
avoided life's comforts. Many great scholars and saints
appeared among them, and their examples are still followed.

The Messenger warned people not to lie about him:
"Those who lie about me should prepare their abodes in the
Fire"[293] and: "Whoever relates from me falsely is a liar."[294] In

---

[292] Those people who are the first two or three narrators cited in a
Tradition's chain of authority.

[293] *Bukhari*, "'Ilm," 38; *Muslim*, "Zuhd," 72; *Abu Dawud*, "'Ilm," 4;
Tirmidhi, "Fitan," 70.

[294] *Muslim*, "Muqaddima," 1.

the face of such warnings, would the Companions, who had sacrificed their entire lives for the cause of Islam, even think of lying about the Messenger?

Based on these considerations, the Companions took great care when narrating Traditions so that no mistake or misunderstanding would occur. For example 'Ali used to say: "I fear to narrate a Tradition from the Messenger so much that I would rather fall from Heaven than speak a lie on his behalf."[295]

'Abd Allah ibn al-Mas'ud, one of the most knowledgeable and nearest Companions, was similarly careful. When asked to report from the Messenger, he began with: "The Messenger of God said," stopped and bowed his head, breathed deeply and unbuttoned his collar while his eyes filled with tears. After the narration, he added: "The Messenger of God said this, or something like this, or something more or less like this."[296]

Zubayr ibn 'Awwam, one of the ten Companions assured Paradise, narrated only a few Traditions from the Messenger. When his son asked him why, he replied: "I am so afraid that I might say something contrary to what the Messenger really said. For he declared: 'Those who lie about me intentionally should prepare their abodes in the Fire.'"[297] Anas ibn Malik, who served the Messenger for 10 years, said: "If I were not so afraid of making a mistake, I would relate many more narrations from the Messenger."[298]

---

[295] Bukhari, "Istitaba," 6; Abu Dawud, "Sunna," 28.

[296] Ibn Maja, "Muqaddima," 3.

[297] Bukhari, "'Ilm," 38; Muslim, "Zuhd," 72.

[298] Darimi, "Muqaddima," 25.

'Abd al-Rahman ibn Abi Layla met 500 Companions. When he visited a place, people would say: "The man who met 500 Companions has come to our town." He had a great influence on Abu Hanifa and Imam Abu Yusuf. He reports: "I was personally familiar with 120 Companions. Sometimes all of them were in the same mosque. When they were asked about something, each would wait for the other to answer. If they were asked to narrate a Tradition, no one would dare to. Finally, one of them would place his trust in God and begin to narrate. He would always add: 'The Messenger said this, or something like this, or something more or less like this.'"[299]

Zayd ibn Arqam was one of the first people to embrace Islam. In the early days of Islam, the Messenger would meet with the Muslims secretly in his house. Zayd was appointed superintendent of the public treasury during the caliphates of 'Umar and 'Uthman. When he saw 'Uthman give items from the treasury to his relatives, he told him: "O Commander of the Faithful. People will suspect me and will no longer trust me. Allow me to resign." When 'Abd al-Rahman ibn Abi Layla asked him to narrate a Tradition, Zayd answered: "My son, I have become old and forgetful. Narrating about the Messenger is not something easy."[300]

Literal narration

Although the literal narration is better and always preferable, narration of meaning is allowed if the narrator has an expert command of Arabic, if the word used is appropriate in the given context, and if the original has been forgotten. However, the Companions always narrated Traditions literally despite this permission. For example, one day 'Ubayd ibn

---

[299] Dhahabi, *Siyar A'lam al-Nubala'*, 4:263.

[300] Ibn Maja, "Muqaddima," 3.

'Umayr narrated: "A hypocrite resembles a sheep left between *rabidayn* (two flocks)." 'Abd Allah ibn 'Umar objected: "He did not say so. I heard the Messenger say: 'A hypocrite resembles a sheep left between *ghanamayn* (two flocks).'"[301] The meaning is the same; the difference is only between the words *rabidayn* and *ghanamayn*.

This same care was adopted by the scholars or narrators of the generation immediately following the Companions: the Tabi'un (those who follow). For instance, someone narrated in the presence of Sufyan ibn 'Uyayna: "The Messenger forbade leaving the juice (of grapes, dates, and the like) to ferment (*an yuntabadha*) in bowls made of pumpkin and lined with pitch." Sufyan objected: "I heard Zuhri narrate: 'The Messenger forbade leaving the juice (of grapes, dates, and the like) to ferment (*an yunbadha*) in bowls made of pumpkin and lined with pitch.'"[302] There is no difference in meaning, only in the verb's conjugation.

Bara ibn 'Adhib related:

> The Messenger advised me: Perform *wudu'* before going to bed. Then lie on your right side and pray: "O God, I have submitted myself to You and committed my affair to You. I have sheltered in You, in fear of You, and in quest of You. There is no shelter from You except in You. I believe in Your Book You sent down, and Your Prophet You raised." To memorize this immediately, I repeated it to the Messenger and said at the end of it "Your Messenger You raised." He corrected the final sentence, saying: "and Your Prophet You raised."[303]

---

[301] Abu Dawud al-Tayalisi, *Musnad*, 248.

[302] Khatib al-Baghdadi, *Al-Kifaya fi 'Ilm al-Riwaya*, 178.

[303] *Bukhari*, "Da'awat," 6.

People dream when they sleep. True dreams constitute 1/46 of Prophethood, for the Messenger had true dreams during the first 6 months of his 23-year period of Prophethood. As they are related to Prophethood, not to Messengership,[304] the Messenger corrected Bara. This care was shown by almost all Companions, who studied the Traditions they heard from the Messenger and then discussed them. The Messenger told them: "Memorize and study the Traditions, for some are related to others. Therefore, come together and discuss them."[305]

Verification

The Companions strove to verify the Tradition's meaning. None of them lied, for their fear of Divine punishment was too great. However, reporters might have misunderstood the Tradition, missed an important point while receiving it from the Messenger, or misinterpreted it. With no intention to oppose the Messenger, they exerted themselves to understand his true purpose and discussed what they received from him.

A woman asked Caliph Abu Bakr if she could inherit from her grandchildren. He answered: "I have seen nothing in the Qur'an that allows this, nor do I remember the Messenger saying anything on this point." Mughira ibn Shu'ba stood up and said: "The Messenger allowed the grandmother to receive one-sixth (of the estate)." Abu Bakr asked Mughira if he could produce a witness to testify to this. When Muhammad ibn Maslama testified to it, Abu Bakr gave the woman one-sixth of her grandson's estate.[306]

---

[304] A Prophet is one who receives revelation but is not given a Book, and so follows the way of a previous Messenger. A Messenger is one who usually receives a Book or Pages and sets a way to follow. (Tr.)

[305] *Darimi*, "Muqaddima," 51.

[306] *Tirmidhi*, "Fara'id," 10.

When the Messenger declared: "Those called to account for their deeds on the Day of Judgment by God will be ruined," 'A'isha asked: "What about the Divine declaration in the Qur'an: *Then they will be called to account (for their deeds), and it will be an easy act of giving account?* The Messenger answered: "It is about presentation. Everyone will give account to God for their deeds. If those who did evil deny their evil deeds, God will inform them of their deeds. Such people will be ruined."[307]

As recorded in Bukhari, 'Umar narrates:

> I heard Hisham ibn Hakim pronounce some words of Surat al-Furqan somewhat differently from the way the Messenger taught me. I waited patiently until he had finished praying, and then asked him: "Who taught you such a recitation?" When he told me that he had learned it from the Messenger, I took him to the Messenger and explained the situation. The Messenger asked Hisham to recite the sura, which he did. The Messenger nodded, saying: "This is the way it was revealed to me." Then he asked me to recite, which I did. Again he nodded and said: "Thus it was revealed." He added: "The Qur'an is revealed in seven different ways. Recite it in the way easiest for you."[308]

The Companions were so devoted to the Sunna that they would travel long distances to learn just one *hadith*. For example, Abu Ayyub al-Ansari traveled from Madina to Egypt to check one hadith's exact wording. Among those who

---

[307] *Bukhari*, "'Ilm," 35; *Muslim*, "Janna," 79.

[308] *Bukhari*, "Khusuma," 4; *Muslim*, "Musafirin," 270; *Abu Dawud*, "Witr," 22. Some words of the Qur'an can be pronounced with slight differences. For example, in *Surat al-Fatiha*, the word *Mâlik* also can be pronounced as *Melik* with no significant difference in meaning. As another example, the word *heyte* in 12:23 also can be pronounced as *hîte* with no difference in meaning. This is a difference of accent only. (Tr.)

had received it from the Messenger, only 'Uqba ibn Amir was still alive and living in Egypt. Abu Ayyub arrived in the capital city and, calling on its governor Maslama ibn Mukhallad, found a guide to take him to 'Uqba. When he found this Companion in a street, he asked him about: "Whoever covers (hides) a believer's defect in the world, God will cover his (or her) defects in the Hereafter."[309] Being told by 'Uqba that his memory was correct, Abu Ayyub took his leave, saying: "I came just to ask about this *hadith*. I wouldn't like to make my intention impure [by staying] for some other reason."[310]

As related in Bukhari, Jabir ibn 'Abd Allah traveled for a whole month just to receive a *hadith* directly from its narrator, 'Abd Allah ibn Unays. Finding 'Abd Allah, he said: "I've been informed that you relate a *hadith* that I didn't hear from the Messenger. Fearing that one of us may die before I learn it, I have come to you." Jabir learned the *hadith* and returned to Madina.[311]

Such journeys continued throughout the following centuries. Sa'id ibn al-Musayyib, Masruq ibn Ajda, and others made long journeys to learn a single *hadith* or even to confirm a single letter of one *hadith*. Kathir ibn Qays relates that one such lover of knowledge traveled from Madina to Damascus to learn one *hadith* from Abu al-Darda'.[312]

The Tabi'un exhibited the same degree of caution as the Companions when narrating a Tradition. As stated by

---

[309] *Bukhari*, "Maghazi," 3; *Muslim*, "Birr," 58.

[310] Khatib al-Baghdadi, "Al-Rihla fi Talab al-Hadith," 118-24.

[311] Ibn Sa'd, *Tabaqat*, 3:178; Bukhari, *Al-Adab al-Mufrad*, 337.

[312] Al-Baghdadi, "Al-Rihla fi Talab al-Hadith," 78; Ibn Maja, "Muqaddima," 17.

A'mash, they would prefer the sky to collapse on them than to add so much as a wrong vowel to a *hadith*.[313]

The Ahl al-Sunna wa al-Jama'a agree on the absolute truthfulness of the Companions.[314] However, after internal conflicts broke out among the Muslims, the Tabi'un began to scrutinize whatever *hadith* they heard and to inquire about their narrators' truthfulness. Muhammad ibn Sirin says: "Before, we didn't ask about the narrators. But after the internal conflicts broke out, we began to ask."[315]

People of weak character and ungrounded faith fabricated Traditions to promote their sectarian beliefs. The Nasiba (the Umayyads and their supporters who opposed 'Ali) forged Traditions in favor of 'Uthman and Mu'awiya and against 'Ali, and the Rafidites (Shi'a extremists) forged Traditions against 'Uthman and Mu'awiya and for 'Ali. This caused meticulous, truth-seeking scholars to undertake a detailed and careful examination of each reported *hadith* and its narrators' character. Abu al-'Aliya says:

> We were no longer content with what was reported to us from a Companion. We traveled to receive it directly from the Companion or Companions who had narrated it, and to ask other Companions who knew about it."[316]

---

[313] Khatib al-Baghdadi, *Al-Kifaya fi 'Ilm al-Riwaya*, 178.

[314] The Ahl al-Sunna wa al-Jama'a (the People of Sunna and Community) are the great majority of Muslims who follow the way of the Prophet and Companions. Various factions differ from them in matters of belief (such as the Mu'tazila and Jabriya) or the role of the Companions in religion (such as the Kharijites and Shi'a), partly because of political inclinations and partly because they were influenced by ancient philosophies. (Tr.)

[315] Muslim, "Muqaddima," 5.

[316] M. 'Ajjaj al-Khatib, *Al-Sunna Qabl al-Tadwin*, 178.

Imam Muslim relates that Bushayr al-'Adawi narrated a *hadith* to Ibn 'Abbas. Noticing that the latter was not paying attention, Bushayr asked in surprise: "Why aren't you listening to me? I'm narrating a *hadith*." Ibn 'Abbas answered:

> In the past, our hearts would jump for joy and excitement when somebody began to narrate a hadith, saying: "The Messenger said." We would be fully attentive. But after people began to travel from place to place, we only receive from those whom we already know.[317]

Ibn 'Abd al-Barr, the great scholar of Muslim Spain (Andalusia), reports from Amir ibn Sharahil al-Sha'bi, one of the greatest Tabi'un scholars: Rabi' ibn Husayn related to Sha'bi the *hadith*:

> Those who recite ten times: "There is no god but God, One, and He has no partner. His is the kingdom, and His is all praise. He gives life and causes death. He is powerful over everything," may earn as much reward as those who free a slave.

Sha'bi asked Rabi' who had narrated that *hadith* to him. He said that 'Abd al-Rahman ibn Abi Layla' had done so. Sha'bi then left and found Ibn Abi Layla, who was living in another city. Ibn Abi Layla testified to the *hadith*'s authenticity, saying he had heard it from Abu Ayyub al-Ansari.[318]

Such great scholars as Ibn Shihab al-Zuhri, Ibn Sirin, Sufyan al-Thawri, Amir ibn Sharahil al-Sha'bi, Ibrahim ibn Yazid al-Naha'i, Shu'ba, Abu Hilal, Qatada ibn Di'ama, Hisham al-Dastawa'i and Mith'ar ibn Qudam did their best to determine which Traditions were authentic and which were fabricated. When they were unsure of a Tradition's authen-

---

[317] *Muslim*, "Muqaddima," 5.

[318] M. 'Ajjaj al-Khatib, *Al-Sunna Qabl al-Tadwin*, 222.

ticity, they would consult each other. For example, Abu Hilal and Sa'id ibn Abi Sadaqa asked Hisham al-Dastawa'i about one Tradition's exact wording just to be sure. Shu'ba and Sufyan al-Thawri referred to Mith'ar a matter about which they did not have exact knowledge.[319] Such great scholars did not allow fabricated Traditions to spread. Whenever and wherever they heard people known for their sectarian views narrate a Tradition, these Traditionists would ask who had related this Tradition to them.

Those truth-loving and truth-seeking scholars did not refrain from revealing the weaknesses of their families or relatives. For example, Zayd ibn Unaysa warned Traditionists not to receive hadith from his brother, perhaps because of his forgetfulness, carelessness, or sectarianism.[320] When asked about his father, 'Ali ibn al-Madini, the first to write on the Companions, answered: "Ask others about him." When they insisted, he explained: "Hadith means religion. My father is weak on this point."[321]

Waki' ibn Jarrah, who was brought up in the school of Abu Hanifa and was a tutor of Imam Shafi'i, said: "As far as I know, I have never forgotten anything once I heard it. Nor do I remember anything that I had to repeat in order to memorize, if I only heard it once." Despite his keen memory, Imam Shafi'i once complained to Waki' about his poor memory. Waki' answered: "Refrain from sin. Knowledge is a light from God, and so cannot be granted to sinful people." When his father Jarrah was narrating a hadith, Waki' was always nearby. When asked why, he answered: "My father works in

---

[319] Ibid., 229.

[320] *Muslim*, "Muqaddima," 5.

[321] Ibn Hajar, *Tahdhib al-Tahdhib*, 5:176; Dhahabi, *Mizan al-I'tidal*, 2:401.

the state's finance department. I am afraid he might soften some Traditions in favor of the government. I accompany him to prevent such a lapse."[322]

While the Traditions were being written down, they also were being memorized by some of the greatest Traditionists of Islamic history. For example, Ahmad ibn Hanbal memorized around one million Traditions, including authentic, good, weak, and fabricated ones (some were identical in text but had different narration chains). His *Musnad* contains only 40,000 Traditions out of 300,000 Traditions.

Yahya ibn Ma'in memorized both authentic and fabricated Traditions. When Ibn Hanbal asked him why he did so, he replied: "I inform people of fabricated Traditions so they may choose the authentic ones."[323] Many scholars engaged in this activity and knew hundreds of thousands of them by heart. Among them, the most famous are Zuhri, Yahya ibn Sa'id al-Qattan, Bukhari, Muslim, Daraqutni, Hakim, Dhahabi, Ibn Hajar al-'Asqalani, and Imam Suyuti.

Thanks to the tremendous efforts of such Traditionists, authentic Traditions were distinguished from fabricated ones. In addition to recording authentic Traditions in volumes and memorizing them, many Traditionists wrote on the narrators' character so people would know who was reliable or unreliable, careful or careless, profound and meticulous or superficial, and God-fearing or heedless.

When people warned them that revealing people's defects would bring shame upon those people, they would reply: "Hadith means religion. Therefore it should be given greater

---

[322] Ibn Hajar, *Tahdhib al-Tahdhib*, 6:84.

[323] M. 'Ajjaj al-Khatib, *Al-Sunna Qabl al-Tadwin*, 229.

care than the hiding of the narrators' defects."[324] Yahya ibn Sa'id al-Qattan, renowned for being alert to sins, used to say: "In the presence of God I would rather have them as enemies than the Messenger."[325]

Ensuring authenticity

There were several ways to tell whether a Tradition had been fabricated or not. One was to encourage the narrators to confess. This was not uncommon among those who had fallen into sectarianism and then, being guided to the truth, acknowledged the Traditions they had fabricated.

In addition, the Traditionists were extremely sensitive to lying. If it could be proven that a narrator had lied even once, all Traditions coming from that source were rejected. Narrators had to be completely truthful, have a keen memory, be very careful in practicing Islam, and not be involved in sectarianism. Moreover, if reliable narrators became forgetful or had similar mental difficulties, their Traditions were no longer accepted. For example, when Ibn Abi Lahi'a, famous for his austerity and God-consciousness, lost the notebook from which he used to relate Traditions, Imam Bukhari restricted himself to those of his narrations confirmed or reinforced by other reliable narrators.

It is said that one's literary style is identical with that particular person. So if you are a careful reader, you can identify an author by his or her style and distinguish him or her from others. Traditionists dedicated themselves to Hadith, and were so could distinguish easily between the Prophet's sayings and those of everyone else, no matter how gifted.

---

[324] Ibid., 234.

[325] Ibn Salah, *'Ulum al-Hadith*, 389.

Another way was to judge them according to the Qur'an and the *mutawatir hadith*. If three or more Companions reported a *hadith* from the Prophet, which was then handed down by several transmission chains of reliable narrators, it is *mutawatir*. Traditions reported from the Prophet by one Companion are called *ahadi*. Such Traditions usually were accepted as authentic after judged according to the Qur'an and *mutawatir* Traditions.

Although not an objective method, some saintly scholars saw the Messenger while awake and received directly from him. The *hadith qudsi*: "I was a hidden treasure. I wished to be known, and so created the universe" is reported to belong to this class.[326] Jalal al-Din al-Suyuti is reported to have met with the Messenger several times while awake. Before writing down a *hadith* he considered authentic, Imam Bukhari performed *wudu'*, referred it to the Messenger, and recorded it in his notebook only after receiving the Messenger's approval.[327] Some Traditionists saw the Companion who had narrated the *hadith* from the Prophet.

The Traditionists wrote multi-volume works about narrators, in which they detailed these people's biographies: where and when they were born, where they emigrated and lived, their teachers, from whom they received and to whom they narrated Traditions, and when and where they died.

The first book of this genre was 'Ali ibn al-Madini's *Kitab al-Ma'rifat al-Sahaba* (The Book of Knowledge about the Companions). Among the most significant are the following: Ibn 'Abd al-Barr's *Al-Isti'ab fi Ma'rifat al-Ashab*

---

[326] Ajluni, *Kashf al-Khafa'*, 1:132; 'Ali al-Qari, "Al-Asrar al-Marfu'a," 269.

[327] Ibn Hajar, *Tahdhib al-Tahdhib*, 9:49.

(The Comprehensive Book of Knowledge about the Companions), Ibn Hajar al-'Asqalani's *Al-Isaba fi Tamyiz al-Sahaba* (Finding the Truth in Judging the Companions), Ibn al-Athir's *Usd al-Ghaba* (The Lions of the Forest), Ibn Sa'd's *Al-Tabaqat al-Kubra'* (a most comprehensive biographical dictionary of the leading Companions and of the Tabi'un scholars), and *Tarikh Ibn 'Asakir* (History by Ibn 'Asakir), *Tarikh al-Bukhari* (History by Bukhari) and Yahya ibn Ma'in's *Al-Tarikh al-Kabir* (The Great History).

The greatest Traditionists, among them Bukhari, Muslim, Tirmidhi, Abu Dawud, Nasa'i, Ibn Maja, and Ahmad ibn Hanbal, collected authentic Traditions in voluminous books. Others, such as Maqdisi, collected fabricated Traditions. Still others, who came later, tested once more the authenticity of all previously collected Traditions.

For example, Ibn al-Jawzi (d. 597 AH) judged several Traditions in Ibn Hanbal's *Musnad* to be either weakly transmitted or fabricated, although he belonged to Ibn Hanbal's legal school. Later, Ibn Hajar al-'Asqalani made a detailed examination of the same Traditions and, with the exception of thirteen, proved their authenticity. Jalal al-Din al-Suyuti (d. 911 AH) scrutinized them once more and concluded that none were fabricated, although a few may have weak chains of transmission. He also reviewed Ibn al-Jawzi's *Al-Mawdu'at al-Kubra'* (A Great Collection of Fabricated Traditions) and sorted out the authentic ones. Thinking that the rest might not be fabricated either, he wrote *Al-Laa'li al-Masnu'a* (The Artifical Pearls).

Other great Traditionists compiled additional compendia. Such leading Traditionists as Bukhari and Muslim, tremendously exacting scholars, did not include many Traditions in their collections. Hakim's *Al-Mustadrak 'ala al-Sahihayn*

(Addendum to The Two Collections of Authentic Traditions) is a voluminous appendix to Bukhari and Muslim. It was reviewed closely by Hafiz Dhahabi, who was famous for his keen memory.

In later centuries, books were written on widespread maxims, wise sayings, or proverbs regarded as Hadith. Sakhawi's *Maqasid al-Hasana* and Ajluni's *Kashf al-Khafa'* examined them one by one and explained which are truly Traditions and which are not. For example, apart from many authentic Traditions and Qur'anic verses encouraging people to learn, such popular sayings as: "Seek knowledge from the cradle to the grave" and "Seek knowledge even if it is in China" were tested by the Traditionists and shown not to be real Traditions.

After such tremendous studies, detailed examinations, and exacting verifications, we can state that the collections of authentic Traditions no longer contain fabricated Traditions. Those who continue to question the Traditions and Sunna act out of nothing more than religious, political, and ideological prejudice, as well as from biased Orientalist scholarship, to cast doubt on this vital source of Islam and its implementation in one's daily life.

Examples

Some examples of fabricated Traditions are the following:

- Abu Hanifa is perhaps the greatest Muslim jurist, and still shines like a sun in the sky of Islamic jurisprudence. But the saying attributed to the Prophet that "Abu Hanifa is the lamp of my nation" is not a *hadith*.[328] It must have been fabricated for sectarian considerations.

---

[328] Ajluni, *Kashf al-Khafa'*, 1:33.

- "Have white cockerels" must have been forged by a white cockerel seller, even though we like white cockerels.[329]

- "Beware of the evil of one to whom you have done good" is another illogical saying wrongly attributed to the Prophet.[330] You can win somebody's heart by being good to him or her. If it were permissible to attribute a saying to the Prophet, I would say: "Do good to the one whose evil you fear," for it is said that "people are the slaves of the good done to them."

- Although rationality is a principle of Islam, Islam does not depend upon rationalism. No one can judge the Qur'an and the Prophet according to the dictates of individual reason. Islam is the collection of principles established by God, the Owner and Giver of all reasoning and intellect. Therefore, the saying: "Discuss among yourselves a saying attributed to me. If it agrees with the truth, confirm it and adopt it as a religious principle. It doesn't matter whether I have uttered it or not," is a fabrication.

- Another saying wrongly attributed to the Messenger is: "I was born in the time of the just king."[331] This was fabricated to exalt the Persian king Anushirwan. No one can confer honor on the Messenger, who himself brought honor to the whole of creation, most particularly to our world.

- Another widespread beautiful saying is also mistakenly thought to be a Tradition: "Cleanliness comes from belief." The meaning is true, but it was not reported from the Messenger through a sound chain of transmission.

---

[329] Ibid., 1:36.

[330] Ibid., 1:43.

[331] Ibid., 2:340.

Instead, he said: "Purity (in body, mind, and heart) is half of belief, and *al-hamdu li-Allah* (all praise be to God) fills up the balance (where the good deeds will be weighed)."[332]

• Aqiq is a place located between Madina and Makka. During a journey, the Messenger told those traveling with him to: "Set up your tents at Aqiq." In Arabic, the word translated as *set up your tents* is *takhayyamu*. Since diacritical points were not used in writing during the early days of Islam, this word was confused with *takhattamu* (wear a ring). In addition, *aqiq* is used for cornelian. All this led to a false Tradition: "Wear a ring of cornelian," with the addition of "because it removes poverty."[333]

• "Looking at a beautiful face is an act of worship" is another false Tradition, one plainly slanderous against the Messenger.

• The saying: "Seek knowledge even if it is in China" is another false Tradition. It may have been fabricated to encourage learning. However, the Prophet has many sayings, and the Qur'an urges Muslims to learn or to seek knowledge: *Only those of His servants fear God who have knowledge* (35:28), and: *Say: "Are they equal— those who know and those who don't know?"* (39:9). In addition, the Prophet said: "Angels spread their wings beneath the feet of those who seek knowledge, because they are pleased (with them)."[334]

Some examples of authentic Traditions labelled as fabricated are the following:

---

[332] *Muslim*, "Tahara," 1; *Tirmidhi*, "Da'awat," 86.

[333] Ajluni, *Kashf al-Khafa'*, 1:299; Daylami, *Musnad al-Firdaws*, 56.

[334] *Abu Dawud*, "'Ilm," 1; *Tirmidhi*, "'Ilm," 19.

- Imam Bukhari relates in his *Sahih*: This is in the Torah: "O Prophet, We have sent you as a witness, a bringer of good tidings and a warner, and a refuge for the unlettered. You are My servant and Messenger. I named you 'the one who places his trust in God.' He is not harsh and rude, nor one who shouts in the streets. He does not repel evil with evil; instead, he pardons and forgives. God will not take his soul until He guides the deviant people to believe that there is no god but God, and thereby opens blind eyes and deaf ears and hardened hearts."[335]

Orientalists and their Muslim followers criticize this *hadith* because it was reported by 'Abd Allah ibn 'Amr ibn al-'As, who sometimes narrated from Ka'b ibn al-Akhbar. What they neglect to consider is that:

- This *hadith* does not contradict the characteristics of the Messenger described in the Qur'an and other Islamic sources.

- Despite their distortions and alterations, the Torah and the Gospels still contain references to the Messenger. The Qur'an points to this in several verses, among them: *Those who follow the Messenger, the unlettered Prophet whom they find written in the Torah and the Gospel with them* (7:157); and: *This is their like in the Torah, and their like in the Gospel is this* (48:29). Husayn Jisri, who lived during the first half of the twentieth century, found 124 allusions to the Messenger in the Torah and the Gospels. *The Gospel of Barnabas* explicitly mentions Prophet Muhammad.

- Ka'b al-Akhbar was a Jew who accepted Islam. Many Christians and Jews embraced Islam, especially during

---

[335] Bukhari, "Tafsir," 48/3; "Buyu'," 50; *Darimi*, "Muqaddima," 2.

its early spread in Africa and Asia. They brought with them their previous knowledge, but that which was contrary to Islam was either corrected or mostly rejected. Such Companions as 'Abd Allah ibn 'Abbas, Abu Hurayra, Anas ibn Malik, and 'Abd Allah ibn 'Amr ibn al-'As listened to Ka'b's narrations from the Torah. It was impossible for them to accept anything contrary to Islam. Would 'Abd Allah ibn 'Amr, an ascetic who was deeply devoted to Islam and the Prophet, lie or fabricate a Tradition when he knew the punishment for such an action?

• During a severe famine and drought, Caliph 'Umar held the hand of 'Abbas, the Prophet's uncle, and prayed: "O God! While he was alive our Prophet prayed to You for rain, and You sent down rain. Now we take his uncle as the means to pray to You for rain, so send down rain."[336]

Some criticize this Tradition based on Jahiz's objection. But Jahiz is not a Traditionist; rather, he sought to deny even the most authentic Traditions. His teacher was Nazzam, a materialist belonging to the Mu'tazila heterodox sect. Jahiz criticizes this Tradition in his *Al-Bayan wa al-Tabyin* as follows:

> In all the Traditions attributed to 'Umar with regard to praying for rain, there are defects making it difficult for us to accept their authenticity. In some versions, he prayed on the pulpit; in others, in an open area; and still in others, after a prescribed prayer. Such confusions show that those Traditions are not authentic.

The science of Hadith requires profound specialty. Jahiz is not a specialist. Neither is Ibn Abi al-Dunya, who, although a blessed ascetic, criticizes this Tradition in his

---

[336] Bukhari, "Istithqa'," 3; "Fada'il al-Ashab," 11.

book, which contains many mistakes and fabricated Traditions. Imam Ghazali is one of the few great revivers of the Islamic religious sciences and one of our greatest religious guides. Yet if you mention him as a reference in a disputed matter of Hadith, Traditionists will laugh at you. A doctor is not asked about engineering, and no one goes to a chemist for medical information or advice.

Second, using somebody or something as a means to reach God, provided you understand that the means do not affect the outcome, is allowed: *O you who believe! Fear God and seek a means to Him* (5:35). The Companions usually asked the Messenger to pray on their behalf. Once during a drought, they asked him to pay for rain. He did so, and it rained so heavily that they had to ask him to pray for it to stop. He prayed on the pulpit, and the people went to their houses in sunlight. After this explicit favor of God, the Messenger said: "I bear witness that God is powerful over everything, and that I am His servant and Messenger."[337]

The Qur'an encouraged the Companions to ask the Messenger to seek God's forgiveness for them, emphasizing that his praying is a means of peace and tranquility:

> We never sent any Messenger, but that he should be obeyed, by the leave of God. If, when they wronged themselves, they had come to you, and prayed forgiveness of God, and the Messenger had prayed forgiveness for them, they would have found God All-Forgiving, All-Compassionate. (4:64)

and: *Pray for them; your prayers are a comfort for them* (9:103). Once a blind man complained to the Messenger

---

[337] *Bukhari*, "Istithqaʿ," 14; *Abu Dawud*, "Istithqaʿ," 2; *Ibn Maja*, "Iqama," 154.

about his blindness. The Messenger advised him to perform *wudu'*, pray two *rak'as*, and say:

> O God, I ask You and turn to You for the sake of Your Prophet Muhammad, the Prophet of mercy. O Muhammad, I turn to my Master for your sake for my need to be met. O God, accept his intercession with You on my behalf!

The man did so and recovered his sight.[338] In conclusion, nothing in the Tradition ruins its authenticity.

- It is reported in almost all of the six most authentic books of Tradition: "If a dog licks your bowl, clean it seven times; the first time with soil, the other six with water."[339]

Some who are unaware of Hadith principles and medical developments doubt this *hadith*'s authenticity, despite its authentic chain of transmission and its being a proof of Muhammad's Prophethood. Had he not been a Prophet taught by God, how could he have known medical facts discovered only centuries later? We now know that dogs may carry microbes of certain diseases in their saliva and excrement, and that these can harm human health if they are transmitted.

Moreover, no one in the Propeht's era knew about disinfection and sterilization. The Messenger, being a Prophet taught by the All-Knowing, recommends soil to clean a bowl licked by a dog. Today we know that soil is a good antiseptic that contains such substances as tetracycline.

---

[338] *Ibn Maja*, "Iqama," 189; Tirmidhi, "Da'awat," 118.

[339] *Muslim*, "Tahara," 91; *Bukhari*, "Wudu'," 33; *Abu Dawud*, "Tahara," 37.

Some interpret *seven times* to mean as many times as needed to clean the bowl. Hanafi jurists regard it as sufficient to clean the bowl three times.

- Some contemporary critics, including the French convert Maurice Bucaille, were quick to criticize the following Tradition, reported by Abu Hurayra: "When a fly falls into one of your bowls, dip it completely in the food before taking it out, for there is disease in one wing [or side] and a cure in the other."[340] This Tradition's narrators are beyond reproach. It was included by Bukhari, Abu Dawud, Nasa'i, Darimi, and Ahmad ibn Hanbal.

  Like the previous Tradition, this one contains a proof of Muhammad's Prophethood. At that time, no one knew that flies carry microbes. Moreover, we now know that when a fly falls into a bowl, it tries to hold one wing off the food so it can take off again. As a result, it leaves its bacteria in the food. But when it is submerged in the food with a slight touch, the tiny bag on the other wing or side (the word *janah* has both meanings) bursts open and scatters anti-bacteria to kill the germs left on the food.

- Another authentic, but criticized, Tradition mentioned in all the authentic books of Tradition is: "It is not worth setting out to visit [intending to gain spiritual reward] any mosque other than al-Masjid al-Haram [the Holy Mosque surrounding the Ka'ba], the Prophet's Mosque [in Madina], and al-Masjid al-Aqsa' [just south of the Dome of the Rock in Jerusalem]."[341] This Tradition is criticized

---

[340] *Bukhari*, "Tib," 58; *Abu Dawud*, "At'ima," 48; *Ibn Maja*, "Tib," 31; *Darimi*, "At'ima," 12.

[341] *Bukhari*, "Al-Salat fi Masjid Makka," 1; *Muslim*, "Hajj," 511; *Tirmidhi*, "Salat," 126.

for being reported by Companions who narrated from
Ka'b al-Akhbar or that it sanctifies al-Masjid al-Aqsa'.
This pretext is completely groundless, for it does not
belong to the Jews. Our Prophet turned to it while praying in Makka.

It is also the symbol of Islam's terrestrial dominion. Our
Prophet was first taken to al-Masjid al-Aqsa' during his
Ascension and led prayer there before the souls of the previous Prophets. God declares that *He blessed the vicinities
of this mosque* (17:1). This blessed land surrounding it was
first captured by Prophet Yusha (Joshua) ibn Nun after the
death of Moses. After Prophet Muhammad, it was recap-
tured during 'Umar's caliphate. Salah al-Din Ayyubi, one
of the greatest Muslim commanders, retook it from the
Crusaders. If the Messenger included it among the three
mosques most blessed and worthy of visiting, despite difficulties of travel, it is because God sanctified it.

Despite their sanctity, however, it is a mistake to assume a
special kind of prayer in those mosques. As reported by
Ibn 'Abbas, a woman promised God that she would pray
in al-Masjid al-Aqsa' if she recovered from her illness.
She recovered and, before setting out, called on Maymuna
(one of the Messenger's wives), who told her:

> Stay here, mind your house, and pray in the Mosque
> of the Prophet. I heard the Messenger say: "Prayer per-
> formed here is 1,000 times better than that performed
> in any other mosque, except that of the Ka'ba."[342]

• The Messenger declared: "Among my Community there
will always be a group who support the truth, until the

---

[342] *Muslim*, "Hajj," 510; *Bukhari*, "Masjid Makka," 1; *Nasa'i*, "Manasik,"
124.

Command of God will come [the Last Day]. Those who oppose them will not be able to harm them."[343]

Despite being recorded in almost all authentic books of Tradition and proved by the long history of Islam, this Tradition has been subjected to unjustifiable criticism. Islam has resisted all attacks. No earthly power has been able to destroy it. Even after the concerted efforts to do so during the last 3 centuries, Islam is the only alternative, stronger and fresher than ever, for true human happiness and prosperity in both worlds.

God has preserved Islam through a devoted self-sacrificing community in every period. This community concentrated, in one period, in Damascus, and in another, in Baghdad or Istanbul; once around 'Umar ibn 'Abd al-'Aziz, and then around Imam Ghazali or Imam Rabbani. While concentrating around a particular person in one place, they may have come together, in another, around someone else. Nor will the world be lacking in such groups in the future.

• Another Tradition denied by some is: "When you get up from your bed, don't put your hand in a bowl [of food or drink] before washing it three times. You don't know where your hands have been while you were asleep."[344]

Ahmad Amin and Abu Rayya, under the influence of the Orientalist Goldziher, ridicule this Tradition, even though it contains principles of hygiene. People often suffer from allergies or an itch. They might have scratched the affect-

---

[343] *Muslim*, "'Imara," 170; *Bukhari*, "I'tisam," 10; *Abu Dawud*, "Fitan," 1.

[344] *Abu Dawud*, "Tahara," 50; *Bukhari*, "Wudu'," 26; *Muslim*, "Tahara," 87-88.

ed places while sleeping, thereby accumulating germs, particularly under their fingernails. If such people eat (from communal bowls) without washing their hands, other people may become infected.

The Messenger always depended on Revelation, whether explicit or implicit. His Companions, famous for truthfulness, followed him as closely as possible and narrated whatever they received from him. Meticulous, truth-loving Traditionists collected the Traditions reaching them through reliable, trustworthy, and upright narrators. Some authentic Traditions predict certain future events and scientific developments. Just as none of these have yet proven to be false, so too no one has been able to falsify any other authentic Traditions.

Creation still holds some mysteries, and will continue to do so, regardless of human scientific and other progress. Psychic events or supernormal phenomena like telepathy and second sight, necromancy and other transcendental experiences, give clues to the existence of worlds or dimensions different from our own. As it is possible to find references to this in the Qur'an, some Traditions also may be dealt with from this viewpoint.

• As recorded in authentic books of Tradition, Tamim al-Dari, a Christian convert, tells of a hairy creature called "Jassasa" whom he saw in a strange island, and of a gigantic man who lives in a cave and introduces himself as the Dajjal (Anti-Christ).[345] We cannot deny this Tradition on positivistic premises, just as we cannot deny that the breast of our Prophet was burst open.

---

[345] *Muslim*, "Fitan," 119; *Abu Dawud*, "Malahim," 15; *Ibn Maja*, "Fitan," 33.

• Another Tradition that we can deal with partly from the same viewpoint is that God enjoined 50 daily prayers during the Ascension of Prophet Muhammad. On his return, Moses warned him about the difficulty of such an order. After the Prophet's repeated appeals, God reduced the number to five.[346]

There are delicate points in this *hadith*. God is All-Forgiving. He knows how many prayers a day His servants can endure, and expects them to pray to Him for forgiveness and to realize their goals. Praying or supplicating is a mystery of servanthood to God and the cornerstone of servanthood. When servants perceive their poverty, inadequacy, and impotence, they come to depend on their Master's absolute and infinite Richness and Power, thereby acquiring immeasurable power and inexhaustible wealth. Servants should be reminded repeatedly of this so that they are not left to their carnal, evil-commanding, and self-conceited selves. If they are not so reminded, they are subject to incurable, unrecoverable helplessness and destitution.

As Prophet Muhammad is the last Prophet, he encompasses all aspects and dimensions of Prophethood and confirms all previous Prophets. If we compare Prophethood to a huge blessed tree with branches spreading throughout the universe, Prophet Muhammad represents it in its entirety. His Prophethood is rooted deeply in the mission of all earlier Prophets. Therefore, it is natural for him to benefit from his roots.

Moses preceded him, so desiring ease for his nation in carrying out its religious duties, Prophet Muhammad justifi-

---

[346] *Bukhari*, "Salat," 1; *Nasa'i*, "Salat," 1; *Muslim*, "Iman," 263; *Ibn Maja*, "Iqama," 194.

ably followed his advice. Although the greatest Prophet, he never allowed his followers to regard the others Prophets as inferior to him.

This matter requires further elaboration, as there is much to be said on it. However, this subject is beyond the scope of this book.

The number of authentic Traditions

Some Orientalists and their Muslim followers try to cast doubt on the Sunna's authenticity on the pretexts that some Companions narrate too many Traditions and that there are vast numbers of Traditions.

First, the Traditions are not limited to the Messenger's words. Rather, they cover his entire life: all his actions, likes and dislikes, and approvals or tacit confirmations of what his Companions said and did. He lived for 23 years among them as a Messenger of God. He taught them Islam down to its minutest details. He led the prayer five times a day, every detail of which was recorded, for he told them: "Pray as you see me praying." He fasted and explained all of its details to them, just as he did for alms-giving and pilgrimage. The essentials of belief and pillars of Islam (prayer, fasting, alms-giving, and pilgrimage) alone are the subjects of countless books.

Being a universal Divine system that includes everything related to human life, Islam has laws and regulations for individual and collective life: spiritual and material, social and economic, political and military, and all other aspects faced during one's daily life. He laid down principles related to all these. He constantly warned his Companions against deviation, and encouraged them to be deeper, more sensitive, and more careful servants of God.

He also told them about former nations and predicted future events. Abu Zayd 'Amr ibn Akhtab reported that sometimes the Prophet would ascend the pulpit after the dawn prayer and address the congregation until noon. He would continue talking after the noon and afternoon prayers, telling them what had happened from the beginning of the world until that time, and what would happen from then until the Last Day. Such addresses would include information on the upheavals of the other world, the grave, the Resurrection, the Great Mustering, balancing people's deeds, the Last Judgment, the Bridge, and Hell and Paradise.[347]

The Messenger commanded armies, heard and tried cases as a judge, sent and received envoys and delegations. He signed peace treaties, waged war, and dispatched military expeditions. He laid down rules of hygiene and principles of good conduct and high morality. His miracles number in the hundreds. As he set an example to be followed by Muslims, and because of the vital importance of Hadith in Islam as well as his Companions' love of him, his life was recorded from beginning to end.

He honored the universe with his Messengership, His servanthood to God, and his exalted, peerless personality. As honored witnesses of his life, the Companions recorded everything related to him. When they scattered throughout the lands conquered by Islam, new converts asked them to relate Traditions from the Messenger. They were so deeply devoted to him that they remained extraordinarily faithful to their memories of him.

Once during his caliphate, 'Umar passed by the house of 'Abbas, the Prophet's uncle, on his way to the Friday con-

---

[347] *Muslim*, "Fitan," 25.

gregational prayer. A few drops of blood fell on his robe from the gutter. He became so angry that he pulled the gutter to the ground, saying to himself: "Who slaughtered an animal on this roof so that its blood should stain my robe when I'm going to the mosque?" He reached the mosque and, after the prayer, warned the congregation: "You are doing some wrong things. I was passing by such and such a wall on my way here, when some blood dropped onto my robe from the gutter. I pulled the gutter to the ground."

'Abbas was upset and sprang to his feet: "O 'Umar, what have you done!? I personally saw the Messenger put that gutter there in person." Now, it was 'Umar's turn to be upset. He said to 'Abbas in great agitation: "By God, I will lay my head at that wall's foot and you will put your foot on it to replace the gutter. Until you do that, I will not raise my head from the ground." Such was their devotion and faithfulness to the Messenger.[348]

The Messenger implanted such a zeal for learning in his followers' hearts that Islamic civilization, under the blessed shadow of which a considerable portion of humanity lived peacefully for centuries, was built on the pillars of belief, knowledge, piety, and brotherhood. In the lands through which the pure water of Islam flowed, innumerable flowers burst open in every field of science, and the scent diffused by them exhilarated the world.

Some of these flowers, like Ibn Hajar al-Asqalani, read in two or three sessions the entire collection of authentic Traditions compiled by Imam Muslim. Imam Nawawi dedicated himself so thoroughly to teaching and writing that he never married—he did not want to assign any time to any-

---

[348] *Ibn Hanbal*, 1:210.

thing other than knowledge. Imam Sarakhsi, a great Hanafi jurist, was imprisoned in a well by a king. During that time, he dictated his monumental 30-volume compendium, *Al-Mabsut*, to his students from memory. When his students told him that Imam Shafi'i, founder of the Shafi'i legal school and regarded by some as the second reviver of Islam, had memorized 300 fascicules of Traditions, he answered: "He knew the zakat (one-fortieth) of what I know."[349]

The works of Ibn Hajar al-Asqalani, Ibn Jarir al-Tabari, Fakhr al-Din al-Razi, Imam Suyuti, and others cover so many volumes that when divided among the days of their lives, we can see that they wrote about 20 pages every day. We cannot study or even read during our lives what each wrote during his lifetime.

Anas ibn Sirin, son of Muhammad ibn Sirin, one of the greatest Tabi'un scholars, says: "When I arrived in Kufa, 4,000 people were attending Hadith courses in mosques; 400 were experts in Islamic jurisprudence."[350] To understand what it meant to be an expert in Islamic jurisprudence, consider the following: Ahmad ibn Hanbal, whose *Musnad* contains 40,000 Traditions chosen from among the one million in circulation, was not considered an expert jurist by Ibn Jarir al-Tabari. Nor was he given the same status as Abu Hanifa, Imam Abu Yusuf, Imam Shafi'i, Imam Malik, and the like. The fact that some did not consider such a great figure an expert jurist shows just what intellectual and scholarly heights a jurisprudent had to reach to be regarded as an expert.

The general atmosphere was extremely propitious for the development of both religious and secular sciences, especial-

---

[349] Sarakhsi, *Muqaddima li-Usul al-Sarakhsi*, 5.

[350] M. 'Ajjaj al-Khatib, *Al-Sunna qabl al-Tadwin*, 150-51.

ly the science of Tradition. Every Muslim strove to acquire knowledge of Islam and recognize its Holy Prophet fully. People had a great aptitude for literature and languages, for poetry was widespread during the pre-Islamic period.

The Qur'an came, first of all, as an absolute and incomparable linguistic miracle. No literary or poetic expert denied its eloquence, and almost all of them gave up poetry after their conversion to dedicate themselves to the Qur'an and the Hadith. One of them, the poetess Hansa, became so deeply devoted to Islam that when her four sons were martyred at Qadisiyah, she praised God, saying: "O God, You gave me four sons, all of whom I have sacrificed in the way of Your Beloved (Prophet). Praise be to You, to the number of thousands."[351]

Life was quite simple in the desert. This enabled people to commit themselves to Islamic sciences. Also, they had very keen memories. For example, the Messenger once asked Zayd ibn Thabit to learn Hebrew; within a couple of weeks, he could read and write letters in it.[352] Ibn Shihab al-Zuhri, Qatada ibn Diama, Sha'bi, Ibrahim ibn Yazid al-Nakha'i, Imam Shafi'i, and many others publicly said that they never forgot a word after they memorized it. They could do this after either reading or hearing something only once.

When Imam Bukhari arrived in Baghdad, ten leading persons in Islamic sciences tested his knowledge of Hadith and memory. Each recited ten Traditions, changing either the

---

[351] Ibn Athir, *Usd al-Ghaba*, 7:90. This blessed woman found eight linguistic or poetic mistakes in a stanza of Hassan ibn Thabit, a famous Companion and poet. After the Revelation, she gave up poetry and focused on the Qur'an and the Hadith.

[352] Ibn Hanbal, 5:186.

order of the narrators in a chain of transmission or the chains with each other. For example, the famous Tradition: "Actions are judged according to intentions..." has the following chain (in descending order): Yahya ibn Sa'id al-Ansari, from Muhammad ibn Ibrahim al-Taymi, from Alqama ibn Waqqas al-Laysi, from 'Umar ibn al-Khattab. When they were finished, Imam Bukhari corrected the chains one by one from memory and repeated each Tradition with its own sound chain of transmission. The scholars then admitted his learning and knowledge of Hadith.[353] Ibn Khuzayma went so far as to say: "Neither Earth or Heaven has seen a second person as knowledgeable as you in this field."[354]

Imam Bukhari never sold his knowledge for worldly benefits. When the ruler of Bukhara invited him to his palace to teach his children, the great Imam refused, saying: "Knowledge cannot be debased by being taken to a ruler. If the ruler desires knowledge, he should personally come to knowledge." The ruler replied by asking him to assign one day a week to his children. Bukhari refused again, saying: "I'm busy with teaching the Umma of Muhammad. So, I cannot waste my time teaching your children." The ruler exiled him, and this greatest figure in the science of Hadith spent his last days in exile.[355]

Recording the Traditions

The first written compilations of Traditions were made during 'Umar ibn 'Abd al-'Aziz's caliphate, at the beginning of the second Islamic century (719-22). However, it should

---

[353] Ibn Hajar, *Hadiy al-Sari'*, 487.

[354] Dhahabi, *Tadhkirat al-Huffaz*, 2:556.

[355] Ibn Hajar, *Tahdhib al-Tahdhib*, 9:52.

be remembered that all Traditions that would be collected and arranged in books were in oral circulation. In addition, most of them already had been recorded in individual collections.

The overwhelming majority of Arabs were unlettered. When the Revelation began, a desire to learn to read and write was aroused and encouraged by the Prophet. Remember that he released literate prisoners captured at Badr only after each of them had taught ten Muslims to read and write.[356] Moreover, the Revelation began with the command:

> Read, in the name of your Master, Who has created. He created man from a clot suspended (on the wall of the womb). Read, Your Master is the All-Munificent, Who taught (to write) with the pen. He taught man what he had not known. (96:1-5)

Despite the importance attached to knowledge and learning, in the early period of his Messengership the Prophet did not allow his Companions to write down what he said. For example, he said: "Don't write down what I say. If you have written down something received from me that is not part of the Qur'an, destroy it."[357] He did not want the Companions to confuse the Qur'anic verses with his own words. The Qur'an was still being revealed and recorded on sheets or fragments of leather or wood; it would assume its final book form at a later date.

This was an understandable precaution, for he wanted to be sure that later generations would not mistake his words for those of God. This is clear from a Tradition narrated by Abu Hurayra: "The Messenger once came near us while some friends were writing down what they had heard him say. He

---

[356] Ibn Sa'd, *Tabaqat*, 2:22.

[357] *Muslim*, "Zuhd," 72; *Darimi*, "Muqaddima," 42.

asked what they were writing, and they replied: 'What we heard you say.' The Messenger warned: 'Do you know that the communities preceding you went astray because they wrote down that which is not found in the Book of God?'"[358]

Another reason for this prohibition is that most of the Qur'anic Revelations came on specific occasions. Thus, some of its verses are concise and clear while others are ambiguous. Allegorical verses appear beside explicit and incontrovertible ones. As a purely Islamic community was still evolving, some commandments came to replace earlier ones.

The Messenger also had to address, on various occasions, people with widely varying temperaments and levels of understanding, as well as "new" and "old" Muslims. For example, when a new Muslim asked what the best deed was, he answered that it was belief and performing the five pre-scribed prayers. However, during a time when jihad had priority, he said it was jihad in the way of God. Further, since Islam is for all time and all people, he frequently resorted to allegories, similes, parables, and metaphors.

These and other factors might have led him to forbid certain individuals to record his words. If everyone had kept a personal account and been unable to distinguish between the real and the metaphorical, the concrete and the abstract, the abrogated and the abrogating, the general and the particular and occasional, the result would have been chaos and misunderstanding. For this reason, 'Umar sometimes warned people not to narrate Prophetic Traditions carelessly.

However, many Traditions state that the Messenger allowed his Companions to write down his words. A time

---

[358] Khatib al-Baghdadi, *Taqyid al-'Ilm*, 34.

came when the Companions attained the intellectual and spiritual maturity to distinguish between the Qur'an and the Hadith. Therefore, they could give the proper attention and importance to each, and understand the circumstances relevant to each Tradition. And so the Messenger encouraged them to record his Traditions.

Abu Hurayra relates: "'Abd Allah ibn 'Amr ibn al-'As is the only Companion who has as many Traditions as I do. I didn't write them down, but he did."[359] 'Abd Allah reported that he wrote down whatever he heard from the Messenger. Some people told him: "You're writing down everything coming from the Messenger's mouth. He is a human being; sometimes he is angry and other times he is pleased." 'Abd Allah referred the matter to the Messenger, who pointed to his mouth and said: "Write down, for I swear by Him in Whose hand is my life that only truth comes out from this."[360]

Whether angry or pleased, the Messenger *never spoke on his own; out of personal caprice or whim. Whatever he spoke, is a Revelation [explicit or implicit] revealed* (53:3-4). As his every word and action had some bearing on Islam, they had to be recorded. The Companions did this holy task either through memorizing or recording what they heard or saw. As a result, his life is the most complete biography ever produced. Every aspect, even its minutest details, has been handed down throughout the generations. This is why we should feel indebted to the Companions and the two or three generations after them, especially the great Traditionists, who recorded and then transmitted his words and actions.

---

[359] Bukhari, "'Ilm," 39.

[360] *Abu Dawud*, "'Ilm," 3; Ibn Hanbal, 2:162; *Darimi*, "Muqaddima," 43.

Someone once complained to the Messenger: "O Messenger of God, we hear many things from you. But most of them slip our minds because we cannot memorize them." The Messenger replied: "Ask your right hand for help."[361] In other words, write down what you hear. When Rafi' ibn Khadij asked the Messenger whether they could write down what they heard from him, he was told that they could.[362] As recorded in al-Darimi's *Sunan*, the Messenger advised: "Record knowledge by writing."[363] During the conquest of Makka, the Messenger gave a sermon. A Yemeni man named Abu Shah, stood up and said: "O Messenger, please write down these [words] for me." The Messenger ordered this to be done.[364]

'Ali had a sheet, which he attached to his sword, upon which was written narrations about the blood-money to be paid for injuries, the sanctification of Madina, and some other matters.[365] Ibn 'Abbas left behind a camel-load of books, most of which deal with what he had heard from the Messenger and other Companions.[366] The Messenger sent a letter to 'Amr ibn Hazm, which dealt with blood-money for murder and injury, and the law of retaliation.[367] This letter was handed down to Abu Bakr ibn Muhammad, his great-grandson.

---

[361] *Tirmidhi*, "'Ilm," 12.

[362] Hindi, *Kanz al-'Ummal*, 10:232.

[363] *Darimi*, "Muqaddima," 43.

[364] *Abu Dawud*, "'Ilm," 3; *Tirmidhi*, "'Ilm," 12.

[365] *Bukhari*, "'Ilm," 39; Ibn Hanbal, 1:100.

[366] M. 'Ajjaj al-Khatib, *Al-Sunna qabl al-Tadwin*, 352.

[367] *Darimi*, "Diyat," 12.

Likewise, a scroll transferred from the Messenger to Abu Rafi' was handed down to Abu Bakr ibn 'Abd al-Rahman ibn Harith, one of the Tabi'un.[368] A leading scholar of that generation, Mujahid ibn Jabr, saw 'Abd Allah ibn 'Amr's compilation *Al-Sahifat al-Sadiqa*. Ibn al-Athir, a renowned historian, writes that it contained about 1,000 Traditions, half of which were recorded in authentic books of Tradition, with the chain from 'Amr ibn Shu'ayb, from his father, and from his grandfather, respectively.

Jabir ibn 'Abd Allah al-Ansari also left behind a voluminous book containing the sayings he had heard from the Messenger.[369] *Al-Sahifa al-Sahiha* is another important source of Hadith from the earliest period. Hammam ibn Munabbih, its compiler, followed Abu Hurayra whenever he went and wrote down the Prophetic sayings reported by him. This compilation, recently published by Muhammad Hamidullah, has been carbondated to a period thirteen centuries ago. Almost all of its Traditions can be found either in *Musnad ibn Hanbal* or the *Sahihayn* of Bukhari and Muslim.

After these first simple compilations, Caliph 'Umar ibn 'Abd al-'Aziz, who reigned between 719-22, decided that all oral and written authentic Traditions should be compiled systematically into books. He ordered Abu Bakr ibn Muhammad ibn 'Amr ibn Hazm, governor of Madina, to supervise this task. Muhammad ibn Shihab al-Zuhri, renowned for his profound learning and keen intelligence, undertook the task and acquired the honor of being the first official compiler of Traditions.[370]

---

[368] Khatib al-Baghdadi, "Al-Kifaya," 330.

[369] Ibn Sa'd, 7:2; Khatib al-Baghdadi, "Al-Kifaya," 354.

[370] Bukhari, "'Ilm," 34.

But such an honor was not restricted solely to him: 'Abd al-Malik ibn 'Abd al-'Aziz ibn Jurayj (Makka), Sa'id ibn Abi 'Aruba (Iraq), Awza'i (Damascus), Zayd ibn Qudama and Sufyan al-Thawri (Kufa), Hammad ibn Salama (Basra), and 'Abd Allah ibn al-Mubarak (Khorasan) also were involved.

This period of official and systematic compilation was followed by the period of classification by such great Traditionists as Abu Dawud al-Tayalisi, Musaddad ibn Musarhad, al-Humaydi, and Ahmad ibn Hanbal, who brought out their *Musnad*s. 'Abd al-Razzaq ibn Hammam and others formed their *Musannaf*s, and Ibn Abi Dhi'b and Imam Malik produced their *Al-Muwatta*s. Yahya ibn Sa'id al-Qattan and Yahya ibn Sa'id al-Ansari also should be mentioned among the pre-eminent figures of this period.

Then came the period of such great Traditionists as Bukhari, Muslim, Abu Dawud, Nasa'i, Tirmidhi, and Ibn Maja, who produced the well-known, six most authentic books of Tradition. These celebrated persons, and such other illustrious people like Yahya ibn Ma'in, included in their collections what they believed to be the most authentic Traditions after judging them according to the strictest criteria.

For example, Imam Bukhari sought a Tradition from a man renowned for his reliability and piety. When he saw that man hold his hat toward his animal as if it contained something to eat, in an attempt to entice it to come to him, he asked the man if the hat contained some food for the animal. When told that it did not, Bukhari took no Traditions from him. In his view, one who could deceive an animal in this way might also deceive people. Such were the exacting criteria applied when judging the reliability of narrators.

In short, the Prophetic Traditions were either written down or memorized during the time of the Companions. When the first Islamic century ended, they were circulating widely in both oral and written form. Caliph 'Umar ibn 'Abd al-'Aziz tasked eminent scholars with producing the first official compilation in different cities. Authentic Traditions were distinguished from fabricated ones according to the most stringent care and criteria. After they were classified, one of the most systematic and accurate compilations or collections was undertaken by the most prominent Traditionists of that time.

Later on, new authentic books of Traditions were produced. Also, such illustrious critics of Tradition as Ibn Hajar al-Asqalani, Ibn Abd al-Barr, Dhahabi, Ibn al-Jawzi, and Zayn al-Din al-'Iraqi reviewed all Traditions and wrote large compendiums about their narrators.

As a result of such scholarly activity, the Sunna has reached us through the most reliable channels. No one can doubt the authenticity of this second source of Islam, which approaches the Qur'an in purity, authenticity, and reliability.

CHAPTER 8

The Companions and the Tabi'un

The Companions

These people constitute the first pure and blessed channel through which the Qur'an and the Sunna were transmitted. God is the All-Trustworthy and Inspirer of Trust. The Qur'an describes Archangel Gabriel as trustworthy and as one obeyed and having power (81:20-21). Prophet Muhammad was renowned for his trustworthiness.

The Qur'an was entrusted to the Companions, who memorized and recorded it so that it could be transmitted. This blessed community, praised in the Torah and Gospel, was the living embodiment of almost all laudable virtues and sought only God's pleasure. In addition to the Qur'an, they absorbed the Sunna, lived disciplined lives in strict accordance with the Prophet's example, and exerted all their efforts to both represent and transmit it with complete accuracy.

According to Ibn Hajar al-Asqalani, scholars define a Companion as "a believer who saw and heard the Messenger at least once and died as a believer."[371] Even though some scholars have stipulated that a "potential" Companion should have lived in the Messenger's company for one or even two

---

[371] Ibn Hajar, *Al-Isaba*, 1:7.

years, most scholars say it is enough to have been present in his radiant atmosphere long enough to derive some benefit.

The Companions varied in rank and greatness. Some believed in the Messenger from the first, and conversions continued until his death. The Qur'an grades them according to precedence in belief and to conversion before and after Makka's conquest (9:100; 57:10).

The same gradation also was made by the Messenger. For example, he reproached Khalid for offending 'Ammar, saying: "Don't bother my Companions."[372] He also frowned at 'Umar when he annoyed Abu Bakr, and asked: "Why don't you leave my Companions to me? Abu Bakr believed in me when all of you denied me." Abu Bakr knelt down and explained: "O Messenger of God, it was my fault."[373]

Hakim al-Nisaburi divided them into twelve ranks, and most scholars accept his ranking:

- The four Rightly Guided Caliphs (Abu Bakr, 'Umar, 'Uthman, and 'Ali), and the rest of the ten who were promised Paradise while still alive (Zubayr ibn al-'Awwam, Abu 'Ubayda ibn al-Jarrah, 'Abd al-Rahman ibn 'Awf, Talha ibn 'Ubayd Allah, Sa'd ibn Abi Waqqas, and Sa'id ibn Zayd).

- Those who believed prior to 'Umar's conversion and met secretly in Arqam's house to listen to the Messenger.

- Those who migrated to Abyssinia.

- The Helpers (Ansar) who swore their allegiance to the Messenger at al-'Aqaba.

---

[372] Ibn Athir, *Usd al-Ghaba*, 4:132.

[373] Bukhari, "Tafsir," 7:3.

- The Helpers who swore their allegiance at al-'Aqaba the following year.

- The Emigrants who joined the Messenger during the hijra before his arrival in Madina from Quba, where he stayed for a short while.

- The Companions who fought at Badr.

- Those who emigrated to Madina between the Battle of Badr and the Treaty of Hudaybiya.

- The Companions who swore allegiance under a tree during the expedition of Hudaybiya.

- Those who converted and emigrated to Madina after the Treaty of Hudaybiya.

- Those who became Muslims after the conquest of Makka.

- Children who saw the Messenger any time or any place after the conquest of Makka.[374]

Muslim scholars of the highest rank, whose minds are enlightened by scientific knowledge and whose souls are illumined by religious knowledge and practice, agree that Prophets are the greatest members of humanity. Immediately after them come the Companions of the Last Prophet, who is the greatest Prophet.

Although some Companions may have the same rank as previous Prophets in a particular virtue, no one can equal a Prophet in general terms. Some of the greatest saints or scholars can compete with or excel some of the Companions in particular virtues. But even a Companion of the lowest rank, such as Wahshi (who killed Hamza), is still greater, in general terms, than all who come after the Companions. All Muslim scholars, Traditionists, theologians, and saints agree upon this.

---

[374] Hakim, *Ma'rifat 'Ulum al-Hadith*, 22-24.

Factors in their greatness

Relation to Messengership. Prophethood is greater than sainthood, and Messengership is greater than Prophethood. Every Prophet is a saint, but no saint is a Prophet. Although every Messenger is a Prophet, not every Prophet is simultaneously a Messenger. Prophet Muhammad is the last and greatest Prophet and Messenger. The Companions are related directly to his Messengership and connected with him due to his Messengership. All who come after the Prophet, however great they may be, are connected with him on account of sainthood only. Therefore, a Companion is greater than a saint to the degree that Messengership is greater than sainthood (the distance between them cannot be measured).

The benefits of company. Nothing can compare with the enlightenment and spiritual exhilaration gained from a Prophet's actual presence or company. No amount of reading what an intellectual, especially a spiritual, master has written can benefit you as much as learning directly from a Prophet. Thus the Companions, particularly those who were with him most often and from the very beginning, benefited so much that they were elevated from crude, ignorant, and savage desert people to the rank of being humanity's religious, intellectual, spiritual, and moral guides until the Last Day.

To be a Companion, one would have to go back to the Makka or Madina of the seventh century CE, listen to the Messenger attentively and observe him speaking, walking, eating, fighting, praying, prostrating, and so on. Since this is impossible, no one can attain the rank of the Companions, who were endowed with Divine coloring in the Messenger's presence.

Truthfulness. Islam is based on truthfulness and the absence of lies. The Companions embraced Islam in its orig-

inal, pristine purity. For them, being a Muslim meant abandoning all previous vices, being purified in the radiant atmosphere of Divine Revelation, and embodying Islam. They
would rather die than tell a lie. The Messenger once declared
that if apostasy were as repugnant to a person as entering fire,
then that person must have tasted the pleasure of belief. The
Companions tasted this pleasure and, being sincere Muslims,
could not lie, as this was almost as serious as apostasy. We
have trouble understanding this point fully, for people in our
own time regard lying and deceit as skills, and almost all
virtues have been replaced by vices.

The atmosphere created by Revelation. The Companions
were honored with being the first to receive the Divine
Messages through the Prophet. Every day they were given
original messages and invited to a new "Divine table" full of
the ever-fresh "fruits" of Paradise. Every day they experienced radical changes in their lives, were elevated closer to
God's Presence, and increased in belief and conviction. They
found themselves in the verses of the Qur'an, and could learn
directly whether or not God approved of their actions.

For example, whenever and wherever *Those who are with
him are hard against the unbelievers, merciful one to another. You see them bowing, prostrating, seeking blessing from
God and good pleasure. Their mark is on their faces, the
trace of prostration* (48:29) was revealed, eyes turned pri-
marily to Abu Bakr, 'Umar, 'Uthman, and 'Ali. After all, they
were famous for being with the Messenger from the very
beginning, their hardness toward unbelievers, their mercy to
fellow Muslims, and for frequent and long bowing and prostration before God while seeking His good pleasure.

When *Among the believers are men who were true to
their covenant with God; some of them have fulfilled their*

vow by death, and some are still awaiting, and they have not changed in the least (33:23) was recited, everyone remembered the martyrs of Uhud, especially Hamza, Anas ibn Nadr, and 'Abd Allah ibn Jahsh, as well as others who had promised God to give their lives willingly in His Way.

While God explicitly mentioned Zayd ibn Haritha in: *So when Zayd had accomplished what he would of her ...* (33:37),[375] He declared in 48:18 that He was well pleased with the believers when they swore fealty to the Messenger under a tree during the expedition of Hudaybiya.

In such a blessed, pure, and radiant atmosphere, the Companions practiced Islam in its original fullness and pristine purity, based on deep perception, profound insight, and knowledge of God. So, even an ordinary believer who is aware of the meaning of belief and connection with God, and who is trying to practice Islam sincerely, can grasp some glimpse of the purity of the first channel through which the Sunna was transmitted to the next generation.

The difficulty of the circumstances. The reward of a deed changes according to the circumstances in which it is done and the purity of the doer's intention. Striving in the way of God in such severe circumstances as fear, threats, and shortage of necessary equipment, and purely for His sake, is far

---

[375] The Messenger declares: "My Companions are like stars; whomever of them you follow, you will be guided to the True Path." This *hadith* is explicitly corroborated by the verse: *Remember you said to him whom God favored...* (33:37) By *him whom God favored*, the verse refers to Zayd ibn Haritha, the Messenger's emancipated slave who is not included among the greatest Companions. God orders all Muslims to follow the way of those whom He favors: *Guide us to the Straight Path, the path of those whom You favored* (1:5). This means that the Companions, especially the greatest among them, are guides by whom one can find the True or Straight Path. (Tr.)

more rewarding than the same action performed in a free and promising atmosphere.

The Companions accepted and defended Islam in the severest circumstances imaginable. The opposition was very inflexible and unpitying. In Muhyi al-Din ibn al-'Arabi's *Musamarat al-Abrar,* Abu Bakr is reported to have told 'Ali after the Prophet's death that the early Companions did not go out except at the risk of their lives—they always feared that a dagger would be thrust at them. Only God knows how many times they were insulted, beaten, and tortured. Those who were weak and enslaved, such as Bilal, 'Ammar, and Suhayb, were tortured almost to death. Young people like Sa'd ibn Abi Waqqas and Mus'ab ibn 'Umayr, were beaten, boycotted, and imprisoned by their families.

Yet none of them ever thought of recanting or opposing the Messenger. For the sake of God, they forsook everything they had—their homes, native lands, and belongings—and emigrated. The believers of Madina welcomed them enthusiastically, protected them, and shared with them everything they had. They fulfilled their covenant with God willingly, sold their goods and souls to God in exchange for belief and Paradise, and never broke their word. This gained them so high a rank in the view of God that no one can attain it until the Last Day.

The severity of circumstances, along with other factors, made the Companions' belief strong and firm beyond compare. For example, the Messenger once entered the mosque and saw Harith ibn Malik sleeping there. He woke him up. Harith said: "May my father and mother be sacrificed for your sake, O Messenger of God! I am ready to carry out your orders!" The Messenger asked him how he had spent the night. Harith answered: "As a true believer." The Messenger said: "Everything that is true must have a truth (to prove it). What is the truth of your belief?" Harith replied: "I fasted during the day and prayed to my Master in utmost sincerity all night long. Now I am in a state as if I were seeing the Throne of my God and the recreation of the people of Paradise in Paradise." The Messenger concluded: "You have become an embodiment of belief."[376]

The Companions became so near to God that "God was their eyes with which they saw, their ears with which they heard, their tongues with which they spoke, and their hands with which they held."

The Companions in the Qur'an. Ibn Hazm voices the opinion of many leading scholars: "All of the Companions will enter Paradise."[377] It is possible to find proofs in the Qur'an testifying to this assertion. The Qur'an describes the Companions as follows:

> Muhammad is the Messenger of God. Those who are with him are hard toward the unbelievers, merciful one to another. [They kept so long vigils that] you see them bowing, prostrating, seeking blessing, bounty (of forgiveness and Paradise) and good pleasure (of God). Their mark is on their faces, the trace of prostration. This is their likeness in the Torah and in the Gospel: as a seed that puts forth its shoot, and strengthens it, and it grows strong and rises straight upon its stalk, pleasing the sowers, that through them it may enrage the unbelievers. God has promised those of them who believe and do deeds of righteousness forgiveness and a mighty wage [He will reward them in Paradise with the things that neither eyes will ever have seen nor ears heard]. (48:29)

---

[376] Haythami, *Majma' al-Zawa'id*, 1:57; Hindi, *Kanz al-'Ummal*, 13:353.

[377] *Ibn Hajar*, 1:10.

And as:

> The Outstrippers, the first Emigrants and Helpers, and
> those who followed them in doing good—God is well-
> pleased with them, and they are well-pleased with
> Him; He has prepared for them gardens underneath
> which rivers flow, therein to dwell forever; that is the
> mighty triumph. (9:100)

Abu Hurayra never missed a discourse of the Messenger.
He was always with him, and stayed in the antechamber of
the Prophet's Mosque. He suffered hunger almost all the
time. Once he went to the Messenger and told him that he had
eaten nothing for days. Abu Talha took him as a guest, but
unfortunately there was little in his house to eat. So, he asked
his wife Umm Sulaym to

> "... put the children to bed early, and put on the table
> whatever we have to eat. When we sit at the table, put
> out the candle pretending to make its light brighter. No
> one sees in the dark whether one is really eating or not.
> I will act as if I am eating, and thus our guest can sat-
> isfy his hunger." After the dawn prayer, the Messenger
> turned to them, smiled, and said: "What did you do last
> night? This verse was revealed concerning you:

> Those who made their dwelling in the abode [Madina],
> and in belief, before them [the Emigrants] love whoev-
> er has emigrated to them, not finding in their breasts
> any need for what they have been given, and preferring
> others above themselves, even though poverty be their
> portion. Whoever is guarded against the avarice of his
> own soul, those—they are the prosperous. (59:9)[378]

We also read of the Companions:

> God was well-pleased with the believers when they
> were swearing fealty to you under the tree, and He

---

[378] *Bukhari*, "Tafsir," 59/6.

knew what was in their hearts, so He sent down peace,
calm and tranquility upon them, and rewarded them
with a nigh victory. (48:18)

The Companions swore many oaths of allegiance to the
Messenger, promising to protect him and carry, by God's
Will, Islam to ultimate victory as best they could. They kept
their promise at the cost of all their belongings and lives.
Most were martyred either during the Prophet's lifetime or
while conveying Islam throughout the newly conquered
lands. It is still possible to find, in almost every part of the
Muslim world, tombs where several Companions are buried.
They also raised numerous scholars in jurisprudence,
Traditions, Qur'anic interpretation, as well as in history and
the biography of the Prophet. The Qur'an states:

> Among believers are those who were true to their
> covenant with God; some have fulfilled their vow by
> death, and some are still awaiting, and they have not
> changed in the least. (33:23)

The Companions in Hadith. The Prophet also praised the
Companions and warned Muslims not to attack or insult
them. For example, Bukhari, Muslim, and other Traditionists
relate from Abu Sa'id al-Khudri that the Messenger warned:

> Don't curse my Companions, don't curse my Compan-
> ions. I swear by Him in Whose hand is my life that
> even if you had as much gold as Mount Uhud and spent
> it in the way of God, this would not be equal in reward
> to a few handfuls of them or even to half of that.[379]

The Companions have such a high value because they
accepted, preached, and protected Islam in the severest circumstances. Besides, according to the rule that "the cause is
like the doer," the reward gained by all Muslims from that

---

[379] *Bukhari*, "Fada'il al-Ashab," 5; *Muslim*, "Fada'il al-Sahaba," 221.

time until the Last Day is being added to the Companions' record, without taking away any of the doers' rewards. Had it not been for their efforts to spread Islam wherever they went, no one would know of it or be able to become Muslim. So, all Muslims after the Companions should feel indebted to them and, rather than thinking of criticizing them, should pray for them:

> As for those who came after them, they say: "Our Master, forgive us and our brothers who preceded us in belief, and put not into our hearts any rancor toward those who believe. Our Master, surely You are the All-Gentle, the All-Compassionate." (59:10)

Tirmidhi and Ibn Hibban quote the warning of 'Abd Allah ibn Mughaffal, which he heard from the Messenger:

> Oh God, Oh God! Refrain from using bad language about my Companions! Oh God, Oh God! Refrain from using bad language about my Companions! Don't make them the target of your attacks after me! Whoever loves them loves them on account of his love of me; whoever hates them hates them on account of his hatred of me. Whoever hurts them hurts me; whoever hurts me "hurts" God.[380]

Imam Muslim relates in his *Sahih* that the Messenger declared:

> Stars are means of security for the heaven. When they are scattered, what was promised for Heaven befalls it. I am the means of security for my Companions. When I leave the world, what was promised for my Companions will befall them. My Companions are means of security for my nation.

---

[380] *Tirmidhi*, "Manaqib," 58; *Ibn Hibban*, 9:189; Ibn Hanbal, 5:57. *Hurt* is used figuratively, in the sense of displeasing, offending, or attracting the wrath of God to yourself.

When they leave the world, what was promised for
my nation will befall it.[381]

As recorded in Bukhari, Muslim, and other authentic
books of Tradition, the Messenger declared:

> The best people are those living in my time. Then come
> those who follow them, and then come those who fol-
> low them. Those will be followed by a generation
> whose witness is sometimes true, sometimes false.[382]

The time of the Companions and the two succeeding generations was the time of truthfulness. People of great righteousness and exacting scholars appeared during these first
three generations. Later generations contained many who lied
and perjured themselves to reinforce false beliefs or attain
worldly aims. It was natural for liars and members of heterodox sects (as it is for biased Orientalists and their Muslim followers) to lie about the Companions and the pure Imams of
the two generations succeeding them, as they were strong-
holds of Islam and strengthened its pillars.

Abu Nu'aym quotes 'Abd Allah ibn 'Umar as saying:

> Whoever desires to follow a straight path should follow
> the path of those who passed away: The Companions of
> Muhammad. They are the best of his Umma, the purest
> in heart, the deepest in knowledge, and the furthest from
> any false display of piety. They are a community whom
> God chose for His Prophet's company and His reli-

---

[381] *Muslim*, "Fada'il al-Sahaba," 207. That is, Heaven is maintained by the
stars' delicate order. When this order collapses, it means the final destruction of the universe. The Prophet was a means of security for his
Companions. Twenty years after his death, people began slandering the
Companions. Their existence, particularly of the leading ones, was a
means of security for the Muslim nation. After their deaths, misfortune
began to visit the Muslims. (Tr.)

[382] *Muslim*, "Fada'il al-Sahaba," 212; *Bukhari*, "Fada'il al-Ashab," 1.

gion's conveyance. Try to be like them in conduct and follow their way. They are the Companions of Muhammad. I swear by God, the Master of the Ka'ba, that they were on true guidance.[383]

As recorded by Tabarani and Ibn al-Athir, 'Abd Allah ibn Mas'ud, one of the first people to embrace Islam in Makka and sent to Kufa as a teacher by 'Umar, said: "God looked at the hearts of His true servants and chose Muhammad to send to His creatures as a Messenger. Then He looked at the hearts of people and chose his Companions as the helpers of His religion and the viziers of His Prophet."[384] He also said:

> You may excel the Companions in fasting, praying, and in striving to worship God better. But they are better than you, for they paid no attention to the world and were most desirous of the Hereafter.[385]

The companions who excelled narrating Traditions. God Almighty created people with different dispositions and potentials so that human social life would be maintained through mutual help and the division of labor. Therefore, some Companions were good farmers, successful tradesmen or businessmen, students, military commanders, and administrators. Some, especially the *Ashab al-Suffa* (those who stayed in the antechamber of the Prophet's Mosque) never missed a teaching of the Messenger and tried to memorize his every word.

These Companions later narrated to people whatever they heard from or saw about the Messenger. Fortunately, they outlived the others by God's Will and, together with 'A'isha,

---

[383] Abu Nu'aym, *Hilya*, 1:305.

[384] Ibid., 1:375.

[385] Ibid., 1:135.

constituted the first, golden channel through which the Sunna was transmitted. The following is a brief description of their characters and lives:

Abu Hurayra was from Yemeni tribe of Daws. He became a Muslim in the early days of 7 AH at the hands of Tufayl ibn 'Amr, the chief of his tribe. When he emigrated to Madina, the Messenger was busy with the Khaybar campaign. He joined him in Khaybar. The Messenger changed his name, 'Abd al-Shams, to 'Abd al-Rahman, saying: "A man is not the slave of either the sun or moon."

Abu Hurayra was very poor and modest. One day the Messenger saw him cradling a cat and nicknamed him Abu Hirr (the father or owner of a cat). People soon began to call him Abu Hurayra. However, he liked to be called Abu Hirr, since this title was given to him by the Messenger.[386]

He lived with his non-Muslim mother. Always praying her conversion, one day he asked the Messenger to pray for this. He did so, and before he lowered his arms, Abu Hurayra ran to his house, so sure was he that the Messenger's prayer would be accepted. When he arrived, his mother stopped him at the door so that she could finish *ghusl* (total ritual ablution). She then opened the door and declared her conversion. After this, Abu Hurayra requested the Messenger to pray that believers should love him and his mother. The Messenger did so.[387] Therefore, love of Abu Hurayra is a mark of belief.

This Companion had an extraordinarily keen memory. He slept the first third of night, prayed and did his daily supererogatory recitations in the second third, and went over

---

[386] *Ibn Hajar*, 4:202.

[387] *Muslim*, "Fada'il al-Sahaba," 158; Ibn Sa'd, 4:328.

the Traditions he had memorized in order never to forget them in the last third. He memorized more than 5,000 Traditions. He never missed a discourse of the Messenger, sought to learn his Traditions, and was a lover of knowledge.

One day he prayed: "O God, grant me knowledge I will never forget." The Messenger heard him and said: "O God, amen."[388] On another day, he told the Messenger: "O Messenger of God, I don't want to forget what I hear from you." The Messenger asked him to take off his cloak and spread it on the ground. The Messenger then prayed and emptied his hands onto the cloak as if filling them with something from the Unseen. He ordered Abu Hurayra to fold up the cloak and hold it to his breast. After narrating this incident, Abu Hurayra used to say: "I folded it up and held it to my breast. I swear by God that [since then] I have not forgotten anything I heard from the Messenger."[389]

Abu Hurayra paid no heed to the world. He usually fasted 3 or 4 days successively because of poverty. Sometimes he writhed with hunger on the ground and said to those passing by: *Istaqra'tuka*, which has a double meaning: "Will you not recite to me some Qur'an?" and "Will you not feed me?"[390] Ja'far Tayyar understood him better than anybody else and took him as a guest.[391]

Abu Hurayra patiently endured such hardship for the sake of Hadith. To those who sometimes warned him that he was narrating too many Traditions, he replied sincerely: "While

---

[388] Hakim, *Mustadrak*, 3:508.

[389] *Muslim*, "Fada'il al-Sahaba," 159; Ibn Sa'd, 4:329, 330.

[390] *Bukhari*, "At'ima," 1.

[391] *Bukhari*, "Fada'il al-Ashab," 10.

my Emigrant brothers were busy in the bazaar and my Helper brothers with farming, I tried to keep my soul and body together to keep company with the Messenger."[392] Sometimes he said: "Were it not for the verse: *Those who conceal the clear signs and the guidance that We have sent down, after We have shown them clearly in the Book, they shall be cursed by God and the curses* (2:159), I would narrate nothing."[393]

Some claim that other Companions were opposed to Abu Hurayra's narrating. This claim is groundless. Many Companions, among them Abu Ayyub al-Ansari, 'Abd Allah ibn 'Umar, 'Abd Allah ibn 'Abbas, Jabir ibn 'Abd Allah al-Ansari, Anas ibn Malik, and Wasila ibn Aslam, narrated Traditions from him. Some asked Abu Ayyub why he narrated from Abu Hurayra despite his earlier conversion, to which he would reply: "He heard from the Messenger many things we did not hear."[394]

Many leading Tabi'un also received numerous Traditions from him, including Hasan al-Basri, Zayd ibn Aslam, Sa'id ibn al-Musayyib (who married Abu Hurayra's daughter so that he could benefit from him more), Sa'id ibn Yasar, Sa'id al-Makburi, Sulayman ibn Yasar, Sha'bi (who received Traditions from 500 Companions), Muhammad ibn Abi Bakr, and Qasim ibn Muhammad (who is accepted as a link in the chain of Nakshbandi spiritual guides). Hammam ibn Munabbih and Muhammad ibn Munkadir are the most famous of the 800 people who received Traditions from him.[395]

---

[392] *Bukhari*, "'Ilm," 42; *Muslim*, "Fada'il al-Sahaba," 159; Ibn Sa'd, 4:332.

[393] Ibn Sa'd, 4:330-1.

[394] *Hakim*, 3:512; Ibn Kathir, *Al-Bidaya*, 8:109.

[395] Ibn Hajar, 4:205.

'Umar appointed Abu Hurayra as governor to Bahrayn. However, when he made a small amount of wealth by trade during his period of office, 'Umar had him investigated. Although he was found innocent and requested to return to office, Abu Hurayra declined, saying: "That is enough for me as a governor."[396]

Abu Hurayra, despite claims to the contrary by such Orientalists as Goldziher and their Muslim followers like Ahmad Amin, Abu Rayya, and 'Ali 'Abd al-Razzaq, was never anti-'Ali and pro-Umayyad. He should have supported 'Ali in the internal conflicts so that sedition would be crushed, but chose to remain neutral, for: "Seditions will appear, during which the one who sits [silent] is better than the one who stands [to participate]; the one who stands is better than him who walks [to participate], and the one who walks is better than him who runs [in them]."[397] This *hadith* might not have been related to the internal conflicts during 'Ali's caliphate, but Abu Hurayra thought that it was and so remained neutral.

Abu Hurayra opposed the Umayyad government. He once stood in front of Marwan ibn Hakam and narrated the *hadith*: "The destruction of my community will be in the hands of a few callow (young) men from the Quraysh."[398] Marwan responded: "May God's curse be upon them," pretending not to understand who was meant. Abu Hurayra added: "If you like, I can inform you of their names and characteristics."

---

[396] Ibn Sa'd, 4:335-6; Ibn Athir, 6:321; Ibn Hajar, 4:210.

[397] *Bukhari*, "Fitan," 9; *Muslim*, "Fitan," 10.

[398] *Bukhari*, "Fitan," 3; Ibn Hanbal, 2:288.

He was frequently heard to pray: "O God, don't make me live until the sixtieth year."[399] This supplication was so famous that whoever saw Abu Hurayra recalled it. He had heard from the Messenger that some inexperienced, sinful young men would begin to rule the Muslims in 60 AH. He died in 59 AH, and Yazid succeeded his father Mu'awiya one year later.

There is no proof that 'A'isha was opposed to Abu Hurayra's narrating. Both 'A'isha and Abu Hurayra lived long lives and, except for the following incident, she never criticized his narrations. Once when he was narrating Traditions near her room while she was praying, she finished her prayer and came out, only to find that he had left. She remarked: "The Messenger's Traditions should not be narrated in this way, one after another,"[400] meaning that they should be narrated slowly and distinctly so that the listeners could understand and memorize them.

Some claim that Imam Abu Hanifa said: "I don't take the opinions of three Companions as evidence in jurisprudence. Abu Hurayra is one of them." This is simply a lie. Allama Ibn Humam, one of the greatest Hanafi jurists, regarded Abu Hurayra as a significant jurist. Besides, there is nothing to prove that Abu Hanifa said that.

Abu Hurayra narrated more than 5,000 Traditions. When gathered together, they make perhaps a volume 1.5 times as long as the Qur'an. Many people have memorized the Qur'an in 6 months or even quicker. Abu Hurayra had a very keen memory and spent 4 years with the Messenger, who prayed for the strength of Abu Hurayra's memory. It would be tanta-

---

[399] Ibn Kathir, 8:122.

[400] *Muslim*, "Fada'il al-Sahaba," 160.

mount to accusing Abu Hurayra of deficient intelligence to claim that he could not have memorized so many Traditions. In addition, all of the Traditions he narrated were not directly from the Messenger. As leading Companions like Abu Bakr, 'Umar, Ubayy ibn Ka'b, 'A'isha, and Abu Ayyub al-Ansari narrated from him, he also received Traditions from them.

While Abu Hurayra was narrating Traditions in the presence of Marwan ibn Hakam at different times, the latter had his secretary record them written secretly. Some time later, he asked Abu Hurayra to repeat the Traditions he had narrated to him earlier. Abu Hurayra began: "In the name of God, the All-Merciful, the All-Compassionate," and narrated the same Traditions with exactly the same wording.[401] So, there is no reason to criticize him for narrating so many Prophetic Traditions.

'Abd Allah Ibn 'Abbas was born 4 or 5 years before the Hijra. He had a keen intelligence and memory, and was an inspired man. The Messenger prayed for him: "O God, make him perceptive and well-versed in the religion, and teach him the hidden truths of the Qur'an."[402] During his lifetime, he came to be known as "the Great Scholar of the Umma," "the Sea" (One Very Profound in Knowledge), or "The Translator (Clarifier) of the Qur'an."[403]

He was a very handsome, tall man endowed with great eloquence. His memory was such that he memorized an 80-couplet poem by 'Amr ibn Rabi'a at one reading. Besides his

---

[401] *Hakim*, "Mustadrak," 3:509-10.

[402] *Bukhari*, "Wudu'," 10; *Muslim*, "Fada'il al-Sahaba," 138.

[403] Ibn Athir, 3:291.

profound knowledge of Qur'anic interpretation, Tradition, and jurisprudence, he also was well-versed in literature, particularly in pre-Islamic poetry. In his *Tafsir*, Ibn Jarir al-Tabari relates either a couplet or verse from him in connection with the interpretation of almost each Qur'anic verse.

He was greatly loved by the Companions. Despite his youth, 'Umar appointed him to his Advisory Council, which consisted of elder Companions. When asked why he had done this, 'Umar tested their level of understanding of the Qur'an. He asked them to explain:

> When comes the help of God, and victory, and you see men entering God's religion in throngs, then proclaim the praise of Your Master, and seek His forgiveness; for He is Oft-Returning [in grace and mercy]. (110:1-3)

The elders answered: "It orders the Prophet to praise God and seek His forgiveness when he sees people entering Islam in throngs after the help of God and victory came." 'Umar was not satisfied, and so asked Ibn 'Abbas the same question. He replied: "This *sura* implies that the death of the Messenger is near, for when people enter Islam in throngs, it means that the mission of Messengership has ended." 'Umar turned to the council and explained: "That's why I include him among you."[404]

Ibn 'Abbas was famous for his deep insight, profound learning, keen memory, high intelligence, perceptiveness, and modesty. When he entered a gathering place, people would stand in respect for him. This made him so uncomfortable that he told them: "Please, for the sake of the help and shelter (you gave the Prophet and the Emigrants), don't

---

[404] *Bukhari*, "Tafsir," 110/3.

stand for me!" Although one of the most knowledgeable Muslims, he showed great respect to scholars. For example, he helped Zayd ibn Thabit mount his horse by holding the stirrup steady and explained: "We have been told to behave like this toward our scholars." In return, Zayd kissed his hand without his approval and remarked: "We have been told to behave like this toward the Messenger's relatives."[405]

As noted above, Ibn 'Abbas did not like people to stand for him to show respect. However, when he was buried, something occurred that was as if the dead had stood in respect for him and the spirit beings welcomed him. A voice was heard from beneath the grave: *O soul at peace! Return unto your Master, well-pleased, well-pleasing! Enter among My servants! Enter my Paradise!* (89:27-30).[406]

Ibn 'Abbas brought up many scholars in every branch of religious knowledge. The Makkan school of jurisprudence was founded by him. Such leading Tabi'un scholars as Sa'id ibn Jubayr, Mujahid ibn Jabr, and Ikrima acknowledged: "Ibn 'Abbas taught us whatever we know." He narrated about 1,600 Traditions.

'Abd Allah Ibn 'Umar was the only one of 'Umar's nine sons to be called Ibn 'Umar (the son of 'Umar). This shows that he had greater worth to be called 'Umar's son or to be mentioned with the name of 'Umar. Although 'Umar is the second greatest Companion, 'Abd Allah may be regarded superior in knowledge, piety, worship, and devotion to the Sunna. His care in following the Prophet's example was such that Nafi', Imam Malik's tutor, narrates: "While we were

---

[405] Ibn Hajar, 2:332.

[406] Ibn Kathir, *Tafsir: Surat al-Fajr,* verses 27-30; Haythami, *Majma',* 9:285.

descending 'Arafat, Ibn 'Umar entered a hole. When he came out, I asked him what he had done there. The Imam answered: 'While descending 'Arafat, I was behind the Messenger. He went down into that hole and relieved himself. I felt no need to do that now, but I don't like to oppose him.'"[407] Also, no one ever saw him take more or less than three swallows of water, for he saw the Messenger drink water in three swallows.

Ibn 'Umar was born in the early years of Islam. He saw his father beaten severely by the Makkan polytheists many times.[408] When the Muslims emigrated to Madina, he was about 10 years old. The Messenger did not let him fight at Badr because he was too young. When he was also prevented from fighting at Uhud, he returned home so grief-stricken that he spent the whole night asking himself: "What sin have I committed that they did not include me in the army fighting in the way of the Messenger?"[409]

Ibn Khalliqan relates from Sha'bi:

> Once in their youth, 'Abd Allah ibn Zubayr, his brother Mus'ab ibn Zubayr, 'Abd al-Malik ibn Marwan, and 'Abd Allah ibn 'Umar were sitting near the Ka'ba. They thought that each should ask God for something special in the hope that the prayer would be accepted. Ibn Zubayr prayed: "O God, for the sake of Your Grandeur, Honor, and Majesty, make me a ruler in Hijaz." Mus'ab stretched out his arms and prayed: "O God, for the sake of Your Honor, Majesty, and Grandeur, of Your Throne and Seat, make me a ruler in Iraq." 'Abd al-Malik raised his hands and prayed: "O God, I ask You to make me a ruler over all the

---

[407] Ibn Hanbal, *Musnad*, 2:131.

[408] Ibn Hisham, *Sira*, 1:374.

[409] *Bukhari*, "Maghazi," 6; Ibn Sa'd, 4:143.

Muslims and secure, through me, Muslim unity even
at the cost of some lives." When 'Abd Allah prayed,
he asked: "O God, don't take my soul before You
guarantee Paradise for me."[410]

The prayers of the first three were accepted: 'Abd Allah
ibn Zubayr ruled for a while in Hijaz and was eventually martyred by Hajjaj the Tyrant, the notorious Umayyad governor.
Mus'ab ruled in Iraq for a short time. 'Abd al-Malik succeeded his father, Marwan, as caliph and secured Muslim
unity of Muslims, though at the cost of many lives and much
bloodshed.

As for Ibn 'Umar, Imam Sha'bi remarks: "Whether the
Imam's prayer was accepted or not will be clear in the Hereafter." Sha'bi knew something: "Ibn 'Umar never opposed
the Prophet's descendants or supported the Umayyads. Hajjaj
was afraid of him. Once, Hajjaj gave a sermon before the
noon prayer that was so long that the noon prayer's time was
almost over. Ibn 'Umar warned him: "O Governor, time is
passing without waiting for you to finish your sermon."
Hajjaj was full of rancor and enmity for Ibn 'Umar. Finally,
during a pilgrimage he found someone to prick Ibn 'Umar's
heel with a poisonous spear while he was in pilgrim attire.
The poison eventually killed him."[411]

'Abd Allah ibn Mas'ud, one of the first five or six people to embrace Islam, also narrated a considerable number of
Traditions. As a youth, he tended the flocks of such Qurayshi
leaders as Abu Jahl and 'Uqba ibn Abi Mu'ayt. After his conversion, he would no longer be separated from the
Messenger. He entered the Prophet's house without asking to

---

[410] Ibn Khalliqan, *Wafayat al-A'yan*, 2:30.

[411] Ibn Sa'd, 4:185-87.

do so and so frequently that people thought he was a family member. During military or non-military expeditions, he carried the Prophet's water bag, wooden sandals, and mat upon which he slept or sat. Eventually, he became known as "the caretaker of the pattens (sandals, like shoes), couch, and water bag."[412]

Ibn Mas'ud worked some wonders. For example, while he was once being tortured in Makka, he became invisible to his torturers. The Messenger called him "the son of the mother of a slave," and advised his Companions: "Whoever wants to recite the Qur'an as if it were being revealed for the first time, let him recite it according to the recitation of the son of the mother of a slave."[413]

One day the Messenger asked him to recite some of the Qur'an to him. Ibn Mas'ud excused himself: "O Messenger of God, shall I recite it to you while the Qur'an is being revealed to you?" However, the Messenger insisted: "I would prefer to hear it from others." Ibn Mas'ud began to recite *Surat al-Nisa'*. When he reached verse 41: *How then will it be, when We bring forward from every nation a witness, and bring you as a witness against those?*, the Messenger, whose eyes were full of tears, stopped him, saying: "Stop, please. This is enough."[414]

Ibn Mas'ud, who was short and weak, once climbed a tree because the Messenger asked him to do so. Those present laughed at his legs. The Messenger warned them, saying:

---

[412] *Bukhari*, "Fada'il al-Ashab," 27; Ibn Sa'd, 3:153.

[413] *Ibn Maja*, "Muqaddima," 11; Hakim, *Mustadrak*, 2:318; Ibn Hajar, *Al-Isaba*, 2:369.

[414] *Tirmidhi*, "Tafsir al-Qur'an," 5.

"Those legs will weigh more than Mount Uhud according to the measure of the Hereafter in the other world."[415]

Caliph 'Umar sent him to Kufa as a teacher and with a letter, in which he said: "O people of Kufa! If I did not prefer you over myself, I would not have sent Ibn Mas'ud to you."[416] Ibn Mas'ud lived in Kufa during the caliphate of 'Umar and trained many scholars. Such great Tabi'un scholars as Alqama ibn Qays, Aswad ibn Yazid al-Naha'i, and Ibrahim ibn Yazid al-Naha'i grew up in the ethos established by Ibn Mas'ud. One of the people attending Alqama's courses asked him who had been his teacher. When Alqama answered that he had learned from 'Umar, 'Uthman, 'Ali, and Ibn Mas'ud, the man responded: "Good! Good!"

Ibn Mas'ud continued to stay in Kufa during 'Uthman's caliphate. However, after 'Uthman summoned him to Madina to investigate a groundless complaint about him, Ibn Mas'ud did not want to go back to Kufa, as he was already very old. One day a man ran to him and said: "Last night I dreamed that the Messenger was telling you: 'They have afflicted you much after me, so come to me.' You answered: 'Alright, O Messenger of God. I will not leave Madina any more.' A few days later Ibn Mas'ud became ill. 'Uthman visited him, and the following conversation took place between them:

> Do you have any complaints?
> I have many complaints.
> Of what?
> Of my sins while going to God.
> Is there something you desire?

---

[415] Ibn Sa'd, 3:155.

[416] Ibid., 157.

God's mercy.

Would you like me to send for a doctor?

The "doctor" has made me ill. So, there is nothing the doctor you will send for can do for me.

Ibn Mas'ud spent about 20 years in the company of the Messenger. He narrated approximately 800 Traditions.[417]

* * *

Besides those four great Companions, 'A'isha, Abu Sa'id al-Khudri, Jabir ibn 'Abd Allah, and Anas ibn Malik are the other Companions who narrated many Traditions.

'A'isha lived with the Messenger for 9 years. She had great talents, a keen intelligence and memory, and a deep insight and perceptiveness. She had a great curiosity to learn new things, and asked the Messenger to explain those matters that she found it hard to understand.

Abu Sa'id al-Khudri lived in the mosque's antechamber and was always with the Messenger. He lived a long life, and a time came when he was regarded as the most knowledgeable person of Madina.

Jabir Ibn 'Abd Allah is the son of 'Abd Allah ibn 'Amr ibn Haram al-Ansari, who was martyred at Uhud. After the Messenger's death, he lived in Madina (where he lectured in the Prophet's Mosque), Egypt, and Damascus. Such leading Tabi'un scholars as 'Amr ibn Dinar, Mujahid, and 'Ata' ibn Abi Rabah attended his lectures.[418] People gathered around him in Damascus and Egypt to learn of the Messenger and his Traditions.

---

[417] Ibn Kathir, 7:183.

[418] Ibn Hajar, 1:213.

Anas Ibn Malik served the Messenger for 10 years in Madina. After the Messenger's death, he lived a very long life, during which he must have taught the Prophetic Traditions to those around him.

All the Traditions recorded in *Kanz al-'Ummal*, including authentic and defectively transmitted ones, number 46,624. It is possible someone to memorize them within a short time. Among the Traditionists of early Islamic ages, many people memorized more than 100,000 Traditions, including fabricated ones. Given this fact, it cannot be claimed by the Sunna's detractors and doubters that the number of Traditions narrated from certain Companions is too great for them to have memorized and narrated.

The Tabi'un

In many of the places where the Qur'an praises the Companions, it also mentions the blessed generations following in their way. For example:

> The Outstrippers (the first to embrace Islam and excel others in virtue), the first of the Emigrants and the Helpers, and those who followed them in doing good, God is well-pleased with them and they are well-pleased with Him. He has prepared for them gardens underneath which rivers flow, therein to dwell forever; that is the mighty triumph. (9:100)

The Tabi'un, first of all, must be among those praised together with the Companions. Like them, they were well-pleased with God regardless of whether He sent them good or bad, blessing or misfortune. Conscious of their servanthood before God, they worshipped Him in deep respect and reverence.

Like the Companions, they loved Him deeply and trusted Him completely. The Messenger praised them, saying:

"Good tidings for those who have seen me and believed in me, and good tidings for those who see those who saw me."[419]

The Tabi'un followed in the Companions' footsteps and showed them due respect. They felt no rancor and enmity against any believer, and wished everyone well:

> As for those who came after them, they say: "Our Master, forgive us and our brothers, who preceded us in belief, and put not into our hearts any rancor towards those who believe. Our Master, surely You are the All-Gentle, the All-Compassionate." (59:10)

As described in 9:100, this blessed generation followed the Companions in doing good (*ihsan*). In addition to meaning respect, being well-wishing and altruistic, one *hadith* says that ihsan also means: "Doing good (*ihsan*) is that you worship God as if you were seeing Him; if, however, you do not actually see Him, surely He sees you."[420]

This generation came at a time when conspiracies and hypocrisy caused great internal dissension. At this critical juncture, they protected, defended, and practiced Islam in deep consciousness and devotion. They became the referents of: *Our Master, in You we trust, to You we turn, and to You is the homecoming* (60:4).

Some of them performed 100 *rak'as* of nightly prayers, recited the whole Qur'an every 2 or 3 days, always did their obligatory prayers in congregation in a mosque, always slept (like Masruq) in prostration before the Ka'ba, and did not laugh loudly during their whole lives.

---

[419] Hakim, *Mustadrak*, 4:86; Haythami, *Majma'*, 10:20; Hindi, *Kanz al-'Ummal*, 11:530.

[420] *Bukhari*, "Tafsir," 31/2; *Abu Dawud*, "Sunna," 16; *Muslim*, "Iman," 5-7.

Uways al-Qarani is generally regarded as the greatest Tabi'un. Although old enough to have seen the Prophet, he had no opportunity to do so. One day while sitting with his Companions, the Messenger advised them: "If you see Uways al-Qarani, ask him to pray for you."[421] During his caliphate, 'Umar asked Yemeni pilgrims about Uways. When he was found one year among the pilgrims, 'Umar requested him to pray for him. Uncomfortable at being identified, Uways was never seen again among people until he was martyred at the Battle of Siffin fighting for 'Ali.[422]

There were many illustrious Tabi'un, among them Masruq ibn al-Ajda', 'Ata' ibn 'Abi Rabah, Hasan al-Basri, Muhammad ibn Sirin, 'Ali Zayn al-'Abidin, Qasim ibn Muhammad, and Muhammad ibn Munkadir, who were peerless in knowledge, piety, and righteousness.

Muhammad ibn Munkadir was called al-Bakka' (the one who cries much), due to his fear of God. Once his mother told him: "O my son, if I had not known you since childhood, I would think you are crying for some sin. Why do you cry so much?" He said that he did so because he was deeply conscious of God's Majesty, of the terror of the Day of Judgement, and of Hell.[423] When asked on his death-bed why he was crying, he replied: *I am afraid I'll be included in the meaning of the verse: Yet there will appear to them from God that they never reckoned with* (39:47).

Masruq ibn al-Ajda' worshipped God very earnestly. He used to sleep in prostration before the Ka'ba. When they

---

[421] Muslim, "Fada'il al-Sahaba," 223-24.

[422] Ibid.

[423] Abu Nu'aym, *Hilya*, 3:146.

suggested that he should lie down during his last illness, he answered: "By God, if someone appeared and told me that God wouldn't punish me, even then I would continue to pray with the same earnestness as before."[424] He did so because he was following the Prophet, who, when asked by 'A'isha why he tired himself so much with praying, answered: "Shall I not be a thankful servant?"

Sa'id ibn Jubayr was a student of Ibn 'Abbas. He spent the day preaching Islam and the night praying. He fought against Hajjaj on the side of 'Abd al-Rahman al-Kindi. When finally he was seized, the soldiers taking him to Hajjaj spent a night in a monastery in a big forest. Sa'id wanted to pray in the forest. The soldiers let him, thinking that wild animals would tear him to pieces. The soldiers watched him pray through a window, and saw wild animals gather around him also to watch.

When his captors used torture to force him to swear allegiance to Hajjaj, he always refused: "You are in the wrong, wronging the Prophet's descendants. I'll never take the oath of allegiance to you." Before he was executed, he recited the verse Muslims recite during the animal sacrifice: *I have turned my face to Him who originated the Heavens and the Earth, a man of pure faith; I am not of those who associate partners with God* (6:79). When they turned his face away from the prayer direction, he recited: *To God belong the East and the West; Wherever you turn, there is the Face of God* (2:115). They struck his neck with a sword and from his lips came out: "There is no god but God, and Muhammad is the Messenger of God."[425]

---

[424] Ibn al-Jawzi, *Sifat al-Safwa*, 3:15.

[425] Abu Nu'aym, *Hilya*, 4:291-5; Ibn Kathir, *Al-Bidaya*, 9:117.

Such were the people who received the Traditions from the Companions and transmitted them to succeeding generations. Among them, the following few are also worth some fuller mention to recognize that blessed generation more closely:

Sa'id Ibn al-Musayyib, the Tabi'un's foremost Traditionist, jurist, and Qur'anic interpreter, was born in 15 AH. He met most of the Companions, including 'Umar, 'Uthman, and 'Ali. Sa'id was renowned for his reflection and memory, as well as for his piety, righteousness, and profound devotion. These characteristics caused everyone to consider him, even during his lifetime, the greatest Traditionist of his time.

At the early age of around 20, Sa'id began to give opinions and deliver legal verdicts, just as Hasan al-Basri had done in Basra. The Companions admired him greatly. 'Abd Allah ibn 'Umar once remarked: "If the Messenger had seen that young man, he would have been very pleased with him."[426]

He was extremely careful about performing his daily prayers in congregation in the mosque. He used to say: "I always have said the opening *takbir* of the daily prayers just after the imam for 50 years."[427] He did not neglect any item of the Sunna. Once when he was ill and doctors advised him to stay in 'Aqiq valley for a month, he objected: "Then how can I come to the mosque for the night and dawn prayers?" He was not content to perform the prescribed prayers anywhere except in the Prophet's Mosque.[428]

---

[426] M. 'Ajjaj al-Khatib, *Al-Sunna qabl al-Tadwin*, 485.

[427] Abu Nu'aym, *Hilya*, 1:163.

[428] Ibid., 2:172.

He did not swear allegiance to Caliph Walid. Although Hisham, governor of Madina, had him beaten daily until the stick was broken, he did not yield. When his friends, such as Masruq and Tawus, advised him to give an oral consent to Walid's caliphate to end the beatings, he always replied: "People do what we do. If we consent, how will we be able to explain this to them?"[429]

Sa'id had married Abu Hurayra's daughter in order to be nearer to him and to improve his knowledge and understanding of Abu Hurayra's Traditions. When Caliph 'Abd al-Malik appealed to him that his son Hisham be allowed to marry Sa'id's daughter, he refused and, in the face of increasing pressure and threats, offered her to Ibn Abi Wada', who stayed in the *madrasa*.[430]

Imam Shafi'i considered all of Sa'id's Traditions unquestionably authentic, even if the Companion from whom he had received it was not mentioned. This means that for Imam Shafi'i, Sa'id was of the same rank as the Companions in knowledge and narration of the Prophetic Traditions. Among those who received Traditions from him, 'Ata' ibn Abi Rabah, Qatada, Muhammad al-Baqir ('Ali's great-grandson), Zuhri, and Yahya ibn Sa'id al-Ansari are worthy of special mention.

Alqama ibn Qays al-Nakha'i. During the time of the Tabi'un, Basra was honored by, in particular, Hasan al-Basri; Yemen by Tawus ibn Qaysan; Madina by Sa'id ibn al-Musayyib; and Kufa by Alqama ibn Qays al-Nakha'i. Kufa was first enlightened by 'Abd Allah ibn Mas'ud during 'Umar's caliphate, and then directly by 'Ali, when he

---

[429] Ibn Sa'd, *Tabaqat*, 5:126.

[430] Ibid., 5:138; Dhahabi, *Siyar A'lam al-Nubala'*, 4:234.

moved the caliphate there. This gave Alqama a splendid opportunity to meet many Companions and to learn about the Messenger's life and Traditions at first hand.

Alqama is the founder of the Kufa school of Islamic religious sciences. Those who saw him remembered 'Abd Allah ibn Mas'ud, for he followed the latter's footsteps in prayer, conduct, and in practicing Islam. 'Amr ibn Shurahbil, among the great scholars who narrated Traditions from Alqama, frequently suggested to those near him: "Let's go to the one who resembles Ibn Mas'ud the most in conduct and attitudes."[431] Ibn Mas'ud represented the Messenger wholly. As the Messenger desired to listen to Ibn Mas'ud recite the Qur'an, so Ibn Mas'ud liked to listen to Alqama.[432]

Imam Abu Hanifa, generally accepted as the greatest Muslim jurist and a man famous for his piety and austerity, admired Alqama so much that he would say: "Alqama is probably more profound in [knowledge] of Tradition and jurisprudence than some Companions."

One day, someone came to Alqama and insulted him greatly. The illustrious scholar showed no indignation and, after the man had finished, recited the verse: *Those who hurt believing men and believing women, without their having earned it, have laid upon themselves calumny and manifest sin* (33:58). The man retorted: "Are you a believer?" Alqama answered humbly: "I hope so."[433]

Alqama struggled with falsehood in his time, and did not obey the misguided Umayyad administrators. As he received

---

[431] Ibn Sa'd, 6:86; Abu Nu'aym, 2:98.

[432] Ibn Sa'd, 6:90-91.

[433] Ibid., 6:86; Abu Nu'aym, 2:100.

Traditions from hundreds of Companions, many leading figures among his own and succeeding generations narrated from
him. Alqama brought up the most illustrious scholars of the
Kufan school, people such as Aswad ibn Yazid al-Nakha'i,
Ibrahim al-Nakha'i, and Hammad ibn Abi Sulayman, and provided Kufa with a propitious ethos for bringing up Sufyan al-
Thawri, Abu Hanifa, and many others.

'Urwa ibn Zubayr ibn al-'Awwam's father was one of
the ten for whom Paradise was promised while alive. 'Urwa's
grandmother was Safiyya, the Prophet's paternal aunt, and
his mother was Asma' bint Abu Bakr, who spent much of her
life with 'A'isha. 'Urwa can be considered a student of his
aunt 'A'isha. He also was taught by Sa'id ibn al-Musayyib,
who was 7 or 8 years his senior.

'Urwa was one of the seven greatest jurists of his time.
He transmitted most of the Traditions narrated by 'A'isha. He
also received Traditions from 'Ali, 'Umar, Ibn 'Abbas, Abu
Ayyub al-Ansari, and many other Companions. Many illustrious figures of succeeding generations, among them Qatada
ibn Di'ama, Ibn Shihab al-Zuhri, Yahya ibn Sa'id al-Ansari,
and Zayd ibn Aslam, narrated from him.

Like his contemporaries, 'Urwa was extremely pious.
For example, one of his feet became infected with gangrene
and he had to have it amputated. While it was being amputated with a saw, he did not complain, but only said: *We
have encountered weariness from this journey of ours*
(18:62).

When one of his four sons died some time later, he
stretched his arms before the Ka'ba and glorified God, saying: "O God, You gave me four limbs, two arms and two legs,
and four sons. You have taken one from both groups and left
to me the remaining three. Many thousands of thanks to

You!"[434] 'Urwa was certainly included in the meaning of: *God is well-pleased with them, and they are well-pleased with Him* (98:8).

Muhammad ibn Muslim ibn Shihab al-Zuhri, known as Ibn Shihab al-Zuhri, narrated one-fourth of the Prophetic Traditions coming from the Tabi'un. His father, Muslim, had struggled against the Umayyads, particularly Hajjaj. As a result, the Umayyad government usually kept him under surveillance. He did not, as alleged, support the Umayyads.

Like others honored by God as the most reliable narrators of the Prophetic Traditions, Ibn Shibab al-Zuhri had an extraordinarily keen memory. He memorized the Qur'an before he was 7 years old (it took him only 8 days). When he was 18 years old, he began to practice *ijtihad* (ruling on Islamic religious or legal matters based on principles laid down in the Qur'an and Sunna). He forgot nothing: "I have betrayed nothing that God put in my heart as a trust."[435]

Ibn Shibab al-Zuhri received his first education from Sa'id ibn al-Musayyib, who taught him for 8 years. He was also taught by 'Ubaydullah ibn 'Abd Allah ibn 'Utba, one of the seven leading jurists of the time. His life was wholly dedicated to Hadith: "I shuttled between Hijaz and Damascus for 40 years for the sake of Hadith."[436]

Some accuse him of flattering the Umayyads. This lie is contradicted by historical facts. It is true that he tutored Caliph Hisham's sons. However, this is not a fault and does not mean that he supported the Umayyads. He should, in fact,

---

[434] Abu Nu'aym, 2:179.

[435] Ibid., 3:364; Dhahabi, *Tadhkirat al-Huffaz*, 1:109.

[436] Ibn Kathir, 9:375.

be praised for trying to guide the future rulers of the Muslim community to truth.

In his first meeting with Ibn Shihab al-Zuhri, Caliph 'Abd al-Malik reminded him that his father had supported 'Abd Allah ibn Zubayr in his dispute with the Umayyads for many years. But Ibn Shihab al-Zuhri never feared to speak the truth to the Umayyad rulers. Some Umayyads alleged that 'Ali was referred to in:

> As for him among them who took upon himself the greater part of it, a mighty chastisement awaits him, coming after: Those who came with slander are a band of you; do not reckon it evil for you; rather it is good for you. Every man of them shall have the sin that he has earned charged to him. (24:11) [This verse was revealed on the occasion of the slander against 'A'isha.]

This was, of course, a great lie against 'Ali. Ibn Shihab al-Zuhri openly stated in the Umayyad court that this verse refers to 'Abd Allah ibn Ubayy ibn Salul, leader of Madina's Hypocrites. When the Caliph frowned, Ibn Shihab al-Zuhri retorted: "May you be left without a father! I swear by God that if a herald were to announce from heaven that God allows lying, I would not lie at all!"[437]

Although Ibn Shihab al-Zuhri defended 'Ali to the Umayyads, he was accused of fabricating pro-Umayyad Traditions by Ya'qubi, a Shi'ite historian. Abu Ja'far al-Iskafi, another Shi'ite historian, made the same claim against Abu Hurayra. According to Ya'qubi's false account, Caliph 'Abd al-Malik had Jerusalem's Masjid al-Aqsa' repaired to encourage the Muslims to circumambulate it instead of the Ka'ba. He asked Ibn Shihab al-Zuhri to fabricate a Tradition

---

[437] M. 'Ajjaj al-Khatib, *Al-Sunna qabl al-Tadwin*, 509-10.

to that effect, which (it was claimed) he did: "It is not worth traveling [for prayer] except to the three mosques: Masjid al-Haram, Masjid al-Aqsa', and my Masjid here [in Madina]."

Earlier in this book, I argued in favor of this Tradition's authenticity. In fact, Ya'qubi laid himself open to ridicule through such an unreasonable account, for:

- No Jewish, Christian, or Islamic history book has record-ed that Masjid al-Aqsa' has been circumambulated as the Ka'ba is.

- The Qur'an extols it and the Muslims therefore revere it; it does not need a fabricated Tradition to secure this rev-erence.

- Caliph 'Abd al-Malik, Caliph 'Umar, Nur al-Din al-Zangi, and Salah al-Din al-Ayyubi all had it repaired.

- Ibn Shihab al-Zuhri could not have met 'Abd al-Malik during his reign and fabricated a *hadith* for him at a time when his own father (along with 'Abd Allah ibn Zubayr) was fighting against the caliph.

- Ibn Shihab al-Zuhri was not a famous Traditionist at this time. He only began to compile the Traditions in a formal manner during the Caliphate of 'Umar ibn 'Abd al-'Aziz.

- 'Abd al-Malik was not the sort of man to attempt such an absurd fraud. Before his caliphate, he was very pious, an authority on Traditions, and well-acquainted with the scholars of his generation. Although he did not succeed, as caliph, in retaining his former reputation among schol-ars for piety, he could not have lowered himself so far to fabricate a *hadith*.

Despite its absurdity, Goldziher used Ya'qubi's account to defame Ibn Shihab al-Zuhri, the first formal compiler of the Traditions and a narrator of one-fourth of them. "Modern" researchers in the Muslim world, such as Ahmad Amin, 'Ali Hasan 'Abd al-Qadir, and Abu Rayya, who are spokesmen for the Orientalists, repeat the same claims.

The science of Hadith is founded on the most secure and sound pillars, and its original sources are there for anyone who wants to study them. Goldziher and his followers, on the other hand, base themselves on folkloric and poetical books, such as *'Iqd al-Farid* and *Al-Aghani* (Songs), and on books dealing with animals, like *Kitab al-Hayawan*. These books, and all similar ones, have nothing to do with Hadith and have no scientific approach.

Ibn Shihab al-Zuhri is one of the greatest Hadith authorities. Leading Hadith experts, such as Ibn al-Madini, Ibn Hibban, Abu Khatim, Hafiz al-Dhahabi, and Ibn Hajar al-Asqalani, agree upon his indisputable authority. He received Traditions from many Companions, and numerous scholars among the first and second generations after the Companions narrated from him.

Among the Tabi'un are many others worthy of mention, like Aswad ibn Yazid al-Nakha'i, Nafi' (who taught Imam Malik, founder of the Maliki legal school), and Tawus ibn Qaysan, who did not sleep for 40 years between the night and dawn prayers. However, the scope of this book does not allow me to go into further detail.

Index

A

'Abd Allah ibn
   'Abbas . .130, 195, 209,
   222, 245, 246, 247, 256,
   260

'Abd Allah ibn
   'Umar 247

'Abd Allah ibn
   Jahsh . . .43, 48, 60, 62,
   66, 232

'Abd Allah ibn
   Jubayr 60, 61

'Abd Allah ibn
   Mas'ud 13, 56, 70,
   74, 106, 165, 239, 245,
   258, 259

Abd Allah ibn Ubayy
   ibn Salul 41, 49, 59,
   99, 262

'Abd al-Muttalib . . .28, 83,
   134, 177

Abraham . . . . .xiv, 132

Abu Bakr 6, 14, 37, 80,
   91, 93, 94, 96, 111, 112,
   113, 139, 140, 143, 146,
   170, 180, 181, 182, 191,
   222, 223, 228, 231, 233,
   245, 260

Abu Dharr 93, 94, 137

Abu Hurayra 20, 205,
   208, 219, 221, 223, 235,
   240, 241, 242, 243, 244,
   245, 258, 262

Abu Jahl 14, 56, 135,
   249

Abu Musa al-Ash'ari . .181,
   182

Abu Sa'id al-Khudri . . .182,
   236, 252

Abu Sufyan 50, 61, 69,
   70, 75, 80, 81, 83, 102

Abyssinia . .17, 18, 93, 154,
   228

'Ali ibn Abu Talib . . .6, 14,
   24, 28, 54, 55, 61, 62, 63,
   74, 78, 80, 88, 90, 93, 96,
   103, 133, 139, 143, 145,
   146, 159, 183, 188, 194,
   196, 199, 222, 228, 231,
   233, 243, 251, 255, 257,
   258, 260, 262, 264

Alqama ibn Qays
   al-Nakha'i 148, 258

'Amr ibn al-'As 66, 80,
   108, 135, 159, 204, 205,
   221

Anas ibn Malik . . .133, 188,
   205, 242, 252

Ansar . . .51, 52, 53, 55, 71,
   76, 99, 228

Arabia 2, 5, 10, 11, 19,
   36, 41, 42, 56, 71, 77, 80,
   83, 84, 85, 86, 87, 108,
   137, 147, 154, 180, 181

B

Badr 43, 47, 48, 49, 51,
   53, 55, 56, 57, 58, 59, 62,
   65, 66, 69, 70, 71, 90,
   101, 103, 104, 131, 219,
   229, 248

belief . . . . .i, 18, 21, 24, 26,
   30, 31, 32, 34, 35, 37, 42,
   52, 53, 55, 64, 65, 68, 82,
   86, 91, 99, 113, 117, 118,
   124, 136, 168, 179, 202,
   203, 213, 215, 220, 228,
   231, 232, 233, 234, 235,
   237, 240, 254

Bible . . . . .xiv, 167

Bilal 93, 111, 115, 137,
   233

Byzantines 38, 84, 85,
   91, 96, 126

Byzantium 73

C

Children of Israel 51

Chosroes 106

Christianity 15, 16, 168

Christians 32, 99, 167,
   168, 204

compassion 123, 124,
   130, 175

D

David 167

Day of Judgment . . .15, 24,
   26, 174, 192

E

Emigrants . . .43, 47, 48, 50,
   52, 53, 71, 72, 99, 100,
   103, 105, 229, 235, 246,
   253

F

Farewell Pilgrimage . . .179

Fatima 170, 180, 181

forgiveness 132

G

Gabriel . . .76, 94, 103, 127,
   144, 162, 169, 227

Goldziher, Ignaz . .210, 243, 263, 264

Gülen, M. Fethullah . . .i, ii, iv, v, vi

H

Hadith . .157, 159, 160, 173, 196, 197, 198, 201, 205, 206, 207, 214, 216, 217, 218, 221, 223, 236, 241, 261, 264

Hamza 43, 48, 55, 60, 61, 62, 90, 96, 175, 229, 232

Heaven 7, 31, 86, 155, 188, 218, 237

Hell 6, 7, 37, 129, 139, 166, 175, 176, 214, 255

Helpers 48, 72, 99, 100, 103, 228, 229, 235, 253

Heraclius 84

Hind 61, 62

Hudaybiya 77, 78, 79, 80, 89, 104, 105, 107, 108, 229, 232

humanity . . . . . .v, xviii, 98

Hunayn . .28, 82, 84, 90, 98, 132, 138

hypocrisy 40, 168, 254

Hypocrites 40, 41, 44, 57, 64, 65, 68, 70, 71, 72, 73, 75, 84, 85, 103, 126, 262

I

Ibn Shihab al-Zuhri . . .195, 217, 260, 261, 262, 263, 264

ignorance 1, 29

Ikrima ibn Abu Jahl 14, 66, 74, 105, 135, 247

J

Ja'far ibn Abi Talib 17, 78, 79

Jabir ibn 'Abd Allah . . .193, 223, 242, 252

Jesus . . . . .xiv, 86, 167, 168

Jews 32, 39, 40, 44, 57, 71, 77, 86, 88, 90, 99, 101, 167, 168, 204, 209

jihad 23, 25, 28, 29

Joseph 9

Juwayriya 179

K

Ka'b ibn Ashraf 40, 57

Ka'ba . . .45, 49, 81, 82, 89, 98, 108, 110, 114, 169, 208, 209, 239, 248, 254, 255, 260, 262, 263

Khadija . .96, 129, 138, 145

Khalid ibn Walid . . .61, 66, 79, 96, 105, 108, 112, 131, 135

Khaybar 70, 77, 78, 88, 89, 90, 96, 104, 110, 133, 176, 179, 240

Khodjaefendi i

knowledge . . . .iv, 196, 199, 200, 218, 245

L

Lamartine 5, 154

Last Day . . . . . . .xv, 30, 36, 127, 136, 173, 210, 214, 230, 233, 237

M

Madina . . . . .x, xiii, xvi, xvii, 20, 23, 27, 32, 38, 39, 40, 41, 44, 47, 48, 49, 50, 51, 55, 56, 57, 58, 59, 64, 65, 69, 70, 71, 72, 73, 74, 75, 76, 77, 79, 80, 84, 85, 90, 95, 98, 99, 100, 101, 104, 107, 108, 109, 125, 130, 131, 140, 143, 148, 180, 181, 192, 193, 203, 208, 222, 223, 229, 230, 233, 235, 240, 248, 251, 252, 253, 258, 262, 263

Makka . .14, 31, 38, 39, 41, 42, 43, 47, 49, 50, 53, 54, 57, 69, 71, 77, 79, 80, 81, 82, 88, 93, 94, 95, 100, 102, 104, 105, 106, 107, 108, 109, 110, 111, 114, 125, 138, 145, 148, 155, 179, 181, 203, 209, 222, 224, 228, 229, 230, 239, 250

Maymuna 179, 209

mi'raj xiv

Moses . . . .xiv, 51, 85, 167, 209, 212

Mu'adh ibn Jabal . . . . .xvii, 135

Mu'awiya 194, 244

Muhajirun 99

N

Nahrawan 133

Negus 17, 106

Noah xiv

O

Orientalists . .204, 213, 238, 243, 264

P

Paradise . . . . .vii, xiii, xviii, 33, 63, 67, 79, 121, 128, 129, 139, 141, 144, 159, 166, 172, 175, 176, 178,

185, 188, 214, 228, 231, 233, 234, 247, 249, 260

Persia 11, 73, 147, 154

polytheism 50, 82, 84

polytheists . . . .xviii, 31, 57, 69, 70, 71, 99, 131, 248

prayer 122, 209

Q

Quraysh . . . .xvi, 39, 41, 42, 43, 44, 47, 49, 50, 51, 53, 54, 55, 57, 58, 65, 70, 71, 74, 76, 77, 79, 80, 89, 98, 104, 105, 106, 107, 108, 109, 111, 243

R

racism 111

S

Sa'd ibn Abi Waqqas 48, 60, 93, 96, 147, 228, 233

Sa'd ibn Mu'adh . . .49, 51, 54, 76

Sa'id ibn al-Musayyib . .257

Sa'id ibn Jubayr . .148, 247, 256

Safiyya . . .73, 78, 179, 260

Said Nursi 66, 136, 142, 150

Salman al-Farisi . . .72, 104

Sassanid 114

science . . .v, x, xv, xvi, 2, 6, 16, 25, 34, 35, 97, 150, 151, 152, 157, 205, 215, 217, 218, 264

Scripture 1, 86, 178

Solomon 167

Spain . .9, 11, 13, 152, 154, 178, 195

Sunna 24, 33, 157, 158, 159, 161, 162, 163, 164, 165, 166, 167, 168, 169, 170, 172, 173, 174, 175, 177, 178, 179, 181, 183, 184, 185, 186, 192, 201, 213, 225, 227, 232, 240, 247, 253, 257, 261

superstition 29

T

Tabi'un 190, 193, 194, 195, 200, 216, 223, 227, 247, 251, 252, 253, 255, 257, 261, 264

Tabuk 83, 85

Tariq 6, 13, 147

Tariq ibn Ziyad . .6, 13, 147

Torah 33, 76, 110, 134, 184, 204, 205, 227, 234

Traditions . .15, 17, 97, 149,
    158, 159, 166, 185, 187,
    188, 189, 191, 194-201,
    203, 205, 206, 211, 213-
    225, 236, 239, 241, 242,
    244, 245, 247, 249, 252,
    253, 257-264

Trench . .70, 71, 76, 77, 89,
    90, 104, 163

U

Ubayda ibn Harith 43,
    48, 55, 112, 147, 184,
    228

Uhud . . . . .xvii, 48, 54, 56,
    59, 60, 61, 63, 64, 68, 69,
    70, 87, 90, 101, 125, 131,
    135, 176, 232, 236, 248,
    251, 252

'Umar ibn al-Khattab 6,
    14, 15, 37, 38, 91, 93, 94,
    96, 103, 107, 111, 112,
    127, 132, 134, 139, 140,
    141, 144, 146, 159, 171,
    176, 181, 182, 183, 184,
    189, 190, 192, 205, 209,
    210, 214, 215, 218, 220,
    223, 225, 228, 231, 238,
    239, 242, 243, 245, 246,
    247, 248, 249, 251, 255,
    257, 258, 260, 263

Umm Habiba 179

Umm Salama .104, 179, 182

unity 21, 24, 25, 27,
    66, 117, 137, 150, 155

'Uqba ibn Nafi' . .6, 13, 147

'Uthman ibn 'Affan 6,
    14, 37, 84, 94, 96, 106,
    108, 128, 146, 175, 189,
    194, 228, 231, 251, 257

Uways al-Qarani 255

V

W

Wahshi 62, 229

wisdom . . . . .xiv, 1, 24, 29,
    150, 163

X

Y

Yarmuk 14, 38, 135

Yemen . . . .xvii, 4, 41, 148,
    258

Z

Zayd ibn Harith . . . .xvi, 12,
    78, 79, 96, 111, 112, 134,
    136, 148, 159, 182, 183,
    189, 196, 214, 217, 224,
    228, 232, 242, 247, 260

Zaynab bint Jahsh 112